Internet Governance

Internet Governance

Infrastructure and Institutions

Edited by
Lee A. Bygrave and Jon Bing

OXFORD
UNIVERSITY PRESS

OXFORD
UNIVERSITY PRESS

Great Clarendon Street, Oxford OX2 6DP

Oxford University Press is a department of the University of Oxford.
It furthers the University's objective of excellence in research, scholarship,
and education by publishing worldwide in

Oxford New York

Auckland Cape Town Dar es Salaam Hong Kong Karachi
Kuala Lumpur Madrid Melbourne Mexico City Nairobi
New Delhi Shanghai Taipei Toronto
With offices in
Argentina Austria Brazil Chile Czech Republic France Greece
Guatemala Hungary Italy Japan South Korea Poland Portugal
Singapore Switzerland Thailand Turkey Ukraine Vietnam

Oxford is a registered trade mark of Oxford University Press
in the UK and in certain other countries

Published in the United States
by Oxford University Press Inc., New York

ISBN 978-0-19-956113-1

Printed in the United Kingdom by
Lightning Source UK Ltd., Milton Keynes

Acknowledgements

The writing of this book would not have been possible without the generous financial support provided by UNINETT Norid AS ('Norid')—the organization responsible for operating the .no TLD. In 2005, Norid commenced sponsorship of a long-term research programme on Internet governance at the Norwegian Research Centre for Computers and Law (NRCCL), University of Oslo. This book is the chief result of the programme so far. It is not the only tangible result. The programme has arranged an international conference, 'Netting the Net: Key Issues on Internet Governance', held 18–19 October 2006, Oslo. It has also generated a comprehensive report (by Dana Irina Cojocarasu) on legal issues regarding 'WHOIS' databases. The report will be published in 2009.

Though jointly responsible for this book, Jon Bing would explicitly like to acknowledge that Lee A. Bygrave has been the main architect of the work and undertaken most of the editing.

The editors have been ably assisted by a reference group that was established at the start of the research programme to provide advice on the book's content and structure. The members of that group have consisted of Hilde Thunem (Managing Director, Norid), Jens C. Koch (Deputy Director, Norwegian Post and Telecommunications Authority), Jens Nørve (Section Director, Agency for Public Management and eGovernment, Norway), and Annebeth Lange (chiefly in her former capacity as Head of Section, Network Addresses and Digital Signatures, Norwegian Post and Telecommunications Authority). Two members of the group—Hilde Thunem and Annebeth Lange—have also written parts of Chapter 5.

At the NRCCL, Terje Michaelsen functioned as research assistant during the first year of the research programme. In that capacity, he gave invaluable input to the initial planning of this book and wrote the first draft of Chapter 3. Susan Schiavetta wrote the first draft of Section 5.2 in Chapter 5. Dana Irina Cojocarasu contributed insight into regulatory issues concerning WHOIS databases. Kamil Karczmarczyk provided speedy research assistance during the final polishing of the manuscript.

The editorial staff at Oxford University Press—particularly Matthew Derbyshire—are to be commended for ensuring that finalization of the manuscript was smooth and congenial. Moreover, the comments of the (anonymous) reviewers they engaged prior to finalization helped sharpen this book's profile.

Last but not least, thanks go to past and present students of the Master's degree programme in Information and Communication Technology Law at the University of Oslo. Much of the initial impetus for writing this book derives from the previous lack of an appropriate introductory text for that part of the Master's degree programme dealing with the history of the Internet and associated governance structures. Thanks go to the students not just for their polite patience in waiting for such a text— a text that we promised would materialize considerably more quickly than it has done—but also for the numerous observations which class discussions with them have generated and which are reflected indirectly, if not directly, in various parts of the book. Amanda Hubbard—a Fulbright Scholar who completed the Master's degree in 2006—deserves special mention in this regard. Indeed, she wrote the first drafts of Chapter 6 concerning the World Summit on the Information Society (a summit that she also attended).

We therefore dedicate this book to our students—past, present, and future.

Lee A. Bygrave and Jon Bing
University of Oslo
. Norway

Contents

Contributors

Harald Alvestrand wrote Section 4.1 in Chapter 4. Harald is an Engineer with Google Norway. He is currently a member of the Board of Directors of the International Corporation for Assigned Names and Numbers (ICANN). He has been active in Internet standardization via the Internet Engineering Task Force (IETF) since 1991, and was IETF Chair 2001–06. He was also member of the Internet Architecture Board 1999–2001. He is the author of several Requests for Comments (RFCs), including RFC 1766 (documenting the first standard for language tags in Internet protocols).

Jon Bing wrote Chapter 1 in addition to helping edit this book. Jon is Professor at the Norwegian Research Center for Computers and Law (NRCCL), University of Oslo. He was, until recently, a member of the Generic Names Support Organization (GNSO) for ICANN.

Lee A. Bygrave co-authored Chapters 3 and 6, and parts of Chapter 5. He additionally undertook most of the editing of this book. Lee is Associate Professor at the Department of Private Law, University of Oslo. He is also attached to the NRCCL, together with the Cyberspace Law and Policy Centre, University of New South Wales, Sydney.

Amanda Hubbard wrote the first drafts of Chapter 6. Amanda is Deputy Legal Advisor, US National Security Council. She has previously worked as Trial Attorney in the Computer Crime and Intellectual Property Division of the US Department of Justice. She was a Fulbright Scholar at the NRCCL 2005–06 and contributed to this book in that capacity.

Annebeth B. Lange co-authored Section 5.4 in Chapter 5. Annebeth is Senior Adviser in Law and Policy, UNINETT Norid AS. She was formerly employed at the Norwegian Post and Telecommunications Authority (NPTA) 2000–07 where she was Head of Section, Network Addresses and Digital Signatures. She contributed to this book in the latter capacity. Whilst with the NPTA she was also the Norwegian representative in the Governmental Advisory Committee of ICANN.

Håkon Wium Lie wrote Section 4.2 in Chapter 4. Håkon is Chief Technology Officer of Opera Software. He worked on the World Wide Web project with Tim Berners-Lee at the European Organization for Nuclear Research (CERN) in the early 1990s and is the originator of the concept of Cascading Style Sheets. He also worked for the World Wide Web Consortium (W3C) 1995–99, helping to establish its European base.

Terje Lundby Michaelsen wrote the first draft of Chapter 3. Terje is an attorney with the Norwegian law firm, Kluge. He was formerly a research assistant at the NRCCL 2005–06 where he worked on Internet governance issues. He contributed to this book in that capacity.

Susan Schiavetta co-authored Section 5.2 in Chapter 5. Susan is Contracts Manager for Nera Networks. Up until 2008, she was a doctoral research fellow at the NRCCL where she successfully completed a dissertation on electronic forms of alternative dispute resolution. She contributed to this book in that capacity.

Lawrence B. Solum wrote Chapter 2. Lawrence is John A. Cribbet Professor of Law, University of Illinois, College of Law, Champaign, Illinois. He was previously Professor of Law at the University of San Diego School of Law 2002–05, and at Loyola Law School, Loyola Marymount University 1998–2002.

Hilde Thunem wrote Section 5.3 and co-authored Section 5.4 in Chapter 5. Hilde is Managing Director of UNINETT Norid AS. She was a member of the executive committee of the Council of European National Top-Level Domain Registries (CENTR) 2005–06. She represents UNINETT Norid at the country-code Names Support Organization (ccNSO) within ICANN.

List of Figures and Table

Figures

Table

Principal Abbreviations and Acronyms

ACM	Association for Computing Machinery
ccNSO	country-code Names Supporting Organization (ICANN)
DARPA	Defense Advanced Research Projects Agency (USA)
DNS	Domain Name System
DOC	Department of Commerce (USA)
GNSO	Generic Names Supporting Organization (ICANN)
HTML	HyperText Markup Language
HTTP	HyperText Transfer Protocol
IAB	Internet Architecture Board
IANA	Internet Assigned Numbers Authority
ICANN	Internet Corporation for Assigned Names and Numbers
ICT	information and communication technology
IEEE	Institute of Electrical and Electronics Engineers
IESG	Internet Engineering Steering Group
IETF	Internet Engineering Task Force
IGF	Internet Governance Forum
IP	Internet Protocol
ISOC	Internet Society
ITU	International Telecommunications Union
ITU-T	ITU Telecommunications Standardization Sector
MOU	Memorandum of Understanding
NOMCOM	Nominations Committee
NPTA	Norwegian Post and Telecommunications Authority
NTIA	National Telecommunications and Information Administration (USA)
NSI	Network Solutions, Incorporated
RFC	Request for Comment

Principal Abbreviations and Acronyms

SLD	second-level domain
SMTP	Simple Mail Transfer Protocol
SNMP	Simple Network Management Protocol
TCP	Transmission Control Protocol
TLD	top-level domain
UDRP	Uniform Domain Name Dispute Resolution Policy
URL	Uniform Resource Locator
WSIS	World Summit on the Information Society
W3C	World Wide Web Consortium

Introduction

Lee A. Bygrave

Governance of the Internet is multifaceted, complex, and far from transparent. It raises contentious issues of public policy and will continue to do so. This is well illustrated by the heated character of many of the policy debates accompanying the United Nations' World Summit on the Information Society (WSIS) which was held in two phases in 2003 and 2005, respectively. It is also well illustrated in the recent meetings of the Internet Governance Forum (IGF) that was the main organizational by-product of the Summit. Yet there is so far little literature providing a detailed, systematic, and non-polemical account of Internet governance, written with the general public in mind at the same time as being academically rigorous. It is hoped that this book will help fill the gap.

The primary aim of the book is to provide insight for a broad range of readers into some of the central issues of Internet governance. Accordingly, this book is addressed to a readership composed of more than just academics and professionals who are expert in the field: students, government bodies, civil society groups, legal practitioners, etc., are also relevant.

A secondary aim—firmly rooted within the first—is to provide an introductory textbook for university students who wish to quickly get up to speed on the Internet and associated governance structures. While the topic of Internet governance is gradually gaining stature as a subject in its own right for tertiary studies, there is still a paucity of appropriate textbooks on the subject.

The broad thrust of the book is descriptive. The various authors do not seek, on the whole, to be overtly polemical in the sense that they take clear sides in ongoing controversies. Their contributions contain, nonetheless, references where necessary to polemical discourse. Moreover, some of the description is enlivened by argument, both theoretical and legal–political.

While 'Internet governance' is a phrase increasingly on people's lips, its precise meaning remains somewhat diffuse. Various attempts at definition have been made. For instance, the Working Group on Internet Governance (WGIG) set up under the aegis of the WSIS proposed the following definition:

Internet governance is the development and application by governments, the private sector, and civil society, in their respective roles, of shared principles, norms, rules, decision-making procedures and programmes, that shape the evolution and utilization of the Internet.[1]

Alternatively, one group of academic experts in the field have defined the phrase as

[c]ollective action by governments and/or private sector operators of TCP/IP networks, to establish rules and procedures to enforce public policies and resolve disputes that involve multiple jurisdictions.[2]

Both of the above definitions are broad. Part of their breadth lies in the fact that the notion of governance embraces more than government and, concomitantly, more than traditional notions of formal regulation by state actors using legal or quasi-legal codes. Governance encompasses a vast range of mechanisms for management and control—of which formal legal codes (treaties, conventions, statutes, regulations, judicial decisions) are but one, albeit important, instance. This book endorses a similar view of governance.

Under both of the above-cited definitions, Internet governance embraces issues concerned not just with the *infrastructure* for transmitting data but also the information *content* of the transmitted data. A large part of this book's focus, however, is on the governance of infrastructure rather than information content. More concretely, special attention is given to the steering and management of currently core elements of the Internet as a specific modality for data transmission, particularly

---

[1] WGIG, *Report of the Working Group on Internet Governance* (Château de Bossey, June 2005), 4, <http://www.wgig.org/docs/WGIGREPORT.pdf>, last accessed 26 April 2008. This definition was adopted in the WSIS *Tunis Agenda for the Information Society*, Document WSIS-05/TUNIS/DOC[6(rev. 1)-E (adopted 18 November 2005], paragraph 34, <http://www.itu.int/wsis/docs2/tunis/off/6rev1.html>, last accessed 26 April 2008.

[2] M. Mueller, J. Mathiason, L.W. McKnight, *Making Sense of 'Internet Governance': Defining Principles and Norms in a Policy Context* (April 2004), 3, <http://dcc.syr.edu/miscarticles/SU-IGP-rev2.pdf>, last accessed 26 April 2008.

- protocols for data transmission in the form of packet switching (Transmission Control Protocol/Internet Protocol—TCP/IP), along with subsequent extensions of these protocols (such as Hypertext Transmission Protocol—HTTP);
- IP addresses and corresponding domain names; and
- root servers.[3]

With this point of departure, content regulation is given relatively modest attention in the book. A range of contentious issues—for instance, privacy of electronic communications, freedom of expression, liability of Internet service providers for dissemination of data with illegal content—are, in the main, only covered insofar as they directly affect, arise out of, or are affected by development and steering of Internet architecture.

This is not to suggest that content issues should be treated as falling outside the discourse on Internet governance. Indeed, as shown in the book, it is usually difficult to maintain a strict separation of the two sets of issues—governance of infrastructure has inevitably an impact on governance of content, and vice versa. That the book devotes considerable space to infrastructure issues is partly because there already exists a great deal of literature on content regulation but relatively little on the shape and shaping of the basic bones of the Internet as infrastructure. In our opinion, that skeleton deserves more intensive study for several reasons.

First, infrastructure and the way it is engineered matter. It embodies policy choices at the same time as it sets limits on policy choices. As Larry Lessig and other scholars have ably emphasized, information systems architecture is a form of normative 'code'.[4] It is, as such, not immutable, value neutral, or necessarily benign.

Second, infrastructure continues to figure prominently among issues currently being debated in national and international forums under the nomenclature of 'Internet governance'. While much of the discourse in the WSIS and first IGF meeting took on a panoply of problems with parameters going beyond engineering standards, discussion at the second IGF meeting held in Rio de Janeiro in November 2007 refocused in large part on infrastructure issues (under the nomenclature of 'Critical Internet Resources'). And within the Internet Corporation for Assigned Names and Numbers (ICANN)—a salient player in the field of Internet

---

[3] For explanations of these terms, see Chapters 1 and 5.

[4] See, for example, L. Lessig, *Code, and Other Laws of Cyberspace* (New York: Basic Books, 1999); J. R. Reidenberg, 'Lex Informatica: The Formulation of Information Policy Rules through Technology', *Texas Law Review*, 1998, vol. 76, 553–93.

governance—infrastructure issues predominate. Issues like the development of the Domain Name System to include an unlimited number of top-level domains, the introduction of Unicode scripts for domain names, the relation between generic and country-code top-level domain names in a liberalized namespace, and the role of 'WHOIS' databases are all currently discussed within ICANN.[5] Some of these issues have festered for considerable time and appear still to be far from satisfactory resolution. At a higher level, there remain question marks against the transnational legitimacy of ICANN operations.

Third, the relative paucity of literature on the work of bodies that have been central to developing core Internet standards partly reflects the fact that their work has largely escaped public controversy. This is particularly so with the Internet Engineering Task Force (IETF) and World Wide Web Consortium (W3C).[6] Yet it is precisely the lack of public controversy and attention which makes their work worthy of focus. What are the features of these bodies that enable them to work largely outside the radar-screen of the general public? Do elements of their work—especially their bottom–up, consensus-oriented decision-making procedures—provide a model for other organizations to emulate? Some scholars answer the latter question in the affirmative.[7] It remains pertinent, nonetheless, to consider the extent to which that answer is justified, particularly given that these bodies' basic approach to decision-making is being adopted in broader international forums for thrashing out Internet policy (primarily ICANN, WSIS, and the IGF). While the application of that approach lends legitimacy to the new processes of policy development, its beneficial effect on the efficiency of these processes is less certain.

An important part of this book's remit is to describe and explain certain fundamental tensions in Internet governance. Some of these tensions may be summed up in terms of authority versus legitimacy; 'digital libertarianism' versus 'digital realism'; commercialism versus civil society ideals; interests of developed countries versus interests of developing countries. These and other tensions run as live wires through various parts of this book. With these tensions as backdrop, the book's overarching theme is the challenges associated with developing and applying governance structures at a global level based on bottom–up, consensus-seeking decisional procedures, without direct foundation in a Treaty framework.

---

[5] See further Chapters 3 and 5.   [6] See further Chapter 4.

[7] See, for example, A. Michael Froomkin, 'Habermas@discourse.net: Toward a Critical Theory of Cyberspace', *Harvard Law Review*, 2003, vol. 116, 749–873.

Chapter 1 (authored by Jon Bing) provides a history of the development of the Internet in terms of its infrastructure, applications, and sources of inspiration. In doing so, it portrays the chief personalities, ideas, and concerns forming the context in which the Internet was created. For the history of the Internet has been much more than just a technical matter of connecting wires, nodes, and networks; powerful visions have also driven its development. The chapter highlights these visions and the personalities behind them. It also provides a simple explanation of the Internet's technical basis, including explanations of protocols, the Domain Name System, and World Wide Web.

Chapter 2 (authored by Lawrence Solum) presents a typology of the various kinds of governance forms that impinge on the Internet. These range from technological forms ('code'/information systems architecture) to non-legal standards (guidelines, recommendations, etc.) to legal norms (legislation, contract, etc.) to market mechanisms. The typology presented draws on theories of the relationship between law and cyberspace. It highlights differences between the governance forms in terms of their respective sources of inspiration, input, and legitimacy, and in terms of their respective forms for enforcement.

Chapter 3 (co-authored by Lee A. Bygrave and Terje Michaelsen) describes the main organizations that are concerned directly with Internet governance. As part of this description, the chapter outlines the relevant responsibilities and agendas of the respective organizations, together with their sources of funding and their relationships with each other. Attention is directed mainly at transnational bodies. The remainder of the chapter describes the various roles played by national governments, alone and in concert, in Internet governance. Using the self-governance ideals of 'digital libertarianism' as foil, it delineates the growing influence of governments in the field.

Chapter 4 elaborates the processes of developing and adopting basic standards for data communication and storage on the Internet. The first part of the chapter (authored by Harald Tveit Alverstrand) focuses on the organizational mechanics of the IETF. The second part of the chapter (authored by Håkon Wium Lie) focuses on the development of standards for the World Wide Web within the framework of W3C.

Chapter 5 explicates the Domain Name System and the governance mechanisms attached to it. The first part of the chapter (authored by Lee Bygrave) introduces the basic elements of the system. The second part of the chapter (co-authored by Susan Schiavetta and Lee A. Bygrave) turns first to governance issues concerning 'WHOIS' databases, and thereafter to dispute resolution processes in relation to domain names, focusing on ICANN's Uniform Domain Name Dispute Resolution Policy. The third part of the chapter (authored by Hilde Thunem) provides an overview of the principal differentiating features of national regimes for allocating domain names under country-code top-level domains. Building on this overview, the final part of the chapter elaborates the domain name allocation regimes for .no and .uk, respectively. Two main lines of analysis inform the descriptions: (*a*) the relationship of the national domain name authority to government and (*b*) the stringency of the respective rules of these authorities for domain name allocation. The account of the .uk regulatory regime is primarily authored by Edward Phillips (with input from Nick Wenban-Smith and Lee A. Bygrave); the .no regime by Hilde Thunem and Annebeth Lange.

Finally, Chapter 6 (co-authored by Amanda Hubbard and Lee A. Bygrave) takes up a number of issues broadly concerned with the possibilities for democratizing governance of the Internet—that is, ensuring broad and equitable participation in governance processes. These are issues that received a great deal of attention in the discussion accompanying the World Summit on the Information Society (WSIS) held in Geneva in December 2003 and Tunis in November 2005. Hence, the WSIS forms much of the focus of Chapter 6. The first part of the chapter provides an overview of the Summit's organizational mechanics, main participants, and principal results. The chief organizational result of the Summit was to establish a new arena for dialogue—the Internet Governance Forum (IGF). The second part of Chapter 6 thus outlines the characteristics of the IGF, in light of its first two meetings, held, respectively, in Athens in October/November 2006 and in Rio de Janeiro in November 2007. The chapter concludes by drawing up some of the lessons to be learned from the WSIS and IGF discussions, for future global dialogue on Internet governance.

Despite its basically descriptive remit, this book does advance a thesis. The thesis is that one of the chief reasons for the spectacular success of the Internet in terms of its functionality lies in the fact that it has been developed in open and democratic decisional cultures dedicated to 'rough consensus and running code'.[8] Concomitantly, Internet governance structures ought to continue, as a point of departure, to cultivate such cultures. The contributors to the book recognize that this aim will not be

---

[8] The phrase 'rough consensus and running code' is a central mantra of the Internet Engineering Task Force (IETF), the main workhorse in development of core Internet standards. See further Chapter 4 (Section 4.1).

easy to achieve. On the one hand, it cuts against the grain of numerous business practices. On the other hand, a considerable number of national governments wish to subject development of Internet standards to more extensive 'top–down' regulatory controls—in other words, to decisively weight Internet governance in favour of Internet *government*. We are not suggesting that 'top–down' regulation has no useful role to play in this area; such intervention may, for example, be necessary to prevent instances of abuse of power through private fiat.[9] Yet its imposition ought to be light-handed, proportionate, and on an exceptional rather than routine basis.

Advocates of increased Internet government sometimes argue that bottom–up, consensus-oriented decisional strategies are insufferably slow and inefficient. Certainly such processes can be slow and inefficient, but legislative or other forms of 'top–down' control can be too. And there is a risk that orders sent down from above will end up not being respected if they are not sufficiently anchored in grassroots sentiment. This risk looms especially large with respect to development of Internet architecture. Not only have the organizational mechanics of such development been traditionally at odds with 'top–down' control models, but the Internet now affects so many different interest groups that, arguably, its governance is likely only to be truly effective in the long-term if the bulk of these various groups are all taken proper account of—which means, precisely, continued embracement of bottom–up, consensus-oriented decision-making strategies.

Unless otherwise stated, all references in the book (including URLs) are current as of 1 July 2008.

---

[9] See, for example, the discussion on 'network neutrality' in Chapter 2 (Section 2.10).

1

Building cyberspace: a brief history of Internet

Jon Bing[1]

1.1. Paul Baran

The history of the Internet is recent; many of the persons taking part in its development are still alive. In spite of this, the history is shrouded in myths and anecdotes. One of the more persistent myths is that the Internet was principally conceived by US military authorities in order to establish a possibility of communication which would withstand a nuclear attack. This is false. Nonetheless, it is true that the problem of communication in a situation of nuclear warfare worried not only the military but also parts of the scientific community. The worry actually posed a challenging problem of communications network construction. And one of the possible starting points for telling the tale of the development of the Internet is this concern—together with one of the men who set out to address it.

The development of computers was intimately connected with development of the atomic bomb. John von Neumann, who has lent his name to characterize the architecture of the electronic computer, was a central figure in the Manhattan Project, especially in designing the 'Fat Man' dropped over Nagasaki.[2] In turn, the development of the atomic bomb ushered in an era of global tension which helped stimulate some of the conceptual work that inspired development of the Internet.

---

[1] In addition to the sources indicated by footnotes throughout the text, the author acknowledges the helpful comments from Håkon Wium Lie, Håkon Styri, Gisle Hannemyr, and Lee A. Bygrave.

[2] See generally Norman Macrae, *John von Neumann* (New York: Pantheon Books, 1992).

By the late 1950s, both of the world's superpowers of that time—the United States of America (USA) and Soviet Union—had developed arsenals of ballistic nuclear missiles with intercontinental reach. The Soviet Union placed some of its rockets on railroad carriages, which haunted its vast and complex railway system and made exact location of the rockets difficult to ascertain. In the United States, missiles like the Minuteman were placed in underground silos. These silos would typically consist of a Launch Control Facility and a Launch Facility, placed approximately 10 miles apart from each other. Housed within each control facility was a communications control console containing an array of radio and telephone equipment to enable the crew to communicate with other facilities, base headquarters, and the Strategic Air Command.[3]

One of the major challenges facing the authorities was how to ensure that the launch control facility was linked by telecommunication to the Strategic Air Command. In a nuclear war, much of the infrastructure, including telecommunication switches, must be presumed destroyed. Reliance on radio transmission might be precarious due to interference, and landlines would be vulnerable.

This problem also met Paul Baran when he came to work for the RAND Corporation.[4] Baran was born in Poland in 1926, and followed his parents to the United States in 1928. He attended Drexel University, Philadelphia, and his first job was with the Eckert-Mauchly Computer Corporation.[5] Taking night classes at the University of California at Los Angeles (UCLA), he earned an engineering Master's degree in 1959; the same year he joined RAND.

RAND was intent on solving the problem briefly indicated above. Paul Baran also considered how to design a robust communication solution. He himself has told why he started this work. His determination can only be understood against the background of the prevailing climate of apprehension.

---

[3] See 'Minuteman Missile, Historic Resource Study', <http://www.cr.nps.gov/history/online_books/mimi/hrs2-4.htm>.

[4] RAND is a non-profit organization functioning mainly as a think tank. Its name is an acronym derived from the term 'research and development'. The organization has traditionally focused on national security issues.

[5] This later became UNIVAC, the first commercial computer company. Both Eckert and Mauchly had worked with the very first electronic computer, ENIAC (Electronic Numerical Integrator and Computer), at the Moore School of Electrical Engineering, University of Pennsylvania.

9

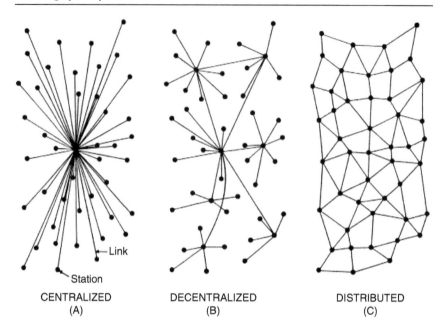

Figure 1.1. Baran's diagrammatic categorization of communications networks: Centralized, decentralized, and distributed networks

It was not done out of intellectual curiosity or a desire to write papers. It was not done in response to a work statement. It was done in response to a most dangerous situation that existed.[6]

Baran worked on the problem for a couple of years, mainly 1961–62, producing 11 volumes in the process.[7] The main results can be summarized in three major points (Figure 1.1).

First, he makes the elementary observation that communication networks can be categorized in one of two forms, either centralized (or star) networks (A) or distributed (or grid or mesh) networks (C), the decentralized networks (B) being one of the types along the spectrum from centralized to distributed. Obviously, a centralized network is highly vulnerable, as the nodes will not be able to communicate if the centre is taken out. Therefore, these were not well suited to ensure secure communication between the central command and a launch control

---

[6] 'An interview with Paul Baran', conducted by Judy O'Neill on 5 March 1990, Menlo Park, California, Transcipt OH 182, *Oral Histories Collection*, Charles Babbage Institute, Center for the History of Information Processing, University of Minnesota, Minneapolis, 13–14.

[7] Available via <http://www.rand.org/about/history/baran.html>.

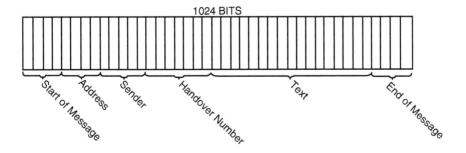

Figure 1.2. Baran's diagram of message blocks

facility. It is possible to calculate network performance as a function of the probability of destruction for each separate node. Baran concludes that: 'It appears that what would today be regarded as an unreliable link can be used in a distributed network almost as effectively as perfectly reliable links.'[8]

Second, Baran suggests the development of standard message blocks, and an algorithm for determining how to forward the blocks through the system (Figure 1.2).

His discussion of the message block system is remarkable—remember this is in the early 1960s:

As we move to the future, there appears to be an increasing need for a standardized message block for all-digital communications networks. As data rates increase, the velocity of propagation over long links becomes an increasingly important consideration...We soon reach a point where more time is spent setting the switches in a conventional circuit switched system for short holding-time messages than is required for actual transmission of the data.

Most importantly, standardized data blocks permit many simultaneous users each with widely different bandwidth requirements to economically share a broadband network made up of varied data rate links. The standardized message block simplifies construction of very high speed switches. Every user connected to the network can feed data at any rate up to a maximum value. The user's traffic is stored until a full data block is received by the first station. This block is rubber stamped with a heading and return address, plus additional house-keeping information. Then, it is transmitted into the network...

The switching process in any store-and-forward system is analogous to a postman sorting mail. A postman sits at each switching node. Messages arrive simultaneously from all links. The postman records bulletins describing the traffic loading

---

[8] Paul Baran, 'On Distributed Communications—I. Introduction to Distributed Communications Networks', Memorandum RM-3420-PR (Santa Monica: Rand Corporation, 1964), 9.

status for each of the outgoing links. With proper status information, the postman is able to determine the best direction to send out any letters. So far, this mechanism is general and applicable to all store-and-forward communication systems.[9]

In addition to these two features—decentralization and what we today would call packet switching[10] and dynamic routing—he added a third: redundancy. Any packet would be sent in triplicate. This would make the network very robust, and his mathematics proved it.

The system may seem complex. Yet calculations indicated that it would handle the long-distance telecommunication within the Department of Defense for an annual $60 million (1964), while such telecommunication cost at that time $2 billion. This seemed too good to be true, and it was not believed, the common assumption being that the big telephone companies would already have realized the concept were it possible.[11]

In this brief look at the early work of Paul Baran, some of the basic concepts of the Internet, as we know it today, have been introduced: distributed networks, packets, and algorithms for routing a package the most efficient way through a distributed network. It is often said that the Internet originated from the attempts of the US Department of Defense to develop a network that would survive an atomic attack. As stated at the start of this chapter, this is a somewhat inaccurate part of cyberspace lore. Yet there is a kernel of truth in it, that kernel being Paul Baran and his fear of the Cold War blossoming into a very hot one. On account of that fear, he designed a robust network that would ensure the Strategic Air Command contact with the Launch Control Facilities for shooting the intercontinental ballistic missiles from their underground silos.

However, Baran's conceived network was never realized as such. It remained in the form of reports written in terse English supported by mathematics and graphs.

The Internet had another beginning. Yet before returning to that story, let us briefly look at another problem, less acute than the perils of the Cold War, but perhaps more intellectually fascinating: the management of large volumes of literature and other data.

[9] Paul Baran, 'On Distributed Communications—I. Introduction to Distributed Communications Networks', Memorandum RM-3420-PR (Santa Monica: Rand Corporation, 1964), 23.

[10] The term 'packet switching' was first used by Donald Davies of the National Physical Laboratory, UK, who independently came upon the same general concept as Baran in November 1963. 'Packet' is an innovative word indicating 'a small package'.

[11] 'Paul Baran, Electrical Engineer', an oral history conducted in 1999 by David Hochfelder, IEEE History Center, Rutgers University, New Brunswick, New Jersey—Transcript, 11–12.

1.2. Melvin Dewey, Paul Otlet, and Vannevar Bush

In our enthusiasm and bewilderment when confronted with the many new possibilities of information technology, we easily forget that even before the arrival of digital computers data crested into waves that threatened to submerge people with information overload. It is claimed that at the time Gutenberg's printing press came into use (approximately 1450),[12] the number of books measured in volumes existing in Europe was 30,000. After the new printing technology had worked for 50 years, the number of books had increased to 15 million.[13] This represents the transition from a time when a scholarly person could read all the books that he (or she, though in that age it typically would be a 'he') came across, regardless of their subject, to a time when one would need tools to navigate in the archives and libraries.

Until the nineteenth century, libraries were organized by classification systems which used a fixed design where each book was given a dedicated slot on the shelf. This was impractical, as the books and shelves had to be reclassified with each addition to the collection. Another problem was that libraries did not use the same system, thus making it difficult for patrons and librarians to use different collections.

This was a problem which Melville Louis Kossuth Dewey (1851–1931) set out to solve.[14]

Dewey grew up in northern New York. His family could hardly afford to send him to college, and when he entered Amherst at the age of 19, he took a job in the library to finance his studies. He remained in libraries for the rest of his life, and gained the title 'father of librarianship'. Dewey devised a system of numbers and decimals to categorize books according to subject. He received permission from Amherst to apply his new system to its library. Amherst published his system in a leaflet entitled *A Classification and Subject Index for Cataloguing and Arranging the Books and*

---

[12] Gutenberg was not the first to print books from moveable metal types; the first such book was *Buljo Jikji*, a Buddhist book printed in Cheongju, South-Korea, in 1372. See further Sun-Young Kwak, 'World Heritage Rights Versus National Cultural Property Rights: The Case of The *Jikji*', *Human Rights Dialogue*, 2005, Spring, <http://www.cceia.org/resources/publications/dialogue/2_12/online_exclusive/5153.html>. However, the printing technology basic to that book did not have the same social consequences as the printing of Gutenberg's Bible.

[13] Sources vary with respect to figures, but the point made in the text does not rely on the exact numbers, which here are cited from Helmer Dahl, *Teknikk, kultur, samfunn: Om egenarten i Europas vekst* (Oslo: Ingeniørforlaget, 1983).

[14] See 'Melvil Dewey, the father of librarianship', <http://www.booktalking.net/books/dewey/> (the different spellings of his first name are intentional).

Pamphlets of a Library. In 1876, Dewey left Amherst and moved to Boston where he founded the Library Bureau. This library supply company was founded 'for the definite purpose of furnishing libraries with equipment and supplies of unvarying correctness and reliability'.

His classification system starts with a division into 10 basic categories.

```
000 Generalities
100 Philosophy and Psychology
200 Religion
300 Social Science
400 Language
500 Natural Science and Mathematics
600 Technology (Applied Sciences)
700 Arts
800 Literature
900 Geography and History
```

Each class has 10 divisions, and these are again further divided until they become very specific. In this way, treatises on 'butterflies' would be classified as[15]

1. Natural Science and Mathematics.
2. Zoological Sciences.
3. Other invertebrates.

```
595.7 Insects
595.78 Lepidopetra
595.789 Butterflies
```

Dewey's classification scheme is now in its 22nd edition, and available in print and Web versions. The Dewey Decimal Classification (DDC) is the world's most widely used library classification system. However, it is unnecessary to dwell here on the details of the scheme or its possible shortcomings. The important point is that by introducing a classification scheme such as Dewey's, a large collection of books or documents may be organized, solving—at least to some extent—the problem created by their abundance.

[15] See 'Let's do Dewey', <http://www.mtsu.edu/~vvesper/dewey2.htm>.

A less-known figure, but with many of the same ambitions as Dewey, is the Belgian Paul Otlet (1868–1944).[16] Taking Dewey's classification system as a starting point, he developed what has become known as the Universal Decimal Classification, recognized as one of the few implementations of a *faceted* classification system. The system today comprises more than 62,000 individual classifications, is translated into 30 languages, and has considerable current use. It has interesting properties but is not the main reason for the present interest in Otlet.

Otlet and his collaborator, Henri Le Fontaine, attempted in 1895 to establish a Répertoire Bibliographique Universel—a master bibliography of the collective knowledge of the world. Otlet wanted to penetrate the books, and disclose the 'substance, sources and conclusions' inside. In 1910, in the wake of the world fair in Brussels, the two of them created an installation, the Mundaneum, in the Palais du Cinquantenaire of the Palais Mondial. They saw the Mundaneum as the centrepiece of a 'city of intellect'. Shortly after the end of World War I, King Albert and the Belgian government gave permission for the Mundaneum to take over 150 rooms in the Cinquantenaire. This may be explained by Belgium at this time lobbying to host the headquarters for the League of Nations, the establishment of which was being planned at the same time.

Inside the Mundaneum, a vast 'documentary edifice' was collected, eventually comprising almost 16 million index cards and documents. The 3 × 5 inch index cards represented the then most recent advance in storage technology—they were standardized, easily handled, and each stored a 'nugget' of information referring to a source.[17] Users would send their queries by mail. The project met with early success, and more than 1,500 requests were processed annually at a fee of 27 francs per 1,000 cards.

However, when the League of Nations was located to Geneva, the Belgian government lost interest in the Mundaneum. In 1924, the Mundaneum had to move, and continued to move until its last remains ended

---

[16] See generally W. Boyd Rayward, *The Universe of Information: The Work of Paul Otlet for Documentation and International Organization* (Moscow: International Federation of Documentation (FID), 1975); Françoise Levie, *L'homme qui voulait classer le monde: Paul Otlet et le Mundaneum* (Brussels: Les Impressions Nouvelles, 2006); W. Boyd Rayward, 'The Origins of Information Science and the International Institute of Bibliography/International Federation for Information and Documentation (FID)', *Journal of the American Society for Information Science*, 1997, vol. 48, no. 4, 289–300; Alex Wright, 'Paul Otlet: Forgotten Forefather', *Boxesandarrows*, 11 October 2003, <http://www.boxesandarrows.com/view/forgotten_forefather_paul_otlet>. The following account builds on these sources.

[17] This sort of index card had actually been instituted by Dewey, and Otlet introduced this standard in Europe.

up in a parking garage, from where they were carted away by the German occupants during World War II.

The story of this first attempt to create a worldwide database of indexing cards would not deserve by itself more than, perhaps, a footnote. Yet as the Mundaneum declined, Otlet's vision became stronger, taking the form of the 'Universal Book', which he elaborated in his treatise, *Traité de Documentation. Le Livre sur le Livre: Théorie et pratique* (1934).[18] For Otlet, 'the only conception which corresponds to reality is to consider all books, all periodical articles, all the official reports as volumes, chapters, paragraphs in one great book... a colossal encyclopedia framed from all that has been published'.[19]

He saw each document in the database, each 'nugget of information', related to all other documents using his classification scheme. He suggested that the database might be consulted at a distance; the end-user equipment was characterized as an 'electric telescope' ('micropho-tothèque', inspired by the emergent technology of television),[20] linked to the database by telephone cables. The user would have an image of the original document projected onto a flat screen at his or her desk. 'Thus, in his armchair, anyone would be able to contemplate the whole of creation or particular parts of it.'[21]

It is the Universal Book that justifies mention of Otlet in the present context. If one had been asked to describe the World Wide Web using the terminology and technology available in the 1930s, it could hardly have been done more precisely than Otlet's attempt in his writings. One may view Otlet both as a unique visionary and as giving voice to a frustration we recognize from our own time—that is, the need for more efficient ways of organizing and retrieving data, and to manage data to permit us to profit from past lessons without being overwhelmed by the avalanche of irrelevant information.

Another person who felt the same frustration, and glimpsed a solution, was Vannevar Bush. He was one of the more prestigious and influential scientists in the United States before and during World War II. He was instrumental in launching the Manhattan Project. He was also, in one way, the direct cause for the development of ENIAC. He had constructed a differential analyser—a form of analogue computer to

---

[18] See *Traité de Documentation. Le Livre sur le Livre: Théorie et pratique* (Liège: Centre de Lecture publique de la Communauté de française, 1934; reprint of 1989).

[19] Cited in Rayward, *The Universe of Information*, 161. [20] Levie, *L'homme*, 272.

[21] Cited in Rayward, 'The Origins of Information Science', 298.

solve differential equations. One such analyser was acquired by Aberdeen Proving Grounds, Maryland, for ballistic tests. This was no longer adequate in 1943, and Aberdeen Proving Grounds made its historic contract with the Moore School of Electrical Engineering for the first electronic computer.

At the end of the war, Vannevar Bush was accordingly familiar with the budding computer technology and the need for organizing data more efficiently. In his elegant essay 'As We May Think', published in the *Atlantic Monthly* of July 1945,[22] he reflects on document management. He considers advances in information technology and projects them in the future. For instance, he discusses the probable development of the technology for microphotographs:

Consider film of the same thickness as paper, although thinner film will certainly be usable. Even under these conditions there would be a total factor of 10,000 between the bulk of the ordinary record on books, and its microfilm replica. The *Encyclopedia Britannica* could be reduced to the volume of a matchbox. A library of a million volumes could be compressed into one end of a desk.

Most impressive, however, is his vision of the imaginary device he calls a 'memex':

Consider a future device for individual use, which is a sort of mechanized private file and library. It needs a name, and, to coin one at random, 'memex' will do. A memex is a device in which an individual stores all his books, records, and communications, and which is mechanized so that it may be consulted with exceeding speed and flexibility. It is an enlarged intimate supplement to his memory.

It consists of a desk, and while it can presumably be operated from a distance, it is primarily the piece of furniture at which he works. On the top are slanting translucent screens, on which material can be projected for convenient reading. There is a keyboard, and sets of buttons and levers. Otherwise it looks like an ordinary desk.

In one end is the stored material. The matter of bulk is well taken care of by improved microfilm. Only a small part of the interior of the memex is devoted to storage, the rest to mechanism. Yet if the user inserted 5,000 pages of material a day it would take him hundreds of years to fill the repository, so he can be profligate and enter material freely.

Most of the memex contents are purchased on microfilm ready for insertion. Books of all sorts, pictures, current periodicals, newspapers are thus obtained and

---

[22] Available at <http://www.theatlantic.com/doc/194507/bush>.

dropped into place. Business correspondence takes the same path. And there is provision for direct entry. On the top of the memex is a transparent plate. On this are placed longhand notes, photographs, memoranda, all sorts of things. When one is in place, the depression of a lever causes it to be photographed onto the next blank space in a section of the memex film, dry photography being employed.

Again, his foresight is striking. If a person in 1945 were asked to describe the working desk of a user of today, the restraints of vocabulary and technology would lead to something very like what Bush envisioned— with the possible exception of the storage medium. Actually, I am tempted to start a small movement to rename the personal computer (PC) as a 'memex'—'personal computer' is, anyhow, a registered trademark originally belonging to IBM.

By this excursion into the years well before the start of the Internet, I have tried to demonstrate the long-term existence of a problem which was thrashing around awaiting a solution in intellectual schemes and technological inventions. The development of the Internet cannot really be understood without an appreciation of this underlying pressure from a generally perceived need to find better ways of organizing and managing data.

1.3. Neal McElroy

Neal McElroy (1904–72) started in Procter & Gamble as a mail clerk in its advertising department in 1925. In 1943, he became Vice President for advertising and President in 1948. He also became the first man with a background in advertising to serve as a US cabinet officer when Dwight Eisenhower appointed him to the post of Secretary of Defense in 1957.

McElroy had considerable success in his career with Procter & Gamble, particularly in linking advertisement for the company with the popular radio serials of the day. The daytime shows targeting the American housewife were actually named after the main products of Procter & Gamble, and became known as 'soap operas'. Procter & Gamble established its own radio production subsidiary in 1940, and produced the first network television soap opera in 1950.[23] One may want to find some sort of

[23] See further generally <http://www.museum.tv/archives/etv/S/htmlS/soapopera/soap-opera.htm>.

allegorical wisdom in the 'father of the soap opera' being named Secretary of Defense, but it was rather McElroy's high-quality management skills which made him the first person without a military background to head the Defense Department.

Before taking on the office, McElroy made a tour to acquaint himself with the organization and some of the persons with whom he would be working. This brought him on Friday 4 October 1957 to Huntsville, Alabama, where President Eisenhower only the previous month had formally renamed the Army Ballistic Missile Agency the George C. Marshall Space Flight Center. McElroy was talking with the new director of the centre, Wernher von Braun,[24] when their conversation was interrupted by an envoi from the Department of Defense who announced that a Soviet radio transmission had been intercepted which originated from an orbit outside Earth's atmosphere—the first human-made satellite, Sputnik I, had been successfully launched.

This was intimidating for the United States; the race for space had been lost,[25] but the race for the first manned space flight and the Moon had just started. This fascinating and exciting tale does not belong here, but important is the political situation it created—extensive funds became available for research and development. Five days after Sputnik I was launched, Neal McElroy assumed his position as Secretary of Defense, and 17 days later he met before the Congress for the first time to present a policy for meeting the Soviet challenge. In this was a plan to create a civil research agency under the Department of Defense, but independent of any of its branches (which competed with each other). His experience from the soap industry had in fact taught him the value of independent research, and he created within his department the Advanced Research Projects Agency (ARPA) to fund long-term research of possible military relevance. He invited cooperation from universities and research institutions outside the defence industries.

The first Chief Scientist appointed at ARPA was the then young physicist Herbert York. He is reported to have placed, soon after his appointment, a picture of the Moon on one of his walls. Beside it, he hung an empty

---

[24] The man behind the German V2 rocket bomb, and who was destined to play a major role in the US space programme.

[25] Both the United States and the Soviet Union had announced during the International Geophysical Year 1957–58 that they would place a human-made object in orbit around the planet.

frame and explained that this was to be filled with a picture of the dark side of the Moon.[26]

This was the context in which the Internet was created. The Cold War was not the direct cause of the developments to follow; more important was rather the race fuelled by the hot exhaust flames of the multistage rockets that eventually would carry Yuri Gagarin into orbit around the Earth and place Neil Armstrong's footprints on the surface of the Moon.

1.4. Joseph Carl Robnett Licklider

J. C. R. ('Lick') Licklider (1915–90) was another man with a vision. He has also been described as the man with the world's most refined intuition.[27] He had a background in psychology and behavioural science, and saw cooperation between man and computer as the key to future development. In 1960, he published the celebrated paper 'Man–Computer Symbiosis', the main idea of which is that computers should be designed 'to enable men and computers to cooperate in making decisions and controlling complex situations without inflexible dependence on predetermined programs'.[28] He was referring, of course, to real-time interactive computer systems. This way of computing would mean that problems would not have to be formulated in depth in advance because the computers would be able to respond to changing variables. The envisaged system would not use traditional batch processing, but rather the time-sharing method, which gives many users at individual terminals access to a large mainframe. Users thus interact directly with the computer instead of relying on technicians and punch cards, and results are obtained immediately.

In 1957, Licklider started to work for the firm Bolt Beranek and Newman (BBN), which designed architectural acoustics. He persuaded the firm to buy a US$25,000 computer without being precisely certain about the purposes for which it could be used. Soon after, BBN acquired its second computer, a PDP-1, from Digital Equipment Corporation for US$150,000, and started to hire young computer engineers. So someone in the firm must have shared Licklider's confidence.

---

[26] Katie Hafner and Matthew Lyon, *Where Wizards Stay Up Late: The Origins of the Internet* (New York: Simon & Schuster, Touchstone ed., 1996), 21.

[27] Ibid. 29.

[28] J. C. R. Licklider, 'Man-Computer Symbiosis', *IRE Transactions on Human Factors in Electronics*, March 1960, vol. HFE-1, 4.

Licklider himself left the firm for ARPA in October 1962 to head up the newly established Information Processing Techniques Office (IPTO). Before Licklider arrived, the focus of research had been on computer-simulated war games. He changed the focus to research in time-sharing, computer graphics, and improved computer languages.

Licklider set up research contracts with the foremost computer research centres, and established a circle of cooperating institutions that his superiors called 'Lick's priesthood', but which Licklider himself dubbed the 'Intergalactic Computer Network'. These projects resulted in the establishment of computer science departments at many universities, including Massachusetts Institute of Technology (MIT), Berkeley, Stanford, and the University of California at Los Angeles (UCLA). Some like to think that this conception of a network of cooperating institutions really is the beginning of the Internet.

Licklider also published *Libraries of the Future* (1965) in which he discussed many of the above-mentioned problems and solutions. He theorized about an information network that he termed a 'procognitive system'. In this connection, he suggested that

... the concept of a 'desk' may have changed from passive to active: a desk may be primarily a display-and-control station in a telecommunication-telecomputation system—and its most vital part may be the cable ('umbilical cord') that connects it, via a wall socket, into the procognitive utility net.[29]

Again, we see how Licklider's imagination projected some of the ideas that were later realized as Internet and World Wide Web.

1.5. IMP

In 1963, one of the persons to be invited to a meeting of the 'Intergalactic Computer Network' was Bob Taylor, who was working in the Office of Advanced Research and Technology in Washington, DC, for the National Aeronautics and Space Agency (NASA). He was somewhat surprised to find that the invitation originated with Licklider, who was Taylor's role model in psychoacoustics—the study of subjective human perception of sound. Early in 1965, Taylor followed Licklider's footsteps and became the third director of IPTO.

[29] J. C. R. Licklider, *Libraries of the Future* (Cambridge, Massachusetts: MIT Press, 1965), 33.

At this time, ARPA was headed by Charles Herzfeld, an Austrian physicist who had fled Europe during World War II. It was also a time when the organization was haunted by the 'terminal problem'. The research institutions contracting with IPTO were all beginning to request more computer power. There was an obvious duplication of effort between the organizations, and computers were expensive. Taylor suggested a solution. Without a memo or preparatory meetings, he took the suggestion directly to Herzfeld. He suggested ARPA should establish electronic links between the computers. In this way, researchers doing similar work at different sites could share resources and results. Rather than spreading resources thinly across the country, ARPA could concentrate on a small number of powerful computers, giving everybody access to them.

It is reported that Herzfeld asked: 'Is it going to be hard to do?', and Taylor responded: 'No, we already know how.' Herzfeld thought it was a good idea, and gave Taylor a budget of $1 million.[30] This is an impressive record for the funding of a research project: the argument for starting building the Internet and the decision to fund its development had taken a total of just 20 minutes![31]

The plan for what eventually would become known as the ARPANET was made publicly known at a 1967 symposium of the Association for Computing Machinery (ACM) in Gatlingburg, Tennessee. The plan was to link 16 sites by an experimental network. The realization of the network was not trivial, in spite of Taylor's assurance to Herzfeld. But Taylor had a suitable candidate for meeting the challenge, Lawrence ('Larry') Roberts, who was recruited to IPTO in December 1966 from the Lincoln Laboratory at MIT. He was 29 years old, and had already gained a reputation as somewhat of a genius. He started working with the plans of the network, and, in that connection, organized an ARPANET Design Session in April 1967 in Ann Arbor, Michigan.[32] At the session, Wesley Clarke, a computer engineer at Washington University, made an important suggestion that the host computers of the sites to be connected should be left out of the network as much as possible, and that a small computer should be inserted between the host computer and the network. This small computer became known as an Interface Message Processor (IMP).[33]

At the Design Session Roberts also learned about the work done by Paul Baran, and he subsequently dug out the RAND reports. He later

[30] See Hafner and Lyon, *Where Wizards Stay Up Late*, 40–2.   [31] Ibid.
[32] See 'IMP—Interface Message Processor', <http://www.livinginternet.com/i/ii_imp.htm>.
[33] The literal meaning of the acronym IMP may not be incidental.

contacted Baran to get advice on distributed communication and packet switching.[34]

Roberts believed that the network should start out with only four sites: UCLA, Stanford Research Institute (SRI), the University of Utah, and the University of California at Santa Barbara. In July 1968 a request for proposals went out to 140 companies. More than a dozen bids were submitted, including bids from IBM and Control Data Corporation. A major defence contractor, Raytheon, was selected for further negotiations in December. Therefore, it came as somewhat of a surprise that the contract was awarded to the small consulting firm Bolt Beranek and Newman (BBN). Licklider, now at MIT, was perhaps not surprised—he was the one who, before his ARPA days, had turned BBN onto the path of computer design and development.[35]

The IMPs were based on Honeywell DDP-516 minicomputers, configured with 12,000 16-bit words of memory, making them among the most powerful minicomputers available at the time.[36] The first IMP was delivered to UCLA on 30 August 1969.[37] It was linked to the SDS Sigma 7 host computer using the SEX operating system.[38] Soon thereafter, IMPs were installed at the other three sites of the experimental network. At SRI, the IMP was linked to an SDS-940 using the GENIE operating system.[39] At the University of California at Santa Barbara, it was linked to an IBM 360/75 using OS/MTV, while at the University of Utah, it was linked to a DEC PDP-10 using the TENEX operating system.[40] Even this small, four-node initial installation illustrates very well how the network was used to battle the incompatibility of data formats, etc., born from the very different operating systems.

---

[34] See, *inter alia*, Judy O'Neill, 'The Role of ARPA in the Development of the ARPANET', *IEEE Annals of the History of Computing*, 1995, vol. 17, no. 4, 76, 78–9; Janet Abbate, *Inventing the Internet* (Cambridge, Massachusetts: MIT Press, 1999), 57.

[35] BBN was (and remains) based in Cambridge, Massachusetts, which is also the home state of Senator Ted Kennedy. Kennedy is reported to have sent the firm a telegram of congratulations for winning a contract to develop an 'interfaith message processor'. See 'IMP—Interface Message Processor', <http://www.livinginternet.com/i/ii_imp.htm>.

[36] Ronda Hauben, 'The Birth and Development of the ARPANET', in Michael Hauben and Ronda Hauben, *Netizens: On the History and Impact of Usenet and the Internet* (Los Alamitos: IEEE Computer Society Press, 1997), 119. A draft version of Ronda Hauben's chapter is available at <http://www.columbia.edu/~rh120/ch106.x08>.

[37] Ibid. 119.

[38] Ibid. 120. However, the draft version of Hauben's chapter, available at <http://www.columbia.edu/~rh120/ch106.x08>, designates GENIE as the operating system used.

[39] Ibid. 120. However, the draft version of Hauben's chapter, available at <http://www.columbia.edu/~rh120/ch106.x08>, designates SEX as the operating system used.

[40] Ibid.

```
Network Working Group                              Steve Crocker
Request for Comments: 1                                    UCLA
                                                   7 April 1969


                     Title: Host Software
                     Author: Steve Crocker
                     Installation: UCLA
                     Date: 7 April 1969
          Network Working Group Request for Comment: 1
```

Figure 1.3. Title of RFC 1

The sites were required to establish the necessary protocols for communication. In 1968, a group calling itself the Network Working Group (NWG) began to establish a set of documents that would be available to everyone involved for consideration and discussion. This group can be seen as an early example of 'Internet governance'. Although the Internet had not yet been established, many of the practices of the NWG form the basis of the governance culture that later developed. For instance, the compilation of documents was introduced in a low key, using the terminology 'Request for Comment' (RFC). The first RFC, dated 7 April 1969, was circulated by Steve Crocker to the other NWG participants—in the form of a paper document, and using the conventional mail system (Figure 1.3).

By the end of 1969 researchers began distributing RFCs in the then operating ARPANET.

Over the ensuing two years, the ARPANET expanded considerably. Below is indicated the first three stages of this network growth, from September 1969 to March 1971 (Figure 1.4).

There has been discussion about the real reason behind the ARPA effort. Was it really only to facilitate cooperation between the institutions working on project budgets extended by ARPA? Or was the real objective a better communication solution, eventually to be used for military purposes? The argument for the latter view is rather convincing,[41] but it may not be necessary to see one explanation as excluding the other. In any case, the network was being constructed with astonishing speed. The original minicomputer was replaced with the less costly Honeywell 316,[42] and by 1973 there were 35 nodes, including a satellite link connecting California

---

[41] See further the review of evidence in Tor Nørretranders, *Stedet som ikke er: Fremtidens nærvær, netværk og internet* (Copenhagen: Aschehoug, 1997), 53–9.

[42] Which led to the IMP being renamed TIP for 'Terminal IMP'.

24

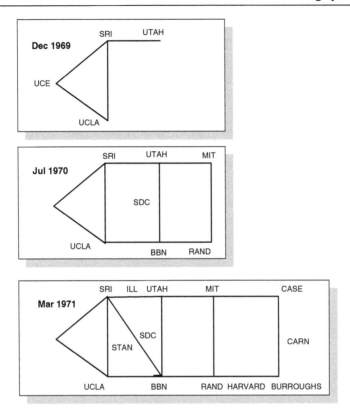

Figure 1.4. Initial growth of ARPANET

with a node in Hawaii. The Hawaiian connection constituted the first link-up of ARPANET to another communications network, this being the wireless ALOHA network developed at the University of Hawaii.[43]

1.6. Vinton G. Cerf and Robert E. Kahn

In 1972, Larry Roberts recruited Robert E. Kahn from BBN, where he had been important in the design of the IMP, to work on network technologies at ARPA. Later that year, Kahn played a pivotal role in Roberts' plans to make ARPANET more widely known. In October 1972, ARPANET was

[43] See Hafner and Lyon, *Where Wizards Stay Up Late*, 220. Norman Anderson and Franklin Kuo were the primary architects of the ALOHA network, with funding provided by ARPA. ALOHA was a packet-switched network using signals from small radios as communications medium. The network was an important forerunner to the Ethernet.

displayed to the public at the first International Conference on Computer Communication (ICCC) held at the Hotel Hilton in Washington, DC. A node was installed in the hotel via which Kahn was able to connect to 40 different computers, thus bringing the project into the limelight for researchers around the globe.

At around the same time, Vinton G. Cerf, a researcher working on an ARPA project at Stanford University, became chairman of the International Network Working Group (INWG), inspired by the earlier NWG. The charter of the group was to establish common technical standards to enable any computer to connect to the ARPANET.

The cooperation between Kahn and Cerf seems to have been one of those rare combinations which make the product larger than the sum of the components. Starting in early 1973, they addressed the problem of designing a general communication protocol for the packet-switched networks to replace the Network Control Protocol of ARPANET. Part of the problem was that the networks themselves would be autonomous, and linking them would need some type of universal joint. Cerf and Kahn found this joint in using gateway computers, and most importantly, transmission control protocol (TCP) messages. Under the framework described by Cerf and Kahn, messages were encapsulated and de-capsulated, the capsules only read by the gateways, while the contents would be read by the receiving hosts. The system is comparable with shipping containers. The container may be loaded with anything, but has a standard text indicating its address and a few other data. Exactly which mode of transporting the container is used—ship, rail, or truck—does not matter. All that is necessary is specialized equipment to move the container from one mode of transport to another. Similarly, the TCP can move across different networks on its journey from sender to addressee.

The new protocol presumed that the networks were unreliable. Packets might be lost or duplicated. If a packet failed to arrive or was garbled on arrival, and the sending host did not get an acknowledgement, an identical twin was re-transmitted. Reliability was shifted to the destination host, the system focusing on end-to-end reliability.

This scheme was described in the paper 'A Protocol for Packet Networks Intercommunication' which was finished by the end of 1973, and published in April 1974[44] (Figure 1.5).

---

[44] See *IEEE Transactions on Communication Technology*, May 1974, vol. Com-22, No. 5, 627–41. One will note that the term 'internetwork' occurs in the abstract, but the term 'Internet' had not yet been created with the meaning used today.

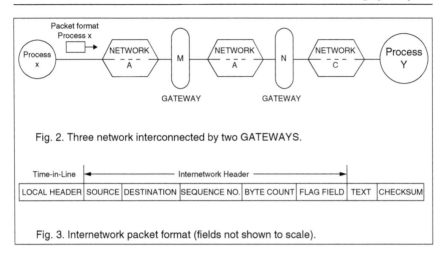

Fig. 2. Three network interconnected by two GATEWAYS.

| LOCAL HEADER | SOURCE | DESTINATION | SEQUENCE NO. | BYTE COUNT | FLAG FIELD | TEXT | CHECKSUM |

Fig. 3. Internetwork packet format (fields not shown to scale).

Figure 1.5. Cerf and Kahn's diagrams of TCP functionality

Abstract—A protocol that supports the sharing of resources that exist in different packet switching networks is presented. The protocol provides for variation in individual network packet sizes, transmission failures, sequencing, flow control, end-to-end error checking, and the creation and destruction of logical process-to-process connections. Some implementation issues are considered, and problems such as Internetwork routing, accounting, and timeouts are exposed.

The TCP was introduced in 1977 for cross-network connections, and slowly began to replace the NCP within the original ARPANET. The TCP was faster, easier to use, and less expensive to implement than NCP. In 1978, IP (Internet Protocol) was added to TCP, and took over the routing of messages. The two protocols are so closely related that they generally are referred to as TCP/IP. From 1983, any system not using the TCP/IP protocol was not accepted (see below).[45]

[45] Cerf (with Yogen Galai and Carl Sunshine) wrote RFC 675, which gives the first complete specification of TCP in December 1974. In 1976, Ray Tomlinson (with Jerry D. Birchfiel and William Plummer) suggested revisions to the specification. Cerf wrote the specification for TCP 2 in March 1977, and three networks were linked up using the protocol—packet radio, ARPANET, and SATNET. In January 1978, Cerf and Jon Postel wrote the TCP version 3 specifications, in which IP split from TCP—IP taking care of routing the packets, and TCP taking care of packeting, error control, re-transmission, and re-assembly. Jon Postel wrote the fourth specification for both protocol elements later in 1978, revising it again in 1979. RCF 760 and 761 of January 1980 outline the specification, and, in February

In the early 1970s—particularly after the ICCC in 1972—researchers in a number of other countries began taking an active interest in ARPANET. The bias of the author makes it natural to mention that Lawrence Roberts and Robert Kahn visited Norway in October 1972, and met with members of the Norwegian Defence Research Establishment at Kjeller just outside Oslo. One of the major objectives of ARPA was the monitoring of seismic disturbances indicating a nuclear explosion for research purposes. This was a reason for the interest in Norway, as a granite formation starting in Russia surfaces close to the city of Hamar in southern Norway, and was monitored by the Norwegian Seismic Array (NORSAR), a neighbour institution to the Defence Research Establishment at Kjeller. In June 1973, an agreement was concluded to establish a link from ARPANET by satellite to the ground station Tanum on the Swedish west coast close to the Norwegian border, and by wire from there to Kjeller.[46] Shortly afterwards, a link was established between Kjeller and University College, London (UCL). Norway therefore became the first country outside the United States to have a node to the ARPANET, just ahead of the UK. The University of Oslo and Technical University in Trondheim were also soon thereafter linked to the network.[47] In this way, Norwegian researchers were among the first outside the United States to start using the ARPANET and gain experience in the possibilities of the new network technology.

1.7. Ray Tomlinson and E-mail

The ARPANET was not designed for sending messages but for sharing resources. The two characteristic services for the net were Telnet and FTP (file transport protocol). Telnet made it possible to sit at one location working on a computer located somewhere else. The file transport protocol allowed files to be moved from one computer to the other.[48]

There are stories of how ARPANET was used for trivial tasks, like when an attendee at a conference at the University of Sussex, UK, on arrival

1980, TCP/IP became the preferred military protocol. Further on the basic elements of TCP/IP, see RFC 1180: A TCP/IP Tutorial (authors: T. Socolofsky and C. Kale) (January 1991), <http://www.ietf.org/rfc/rfc1180.txt>.

[46] On the Norwegian side, Yngvar Lundh and Pål Spilling—then researchers at the Defence Research Establishment—were particularly instrumental in forging this development.

[47] See generally Arild Haraldsen, *50 år—og bare begynnelsen* (Oslo: Cappelen, 2003), 250–1.

[48] See Nørretrander, *Stedet som ikke er*, 69.

home in Los Angeles discovered that he had left his electric shaver at the conference, and was then able to use a program to identify who was logged onto the network in Sussex and the associated teletype number, and in this way send a message that succeeded in bringing his shaver back home.[49] In telling the tale, there is an undertone similar to an anecdote of a schoolboy using a piece of expensive laboratory equipment for a prank—the communication was possible, but it was not what really should be transmitted through expensive cables and satellite links.

Yet e-mail of a sort had already been developed for time-sharing computers, making it possible for users of the shared computer to exchange messages. Ray Tomlinson[50] of BBN had written a mail program running under TENEX, the operating system which BBN had developed for PDP-10, and which was running on most of ARPANET's PDP-10 computers. The program was in two parts, SNDMSG and READMAIL. BBN had two PDP-10 computers in Cambridge, Massachusetts. Tomlinson had written an experimental file transfer protocol called CPYNET, and it occurred to him that this program could be modified to carry a mail from one machine and store it as a file on the other. This was the breakthrough for e-mail. When finalizing the specifications for ARPANET's file transfer protocol, it was decided to slap Tomlinson's programs onto the protocol. The result was MAIL and MLFL, the first electronic mail twins of ARPANET.[51]

ARPANET was never designed for electronic mail but for more serious and sombre research needs. However, the use of the network had fallen somewhat short of what had been expected. The net at this time was sometimes described as an impressive cathedral where the congregation was missing. However, e-mail (and usegroups, see below) soon filled the pews.

Tomlinson became well known for his mail system. Yet his real fame is related to a single sign. While there are many who become famous for a single novel or a single tune, Tomlinson is one of the few to become famous for a single sign. This sign is, of course, the '@'.

For his program, Tomlinson needed a way to separate in an e-mail address the name of the user from the machine on which the user was working. He wanted a character that could not be found under any conceivable circumstances in the name of the user. Studying his teletype

---

[49] See Hafner and Lyon, *Where Wizards Stay Up Late*, 187–8.

[50] Tomlinson is mentioned above (footnote 45) as one of the co-authors of the TCP amendments suggested in 1976.

[51] Hafner and Lyon, *Where Wizards Stay Up Late*, 191–2.

keyboard, there were about a dozen characters for termination of sentences and other syntactical functions. He picked '@'. This also had the advantage of meaning 'at' the designated machine or institution.

The origin of the character itself remained unknown for quite a while. In 2000, Professor Giorgio Stabile of La Sapienza University in Rome found a letter written by a Florentine merchant, Fransesco Lapi, in 1536.[52] This contains the oldest known document using the sign '@'. Lapi tells of the arrival to Spain of three ships loaded with gold and silver from Latin America. He writes that 'there, an @ with wine, which is one thirtieth of a barrel, is worth 70 or 80 ducats'. In his letter, '@' is an abbreviation for 'amphora', which was a measure of capacity used in transport around the Mediterranean. Earlier theories held that the sign originated in the late Middle ages as a 'd' written in italics with a left hand curve to indicate 'ad', which means 'at'. In English, the sign is often referred to as 'commercial at', in Spanish as 'arroba'. The measure was for a long time used in the trade between Venice and the north of Europe, here gaining meaning as 'price per unit'. And looking at the form of a typical amphora, one can appreciate that the '@' is a simplified outline of the container, emphasizing the handles.[53]

Apart from simple e-mail, other services emerged. One service emerging in 1975 was network mailing lists, the first being Message Services Group, or MsgGroup. Multiplayer games were developed, like Adventure. News Groups appeared for any topic about which one wanted to share information. Along with this increased use came also informal rules for behaviour and sanctions for violating them—often referred to as netiquette.[54]

---

[52] See further P. Willan, 'Merchant@florence wrote it first 500 years ago', *The Guardian*, 31 July 2000, <http://www.guardian.co.uk/international/story/0,3604,348744,00.html>, last accessed 29 April 2008; B. Giussani, 'A Brief History of @', *The Industry Standard*, 7 May 2001, <http://www.thestandard.com/article/0,1902,24139,00.html>, last accessed 29 April 2008.

[53] While English-speaking users pronounce the sign with little imagination as 'at', it has found an impressive variety in other languages. In Norwegian it is called 'alfakrøll', which means something like 'alpha twirl'. In Swedish it is called 'kanelbulle', a type of traditional sweet roll with cinnamon, or 'elefantöre' (elephant ear), or 'snabel-a' (an 'a' with the trunk of an elephant), the latter expression being perhaps more common. In Finnish is used 'kissanhäntä' (the tail of a cat), or 'miuk-mauku' (which perhaps only means 'meow'). In German it is called 'Klammeraffe' (a monkey clutching to something), and in Dutch 'apestaartje' (tail of a monkey). In Italian it is known as 'chiocciola' (snail), and in Greek 'papaki' (a small duck). In Israel it is called 'shtrudel', which similarly to the Swedish name refers to bakery. In Japanese there are several names, among them 'naruto', which is the name of a fish sausage with a pink spiral pattern, or 'uzumaki', used for the same sausage, but also used for a maelstrom. See further *Lov&Data*, 1999, number 58, 1–2.

[54] See further Chapter 3 (section 3.3).

1.8. The National Science Foundation[55]

The ARPANET was threatening to split the research community into those who had access to it and those who had not. By the end of the 1970s, the number of academic computer science departments in the United States exceeded 100, while only 15 of the then more than 60 ARPANET nodes were located within universities. The computer science departments were generally not allowed to be linked to ARPANET. The latter was meant to remain closed to those not involved in special research funded by government, that research typically being related to defence matters.

In May 1979, on the invitation of Larry Landweber of the University of Wisconsin, discussions were initiated on building a Computer Science Research Network (CSNET). At this time, the National Science Foundation (NSF) emerged as a major player. The NSF was established in 1950 to promote science by funding basic research and strengthening education. At the end of the 1970s, the NSF was taking a strong interest in computer science, and was in a position to act on behalf of the whole scientific community. However, the NSF did not approve the first draft for CSNET. The draft was revised in 1980 in order to make participation affordable, also for the smaller computer science departments.[56] A three-tiered structure was proposed, involving ARPANET, a TELNET-based system, and an e-mail-only service called PhoneNet, connected by gateways.

This was approved by the NSF, which agreed to support the CSNET for a period of five years. A unique governing system was established. For the first two years, the NSF itself would manage the university consortium. After this period, the University Corporation for Atmospheric Research (UCAR) would take over. The UCAR was familiar with advanced computers and had the management experience to handle cooperation between several universities.

By June 1983, more than 70 sites were online, and at the end of the five-year period, nearly all of the computer science departments of the United States, as well as a large number of private computer facilities, were connected—and the network was financially stable. More networks appeared in the wake of CSNET, for instance BITNET,[57] which was a cooperation between IBM systems with no restrictions on membership.

It is in this period—the middle of the 1980s—that a distinction emerged in the use of the term 'Internet'. Spelled with a small 'i', it meant any

---

[55] Much of this section is based on Hafner and Lyon, *Where Wizards Stay Up Late*, 240–56.

[56] At this time, the annual costs for maintaining an ARPANET site exceeded US$100,000.

[57] An abbreviation of 'Because It's Time Network'.

network using the TCP/IP protocol; spelled with a capital 'I' it meant the public, federally sponsored network that was made up of many linked networks, all running TCP/IP. At this time, router vendors started to sell equipment to construct private Internets, and the distinction between these networks and the public network blurred as the private nets built gateways to the public. Also at this time, networks using TCP/IP were established in other countries, particularly Canada and Europe. In Norway, Uninett had been running as a research project since 1978.

In 1985, five supercomputer centres distributed throughout the United States offered a solution for establishing a national network. The NSF agreed to build a backbone network between these sites, to become known as NSFNET. Academic institutions in a given geographical area were offered to establish a community network; the NSF would then give this network access to the backbone network. Not only would the regional networks get access to the backbone but also to each other. The NSF provided the backbone as a 'free good', but grants to connect campuses to regional networks were limited to two years; after that time, the universities had to pay for the regional connections themselves.

ARPANET made the official transition to TCP/IP on 1 January 1983. The funding by the NSF of CSNET led to partitioning in 1984 of MILNET, the part of Internet that carried unclassified military traffic, and ARPANET for research and non-military use.

In 1979, ARPA established a small Internet Configuration Control Board (ICCB), most of whose members belonged to the research community, to help ARPA in shaping Internet design. The establishment of the ICCB was important because it brought a wider segment of the research community into the Internet decision-making process, which until then had been almost exclusively the bailiwick of ARPA. As interest in the ARPA Internet grew, so did interest in the work of the ICCB. In 1984, ARPA replaced the ICCB with the Internet Advisory Board (IAB). The new board was constituted similarly to the old ICCB, but the many issues of network design were delegated to 10 task forces chartered by and reporting to the IAB.[58]

---

[58] See further Robert E. Kahn, 'The Role of Government in the Evolution of the Internet', <http://www.nap.edu/readingroom/books/newpath/chap2.html>. Note that the name of the IAB was subsequently changed twice, eventually ending up as 'Internet Architecture Board' (in 1992). See further 'A Brief History of the Internet Advisory/Activities/Architecture Board', <http://www.iab.org/about/history.html>.

1.9. The War of Protocols

During the 1980s, the status of the TCP/IP protocol as a chief basis for computer network communication was challenged by the International Organization for Standards (ISO), which had started in the late 1970s to develop a network reference model called Open-Systems Interconnection (OSI).[59] The ISO proposed to replace TCP/IP with OSI. Many of the major computer vendors of the time subscribed to the proposal. They saw TCP/IP as having been developed ad hoc and mainly for the requirements of the research community. In their view, OSI constituted a more systematic approach. Critics of OSI maintained, on the other hand, that OSI was bureaucratic and abstract, and more complicated and compartmentalized in its design than TCP/IP. The ISO produced standards for OSI in 1988, with the US government adopting it as its official standard shortly thereafter. One would have thought that this development effectively closed the lid on widespread deployment of the TCP/IP, in spite of its adoption by the US military in 1983.

The UNIX operating system was to prove, however, of crucial importance for further use of TCP/IP. UNIX was developed by AT&T's Bell laboratory in the early 1970s. It became popular with programmers, mainly because it was sufficiently flexible to be tailored for whatever program they were working on, and sufficiently portable to work on many different computers. In the late 1970s, a brand of UNIX was developed in Berkeley, and became very popular for academic institutions around the world. And in 1981, the TCP/IP was written into a version of Berkeley UNIX by Bill Joy.

Joy joined a couple of graduates from Stanford in 1982 who were starting a company which would be selling 'workstations' more powerful by several magnitudes than the personal computers launched by IBM. The company was called SUN Microsystems, SUN being an acronym of Stanford University Network. The first SUN computers were sold with Berkeley UNIX, including the integrated TCP/IP—network software was included without extra costs.

This was the time of the distribution of computer solutions. At the beginning of the 1980s, computer systems were generally based on terminals hooked into a mainframe or a departmental mini-computer. This was also the basic structure for the ARPANET, CSNET, and other

---

[59] See further Andrew L. Russell, "Rough Consensus and Running Code' and the Internet-OSI Standards War', *IEEE Annals of the History of Computing*, 2006, vol. 28, no. 3, 48–61.

networks—the end user accessed these networks through terminals which were connected to larger computers, which again were connected to the network.

Then the PC came along. On 12 August 1981, IBM released its first PCs. The 'PC' stood for 'personal computer', PC being really a trademark of IBM. The first IBM PC ran on a 4.77 MHz Intel 8088 microprocessor. It came equipped with 16 kb of memory, expandable to 256 k, two 160 k floppy disk drives, and an optional colour monitor. The price tag started at US$1,565. What really made the IBM PC different from other computers was that it was the first to be built from off-the-shelf parts and marketed by outside distributors. The Intel chip was chosen because IBM had already obtained the rights to manufacture the chips.[60]

The PC rapidly automated offices. One lifted the traditional typewriter off the desk, and placed a PC onto the empty space. The microcomputers were not, like the terminals, hooked up to a central computer. The resources for processing and storage were on the desk of the user. This was attractive, though not necessarily a functional improvement. Communication was a headache; even sharing a printer between two PCs could be cumbersome. The PCs were used for tasks which the terminals had not been used for, like word-processing and spread-sheets. On the other hand, the communication which was necessary for a terminal to function was not essential for a PC, and therefore communication was lost—at least for a while. The emergence of the PC constituted initially a rather abrupt change of paradigm, and the focus of development shifted for a while towards the distribution of computer resources and office automation.

In 1973, Bob Metcalfe and his team at Xerox PARC had designed a local area network called Ethernet. It was an efficient solution for tying computers together, either on a campus or within a company. By 1980, Xerox started to market Ethernet as a commercial solution. This snowballed with other companies joining in; the workstations became interconnected through local area networks (LANs). Ethernet made it possible to connect a LAN to the ARPANET. Two LANs using Ethernet could interconnect through the ARPANET hub.

Thus, a situation was built up step by step, first introducing separate PCs or workstations, then connecting them together to a LAN, and then connecting the LANs through ARPANET. The TCP/IP protocol made this

---

[60] See Mary Bellis, 'Inventors of the Modern Computer—The History of the IBM PC', <http://inventors.about.com/library/weekly/aa031599.htm>, last accessed 29 April 2008.

easy. The TCP/IP was open—software was freely available. Also, a simple mail transfer protocol (STMP) was brought out. Together, these factors made TCP/IP come out on top as the preferred way to communicate.

1.10. The Domain Name System

The growth of the networks created a new problem. Craig Partridge, a chief scientist at BBN, is quoted as saying that this problem started to become evident when the number of host computers rose above 2,000. Each host computer had to be given a name, and 'everyone wanted [their host computer] to be named Frodo'.[61]

To sort out the problem, Jon Postel, Paul Mockapetris, and Craig Partridge devised the Domain Name System (DNS).[62] Using three months to work out the details, they introduced the scheme in November 1983, using tree-branching as metaphor. Each address had a hierarchical structure, and after some debate, a specific-to-general addressing scheme was adopted. Eventually, a committee agreed on seven top-level domains: .edu, .com, .gov, .mil, .net, .org, and .int. ARPA began requiring adoption of the DNS in 1985. In January 1986, general acceptance for the DNS was secured at a grand summit meeting on the US West Coast at which all major networks were represented.

The Internet Assigned Number Authority (IANA) was informally established in the early 1980s. It succeeded the first central numbering authority of the network, the Network Information Center (NIC), which was located at the Stanford Research Institute and which would assign host names and distribute a HOSTS.TXT-file. IANA was primarily managed by Jon Postel at the Information Sciences Institute, University of Southern California, under a contract with ARPA. IANA was generally responsible for allocation of all globally unique names and numbers used in Internet protocols, published as Requests for Comments (RFCs). Postel managed IANA from when it was established until his death in October 1998,[63] and became a legend in his own time. He was able nearly single-handedly to exercise the central function and authority of IANA partly for historical reasons and partly because he did it well.[64]

---

[61] Quoted in Hafner and Lyon, *Where Wizards Stay Up Late*, 252. Frodo is, of course, the protagonist in the trilogy, *The Lord of the Rings*, by J. R. R. Tolkien.

[62] Mockapetris is often named as the central person in designing the scheme. The DNS is described in more detail in Chapter 5 (Section 5.1.2).

[63] Postel was also the RFC editor.   [64] Further on IANA, see Chapter 3 (Section 3.2.7).

The Defense Data Network-Network Information Center (DDN-NIC) at Stanford Research Institute handled the actual registration services, including the top-level domains, and Internet number assignment under a contract with the Department of Defense. In 1991, responsibility for the administration and maintenance of DDN-NIC was given to Government Systems, Inc., which, in turn, subcontracted the function to a small company in the private sector, Network Solutions, Inc. As Internet growth at this time occurred mainly outside the military sector, it was decided that the Department of Defense would no longer fund the registration services outside the .mil top-level domain, and, in 1992, the NSF created Inter-NIC to manage the allocation of addresses and address databases. Inter-NIC was a cooperation between three organizations: Network Solutions (which provided registration services); AT&T (which provided directory and database services); and General Atomics (which provided information services).

In January 1998, an agency of the US Department of Commerce, the National Telecommunications and Information Administration, issued a proposal to largely privatize DNS management under the umbrella of a non-profit corporation. That corporation emerged in September 1998 in the form of the Internet Corporation for Assigned Names and Numbers (ICANN). In December 1998, the University of Southern California made an agreement with ICANN to transfer the IANA function to ICANN, effective 1 January 1999. Thus, from that time on, ICANN assumed the functionalities of both IANA and InterNIC.[65]

1.11. End of 'Act One'

By the close of the 1980s, the Internet was no longer a star configuration with ARPANET as the hub. It was more like a decentralized network, like ARPANET itself. The NSFNET had made the network even more available than CSNET—anyone on a college campus could become an Internet user. The NSFNET was becoming the backbone of the Internet, operating connections more than 25 times as fast as the ARPANET. The number of computers in the world connected to each other through the NSFNET far outnumbered those connected by ARPANET, which became just one of hundreds of networks.

[65] Further on ICANN and the process leading to its formation, see Chapter 3 (Section 3.2.8) and references cited therein.

At the end of 1989, ARPANET itself was decommissioned—to use the jargon then favoured by the Department of Defense. There was a certain melancholy in turning off the IMPs and TIPs, progressing to new network technology. It has been mentioned that this brought to mind the scene from Stanley Kubrick's film '2001: A Space Odyssey', where HAL, the huge artificial intelligence computer of the spacecraft,[66] is dismantled circuit by circuit.[67] The network may have been decommissioned, but its parts lived on, as the clusters of ARPANET sites were taken over by regional networks.

The year 1989 was also the twentieth anniversary for ARPANET's creation. To mark the occasion, UCLA sponsored a symposium called 'Act One'. More acts were, of course, to follow.

The policy of NSF was to reserve the Internet for scientific or research use; commercial activities were not permitted. This was generally approved, but—as any lawyer would readily explain—'commercial' is an ambiguous criterion. Other networks did not have this restriction, especially the UUCPNET, which was the store-and-forward network consisting of all of the world's connected UNIX machines and others running some clone of Unix-to-Unix CoPy software. Any machine reachable only via a bang path (an old-style UUCP electronic-mail address specifying hops to get from some assumed, reachable location to the addressee) was on UUCPNET. This led to the barring of UUCPNET from ARPANET and NSFNET, but some links remained open, and a blind eye was turned towards these links. Internet service providers (ISPs) started to be formed in the late 1980s to provide services to the regional research networks and alternative network access. The first dial-up ISP—world.std.com—opened in 1989, and the final commercial restrictions ended in March 1991.

The abolition of these restrictions caused controversy among the traditional users of the Internet, who resisted the network becoming available to sites not working with education or research. By 1994, NSFNET—which by now had been renamed ANSNET (Advanced Networks and Services), and which allowed non-profit corporations to access the network—lost its standing as the backbone of Internet. Both government institutions and competing commercial providers created alternative backbones and interconnections. Regional network access points (NAPs) became the primary interconnections between the many networks.[68]

---

[66] HAL is a pun on IBM, using the adjacent letters of the alphabet.

[67] According to Mark Pullen of the ARPA, cited in Hafner and Lyon, *Where Wizards Stay Up Late*, 255.

[68] See generally <http://en.wikipedia.org/wiki/History_of_the_Internet>.

This is the overture to Act Two, and 1995 is often named as the year when the Internet emerged as a commercial environment. To appreciate the reasons for this commercialization, one should look at the services available on the net. In the discussion above, only e-mail has been singled out. There were, however, many other services—like Internet Relay Chat (IRC), newsgroups, Gopher, and so on—in addition to those already briefly mentioned like File Transfer Protocol (FTP) and telnet. And there were new shareware applications, such as Trumpet Winsock, which facilitated easy access by ordinary PC users to the net.[69] It was the combination of the utility of the services and the availability through the net that explained the further development. In this development, one application—the 'killer application'—was crucial: the World Wide Web.

1.12. Inquire Within Upon Everything

In 1856, a 'comprehensive guide to the necessities of domestic life in Victorian Britain' was published. It attempted to explain all the small secrets of daily life then in 2,775 entries. It tells one if food is fresh and when it is in season, how to dance, the difference between dialects, the rules of games and puzzles, and so on. Whatever one's question, this book gives an answer, often to the most surprising things. However, to a modern reader, the items are organized in a rather puzzling manner; a systematic approach like that of Dewey or Otlet, mentioned above, had not been adopted. The best search function is the alphabetic list of keywords in the back of the book. One favourite entry, confirming the prejudice of some persons against English cuisine, starts in this way:

> **2274. English Champagne**—Take fifty pounds of rhubarb and thirty-seven pounds of fine moist sugar. Provide a tub that will hold fifteen to twenty gallons, taking care that it has a hole for a tap near the bottom . . . [70]

---

[69] The PC had initially limited possibilities to run Internet applications; in practice, one had to link into the net via a minicomputer or a workstation. However, in the early 1990s, Peter Tartan, working at the University of Tasmania, wrote a shareware program called Trumpet Winsock that gave a PC using Microsoft Windows a point-to-point connection using dial-up servers offered by the emerging Internet Service Providers. The program was a great success, and in the mid-1990s constituted the primary way for PC users to access the net. See further Jonathan Zittrain, *The Future of the Internet and How to Stop It* (New Haven: Yale University Press, 2008), 29.

[70] Taken from the 82nd edition published in 1880. This is available in facsimile from Old House Books, Devon.

The book became immensely popular with more than 1 million copies sold. And it was destined to become a sort of metaphor, bridging the gap between the nineteenth and late twentieth centuries, when Tim Berners-Lee commenced work on development of the World Wide Web. 'With its title suggestive of magic, the book served as a portal to a world of information, everything from how to remove clothing stains to tips on investing money. Not a perfect analogy for the Web, but a primitive starting point.'[71]

In 1980, Berners-Lee joined the European Laboratory for Particle Physics (CERN)[72] as a consultant. The institution is situated in France, just across the border from Geneva, Switzerland. Several documentation systems were available at this time for the collaborative research at CERN, but none that met the standards of Berners-Lee. He wanted a program that could store random links between otherwise unconnected pieces of information. 'Suppose all the information stored on computers everywhere were linked', I thought. 'Suppose I could programme my computer to create a space in which anything could be linked with anything.'[73]

His first program, Enquire, was made for a ND[74] computer and had a simple sign-on:[75]

```
At SINTRAN III command level, type
@(GUEST)ENQUIRE < params >
and the system should respond
Enquire V x.x
Hello!
```

The Enquire program facilitated some random linkage between information and proved personally useful for Berners-Lee. However, it could not cope with a wide area network and, accordingly, could not facilitate the collaboration that was desired for in the international high-energy physics research community. Tim Berners-Lee thus set about revising and

[71] Tim Berners-Lee, *Weaving the Web* (London/New York: Texere, 2000), 1.
[72] CERN is derived from the original French name for the laboratory, Conseil Européen pour la Recherche Nucléaire. The official English name is European Organization for Nuclear Research.
[73] Berners-Lee, *Weaving the Web*, 4.
[74] 'ND' stands for 'Norsk Data', a Norwegian manufacturer of minicomputer systems, which came with their own SINTRAN operating system. The company went bankrupt at the end of the 1980s.
[75] From Tim Berners-Lee, 'The ENQUIRE System—Short Description', manual version 1.1 of October 1980, <http://infomesh.net/2001/enquire/manual/>, last accessed 29 April 2008.

refining the ideas behind Enquire. This work bore fruition in a proposal for information management at CERN which he initially put forward in March 1989. The proposal may be seen as an extension of the idea behind the Internet service Gopher, but was also inspired by some of the work done on hypertext by Ted Nelson in his Xanadu project.[76] The proposal, which was not embraced at first sight, was revised by Tim Berners-Lee and Robert Cailliau in May 1990.[77] The proposal included the use of HTML (HyperText Markup Language) to write documents,[78] HTTP (HyperText Transfer Protocol) to transmit the pages,[79] and a browser client to interpret and display the received results. An important feature was that the client's user interface should be consistent across all types of computer platforms, making it possible for the user to access data from many types of computers.[80]

The CERN eventually decided to sponsor the project, which Berners-Lee named 'World Wide Web'. The interface was used in March 1991 on a minor network of NeXT computers. By August of that year, Berners-Lee released basic web server software for any machine.[81]

1.13. The Web Illustrated

At the time the World Wide Web was starting to become known, Marc Andreessen was a student at the National Center for Supercomputing Applications (NCSA) at the University of Illinois. He became familiar both with the Internet and with the World Wide Web. At this time, the

[76] Ted Nelson coined the term 'hypertext', and his Xanadu project, begun in 1960, was the first research project focused on developing a hypertext-based software system. See further <http://en.wikipedia.org/wiki/Project_Xanadu>.

[77] The proposal (as revised) is set out in an appendix to Berners-Lee, *Weaving the Web*.

[78] HTML is a mark-up language related to SGML, usually rendered as an acronym for Standard General Markup Language, but GML is composed of the initials to the three persons behind the formalism: Charles F. Goldfarb, Ed Mosher, and Ray Lorie. Goldfarb was a lawyer who started to work for IBM in 1967. As different printers were using different formats, Goldfarb tried to solve this by marking up a text in a general way, and replacing the printer-specific codes on the selection of the printer. The first comprehensive user guide to GML was published by Goldfarb in 1978. This was picked up by standardizing organizations, and SGML was adopted as ISO 8879:1986. In the latter part of the work, Anders Berglund of CERN played a prominent part, and in this way the SGML became also a basis for HTML. See, inter alia, 'SGML 30 år: Det sto en jurist bak', *Lov&Data*, 2004, no. 77, 10.

[79] Further on HTTP, see RFC 2616: Hypertext Transfer Protocol—HTTP/1.1 (authors: R. Fielding, J. Gettys, J. Mogul, H. Frystyk, L. Masinter, P. Leach, and T. Berners-Lee) (June 1999), <http://www.ietf.org/rfc/rfc2616.txt>.

[80] See further T. Berners-Lee, 'The World Wide Web: Past, Present and Future' (August 1996), <http://www.w3.org/People/Berners-Lee/1996/ppf.html>.

[81] Berners-Lee, *Weaving the Web*, 50–1.

latter was used mainly by those for which it was developed: academics and engineers. The browsers were mainly designed for UNIX computers; they were expensive and not very user-friendly. Marc Andreessen set out to develop a browser that was easy to use and richer in graphics. He recruited a colleague, Eric Bina, and together they developed Mosaic. It permitted richer formatting with tags like 'center', and included an 'image' tag that allowed the inclusion of images on web pages. It also had a graphical interface and—like most of the early web browsers (though not the original CERN 'linemode browser')—clickable buttons and hyperlinks; rather than using reference numbers which the user had to type in for accessing the linked documents, hyperlinks allowed the user simply to click the link.

Mosaic 1.0 was publicly released in April 1993.[82] Its success was immense and immediate: within weeks, 10,000 copies of the browser had been downloaded. The original version had been for UNIX, but Andreessen and Bina set up teams to develop versions for Windows and Macintosh through the summer of 1993. By December of that year, the news on Mosaic made it to the front page of the *New York Times* business section. Andreessen graduated the same month and moved to Palo Alto, California. There he met one of the major investors in the computer industry, Jim Clarke, the founder of Silicon Graphics, Inc. Together they created a new company, Mosiac Communications Corp., which started to develop a browser superior to Mosaic. On 13 October 1994, Netscape was posted for downloading on the Internet. Within weeks it was the browser of choice for the majority of web users. It included new HTML tags that allowed web designers greater control and creativity. However, there was a legal tangle with the University of Illinois, which claimed infringement of rights. The company changed name to Netscape Communications, and a settlement with the university was reached in December 1994.

The technology and trademarks behind Mosaic were licensed by the University of Illinois to a company called Spyglass, Inc., a company founded in 1990 to utilize intellectual property rights originating with the university. In 1995, Spyglass licensed the source code for Mosaic to Microsoft, which used the code as basis for developing Internet Explorer.[83] Thus, both Netscape and Internet Explorer have a common source.

Internet Explorer version 2 was launched in November 1995. It did not become very popular, but version 3, released in August 1996, rapidly

---

[82] The beta version had been publicly available from January 1993.

[83] See Sandi Hardmeier, 'The History of Internet Explorer', <http://www.microsoft.com/windows/ie/community/columns/historyofie.mspx>, last accessed 29 April 2008.

gained popularity. This browser was nearly a full rewrite of the program; little of the source code from Mosaic survived in this version.

One of the reasons for the rapid rise in popularity of Internet Explorer was that it came free of charge with the Windows operating system. This has given rise to legal issues: on the one side, claims have been made that the bundling is an unfair business practice, while Microsoft has counterclaimed that Internet Explorer constitutes an integrated part of its operating system, enabling, for instance, help-functions for its programs.[84]

By the late 1990s, Internet Explorer had decisively become the market leader. Netscape was acquired by America Online in 1999 and then formally closed down in 2003.[85] However, several other browsers continue to exist which compete fairly successfully with Internet Explorer. One example is Mozilla Firefox, which is developed by an open-source offshoot of Netscape. Another is Opera, which is developed by a Norwegian company and designed particularly for mobile telephone interfaces.

1.14. A Web with a View

In the spring of 1995, the research laboratory of Digital Equipment Corporation (DEC) in Palo Alto, California, introduced a new system based on the Alpha chip which was able to operate databases much faster than competing systems. To demonstrate the technology, it decided to index the World Wide Web.

The idea is basically simple, and one well known to lawyers, as the method is basic for all legal information services using text retrieval. Text retrieval may be related to the efforts of Dewey, Otlet, and Vannevar Bush discussed above. Traditional retrieval systems relied on an index of intellectually assigned terms—an indexer would consider a page, and decide which terms best characterized its content, often selecting terms from a pre-defined vocabulary. This was the way in which documents were indexed according to Dewey's or Otlet's classification systems.

Computers made possible an alternative approach. Each word of the text would be sorted alphabetically, retaining a reference ('address') to the location within the text. A user would then specify a search term, this would be matched to the index, and the pages containing those

---

[84] See, for example, the US litigation on point, manifest in *United States v. Microsoft Corp.*, 84 F.Supp.2d 9 (DDC 1999); *United States v. Microsoft Corp.*, 87 F.Supp.2d 30 (DDC 2000); *United States v. Microsoft Corp.*, 253 F.3d 34 (DC Cir. 2001).

[85] See <http://en.wikipedia.org/wiki/Mosaic_Communications_Corporation>.

words could be displayed. Or rather, the preferred format would be KWIC ('keyword in context'), showing the occurrences of the search term with its adjacent text. This format made relevance assessment easier: if the word occurred in a context relevant for the problem of the user, the address made access to the source readily available. More sophisticated search strategies were devised, typically using Boolean logical operators— e.g. find a text in which both the word 'Digital' and 'Equipment' occurs, or augmented to a requirement for these words to occur in the same sentence or adjacent. Ranking of retrieved documents according to different principles was also added.[86]

The first such system was successfully demonstrated by John F. Horty of the Health Law School, University of Pennsylvania, at an American Bar Association conference in 1960. It is far from coincidental that lawyers were the first to use such systems professionally. The intimate relationship between exact wording of a statute or regulation and interpretation for use in legal argument required access to the original, authentic text— solutions as abstract journals like 'Chemical Abstracts' were not viable. Although lawyers are not well known as figuring in the *avant garde* in technology use, they somewhat reluctantly pioneered text retrieval; major systems like Reid-Elsevier's LEXIS-NEXIS are examples of what has come out of this development.

The first Internet search engine was developed by a team led by Louis Monier at DEC's Western Research Laboratory. In August 1995, this search engine conducted its first full-scale 'crawl' of the World Wide Web. Using the Domain Name System, the crawler visited websites, utilizing the HTML-coding to identify interesting bits of a page, and communicating copies of these back to the home site for further processing. In its first trial, the crawler brought back some 10 million web pages.

The new service was called AltaVista—'the view from above'. It became available to the public on 15 December 1995 with an index of 16 million documents. It was an immediate success, with more than 300,000 searches being conducted the first day. At the end of 1996, it was handling 19 million requests daily.[87]

The miraculous quality of AltaVista and other search engines is not the search logic. Compared to the sophistication of professional text retrieval

[86] The history and theory of text retrieval is discussed in J. Bing, *Handbook of Legal Information Retrieval* (Amsterdam: North-Holland, 1984).

[87] See further 'AltaVista: A brief history of the AltaVista search engine', <http://www.websearchworkshop.co.uk/altavista_history.php>.

systems, the search 'language' is not very advanced. The miracle is the vast number of websites indexed, and the maintenance of this index.

Several other major search engines have been launched, including MSN, Lycos, and Yahoo! The latter swallowed Alta Vista in 2003. However, of all current search engines, the most popular is Google.

Larry Page and Sergey Brin, both graduates from Stanford University, started up Google in 1998 literarily in a garage in Menlo Park, California. The story of this company is yet another story of innovation and intuition. The first search engine they built was called BackRub, named for its ability to analyse the 'back links' pointing to a given website through hyperlinks.[88] Using citation frequency as a ranking criterion was well known for retrieval purposes,[89] but the integration of such links in the World Wide Web made them different from the formal references to literature, etc., in conventional texts. The ranked results improved performance considerably, increasing the probability of the first document presented to the user being relevant. Today, Google has not only become the most popular search engine by far, it has initiated numerous additional and often innovative services supplementing the basic search function. Its popularity is reflected in the trade name having graduated to an accepted, English language word—'to google'.[90]

1.15. A Space Odyssey

Since 1981, about the time NSF started to take an interest in network solutions and Tim Berners-Lee wrote his Enquire program, the number of host computers for the Internet has grown exponentially. There are obviously several reasons for this. One reason is briefly discussed above—the revolution of office automation had distributed computer resources throughout the 1980s, rendering typewriters into museum pieces. Local area networks were established for sharing resources, but there were few reasons—perhaps apart from e-mail—to find a solution to international connections. And when such solutions were found, they were typically for a business-specific purpose. At the same time, the office programs started to become really interesting and versatile. The MS-DOC character-driven interface was replaced by the more user-friendly Windows graphical interface introduced by Apple's Macintosh. This made graphics and

---

[88] See <http://www.google.com/corporate/history.html>.
[89] See further Eugene Garfield, *Citation Indexing* (New York: Wiley, 1979).
[90] Included in the 11th edition of the *Merriam-Webster Collegiate Dictionary* (2006).

interaction using a mouse, clicking for navigation, part of the general office environment.

When the World Wide Web and browsers like Mosaic made this available on the Internet, a potential infrastructure already was in place. The LANs could be hooked up to the Internet through an ISP, and suddenly a large world was on one's desktop. Search engines then made this world accessible in a new way and made it a world of education, communication, and entertainment. Surfing the Internet[91] became a meaningful and enjoyable activity by itself, not only as a process auxiliary to something else, like sending an e-mail.

Although the above factors are insufficient as an explanation, they are part of it. The time was ripe; the world was waiting for the solution.

I remember the first time I saw the World Wide Web demonstrated on a NextStep computer in Chicago 1993—the person on the lectern pointed the cursor to a highlighted term in Mosaic, clicked and *wham!* The screen changed, and the feed came from a completely different location. An example (I pride myself that this was to satisfy me) was to click at the citation of an Ibsen play from a US university site, and suddenly the source text was displayed. I found it difficult to believe that an American university stored Ibsen in the original Norwegian, and then—with a sinking feeling—I saw that the site from which the text was displayed was the University of Bergen in Norway. The world had shrunk. I could not believe it. Literarily, I could not believe it; I thought it was a sham; my scepticism based on nearly 20 years of struggling with computer communication. It really was a fairytale technology I experienced at that time.

Let me indulge in another personal experience from the beginning of the commercialization of Internet in 1995. I was visiting the Swedish Data Delegation, and sharing the enthusiasm of the new technology. They told me of this small company in the North of Sweden which specialized in reindeer products. Among these were cured sausages, somewhat like salami. The company had the same autumn launched a website, including an English language home page. And to its amazement, the company has found that it had become an international trader—orders from all over the world were received from buyers who wanted their slice of Rudolph for Christmas.

I also remember the first landing on the Moon. On the evening of 20 July 1969, I was listening to a portable radio following Eagle, the lunar

---

[91] 'Surfing the Internet' is a phrase first popularized by Jean Armour Polly in an article from 1992 bearing the phrase as its title. The article is available at <http://www.gutenberg.org/etext/49>.

entry module of Apollo 11, as it landed. As a child, I had been fascinated by space and the possibility of voyages between the planets and the stars. But during the 1970s the dream faded somewhat. The last time a human set a footprint in lunar dust was 1972. We still have not made it to Mars.

It has occurred to me that two months after Armstrong pronounced his famous words upon stepping onto the surface of the Moon, the first IMP was mounted at University of California, Los Angeles. That event can be seen as the beginning of another journey, not through outer space, but through a type of inner space, cyberspace,[92] or the space of information. This space includes knowledge, images, entertainment, facts, personal views—and it is as infinite as the human mind and human thoughts.

On 21 May 1961, President John F. Kennedy made his famous speech promising to place a man on the Moon before the decade was out. The nation was infected with his enthusiasm, and in a great political surge made the necessary resources available. When the pictures were returned from the Moon, some of us had a strange feeling of *deja vù*, as if the television images were reflections from the covers of the pulp magazines featuring voyages to the Moon for decades—the dream of visiting the Earth's satellite is even older, manifesting itself, for instance, in Johannes Kepler's posthumous novel *Somnium* (1634). This gave the race for the Moon a solid basis for imagination, a feeling of it as being part of our destiny. At the very least, it contributed to the acceptance of the political priorities which had to be made.

Perhaps something similar may also be said for the construction of the Internet. There is a history of visionaries suggesting how all human knowledge may be put at our fingertips. This includes not only the visionaries briefly mentioned in the foregoing parts of this chapter but also other stories of fabled libraries—the ashes of Alexandria and the infinite library of Jorge Luis Borges. The booster technology to realize these visions was the combination of computers and telecommunication. When Licklider named his circle of cooperating institutions the 'inter-galactic network', it may have been a joke. Yet it was said by the person whom everyone regards as a visionary, the person who wanted to realize fully the potential of human–computer interaction, and the person who was able to infuse his friends and colleagues with the same enthusiasm for realizing that vision.

Perhaps this is part of the explanation of how Internet came about. Obviously, there are the rational arguments for communication to beat

---

[92] The term was coined by William Gibson in his novel *Neuromancer* (1984).

the lack of compatibility, and the need for improved communication—
and finally, the attractions of the electronic marketplace. Yet there seems
to be something more, something like the imaginary rocket on the maga-
zine cover poised at the surface of the Moon.

It has also been suggested to me that the success of the Internet is
intimately connected to the 'openness' of its architecture—the distributed
network, open formats, delegation of security and policy enforcement to
the end-node, etc. This openness is perhaps best illustrated by the victory
of the TCP/IP over the OSI. Such openness has also given appropriate
conditions for letting us follow the vision of the intergalactic network,
which will take us much further than where we are today.

When surfing on the Internet, one travels in a universe of ideas and facts
which make the journey as exciting as a trip to Mars. There is obviously
no conflict between the exploration of space and cyberspace; outer space
is mirrored in cyberspace as information.

Yet it is in a way somewhat symbolic that when one dream faded,
the other grew and blossomed. And the journeys in cyberspace are not
restricted to a few astronauts; anyone can become a 'cybernaut' on the
Internet. The space odyssey we can make today is not inferior to the one
Stanley Kubrick in 1968 suggested for 2001. However, the future is no
more what it used to be.

2

Models of Internet governance

Lawrence B. Solum

2.1. What is Internet Governance?

Internet governance is a large, complex, and ambiguous topic. When we think about regulation of the Internet, we might be thinking about a narrow but important set of questions about specific institutions, such as the Internet Engineering Task Force[1] (IETF) or the Internet Corporation for Assigned Names and Numbers[2] (ICANN): these institutions can be said to *govern* the technical infrastructure and architecture of the Internet. We might also be thinking about a much broader and perhaps more compelling set of questions about policy issues that implicate the Internet: these questions include the regulation of online gambling, child pornography, freedom of speech, and the future of commerce and implicate nation states and international organizations. For the purposes of this investigation, Internet governance implicates both the narrow questions about Internet infrastructure or architecture and the broad questions about regulation of applications and content. Moreover, the broad and narrow questions are related. Regulation of the technical infrastructure of the Internet has implications for the regulation of applications and content.

Begin with the Internet itself. The Internet is a global network of networks, with communication between networks enabled by a communications protocol suite, currently TCP/IP. The Internet enables computers or servers that are attached to the net to communicate with one another, creating a platform on which software applications can run. The application that is most commonly associated with the Internet is the World

---

[1] See further Chapter 4 (Section 4.1). [2] See further Chapter 3 (Section 3.2.8).

Wide Web, which utilizes HTTP. But the Internet is not identical to the World Wide Web and it provides a platform for a host of other applications, such as email, file transfer protocol, and a variety of peer-to-peer file sharing programs.

In the broad sense, the Internet is a complex entity that includes the hardware and software technical infrastructure, the applications, and the content that is communicated or generated using those applications. In the broad sense, the Internet includes millions of computers running a myriad applications generating, manipulating, and retrieving a vast array of information. More concretely, the Internet in the broad sense includes the personal computer used to write this chapter, fibreoptic cable, routers, servers, web-browsers, Google, Yahoo!, MySpace, YouTube, the online edition of *The New York Times*, millions of weblogs, tens of millions of Internet-enabled mobile phones, and billions of email messages. In the broad sense, the Internet interpenetrates a wide array of ordinary human life—commerce, communications, entertainment, intimate interpersonal relationships, and a host of other activities increasingly occur in and through the Internet.

If the topic of Internet governance were taken as the investigation of the regulation of all these activities when they took place on (or were significantly affected by) the Internet, then 'Internet governance' would be more or less equivalent to 'law and politics' at least in the 'wired' and 'wireless' (or more developed) nations. This definition of Internet governance is simply too broad and ill-defined to be useful for the purpose of this investigation. We need a narrower and more focused conception of Internet governance to gain real traction on the issues.

What then is the 'Internet' for the purpose of investigating 'Internet Governance'? The narrow answer to this question is that Internet governance is about the ordering of whatever technical systems enable the operation of the global network of networks as a platform for applications. The Internet has a history in which particular technical systems have come and gone; there was, for example, an Internet before TCP/IP,[3] and it seems likely that the current version of TCP/IP will have a series of successors, within the existing structure of the Internet.[4] Further, a new global network of networks may supplant the existing Internet—a development

---

[3] See Chapter 1.
[4] See e.g. RFC 2460: Internet Protocol Version 6 (IPv6) (authors: S. Deering and R. Hinden) (December 1998), <http://www.ietf.org/rfc/rfc2460.txt>.

prefigured by Internet2.[5] The fundamental object of a study of Internet governance is the general type—the universal network of networks—and not the specific token—the existing Internet, based on TCP/IP.

Nonetheless, the Internet as it exists today is important both for its own sake and as the most fully developed realization of a global network of networks. Today's Internet is constituted by a set of technical systems, including TCP/IP, the system of IP numbers that identify individual computers or servers on the net, and the Domain Name System (DNS) that provides alphanumeric equivalents of IP number addresses. Those technical systems enable the operation of a hardware layer—with routers, fibreoptic cable, individual servers, cellular systems, and even satellite links. The same technical systems enable the operation of an applications layer, ranging from the familiar (the World Wide Web, browsers, search engines) to the old and obscure (GOPHER) to novel and innovative applications that may become 'the next big thing' or fail to move outside the laboratory.

Thus, the narrow answer to the question 'What is Internet governance?' is regulation of Internet infrastructure, its current operation, and the processes by which it develops and changes over time. In other words, the narrow focus of Internet governance is about the processes, systems, and institutions that regulate things like TCP/IP, the Domain Name System, and IP numbers. These systems are fundamental—they determine the capacities of the Internet.

Yet the narrow answer to the what-is-Internet-governance question is not satisfactory on its own, because Internet governance in the narrow sense is connected in important ways to Internet regulation in the broad sense. The technical infrastructure of the Internet interacts with the ability of governments to regulate applications, content, and the human activities that are enabled and facilitated by use of the Internet. In other words, the technical infrastructure of the Internet is connected to the legal regulation of gambling and child pornography, to the efficiency and transparency of the world economic system, and to fundamental human rights, such as liberty of conscience and freedom of speech.

The broad answer to the question 'What is Internet governance?' is that regulation of the Internet encompasses the policy questions that are *really different* when content and conduct are communicated and acted on and through the Internet. There is a real difference when the role of

---

[5] A consortium made up of a large number of US universities, working together with industry and government, to facilitate development and application of new Internet technologies. Further on Internet2, see <http://www.internet2.edu/>.

the Internet in a policy question is not merely accidental. This point is important. One function of the Internet is its role as a general system for communication between persons. The Internet has various modalities when it serves this role: email, voice, instant messaging, and so forth. The same content that is communicated via the Internet can also be communicated by phone, snail-mail, in-person conversations, teletype, and other media. Almost every imaginable policy problem—from the preservation of endangered species to the regulation of bid rigging— can involve Internet communications, but these problems are not *really* *different* when the only role of the Internet is to substitute for other communications media.

There are, however, a variety of regulatory problems where the archi- tecture or structure of the Internet does make a real difference. Oper- ationally, a real difference is present if the substantive analysis of the policy problem would be significantly altered if the next-best commu- nications technology were substitute for the Internet. For example, in Internet commerce, the question arises whether consumers are bound by form contracts that may be formed by clicking 'I accept' in response to proposed terms (frequently in a scroll-down box)—sometimes called 'click-wrap' agreements.[6] A similar issue arises in mail-order relationships, where the proposed terms may be in small print on the back of the order form. This appears to be a policy question where the Internet does not make a real difference: if a particular contract is binding in the mail-order context, it will be binding in the Internet context, and *vice versa*. On the other hand, there is a structural similarity between the problem of spam[7] and the problem of junk mail, but in this case, the nature of the Internet arguably does make a difference for economic reasons (the costs of snail- mail are internalized to the sender to a greater degree than are the costs of email). Assuming the examples are correctly analysed, spam is a problem within the scope of an analysis of Internet governance, whereas 'click- wrap' agreements are not.

A complete analysis of Internet governance requires that we address both narrow issues implicated by the institutions that govern the techni- cal infrastructure and architecture of the Internet and the broader issues that are implicated by the ways in which the Internet transforms policy

[6] See, for example, Francis M. Buono and Jonathan A. Friedman, 'Maximizing the Enforce- ability of Click-Wrap Agreements', *Journal of Technology Law & Policy*, 1999, vol. 4, no. 3, <http://grove.ufl.edu/~techlaw/vol4/issue3/friedman.html>.
[7] Further on spam and its regulation, see, for example, Credence E. Fogo, 'The Postman Always Rings 4,000 Times: New Approaches to Curb Spam', *John Marshall Journal of Computer & Information Law*, 2000, vol. 18, no. 4, 915–44.

questions that directly implicate applications, communication, and conduct. Because the narrow issues are rarely of substantial intrinsic importance (architectural elegance of network design matters only to network engineers) and the broad issues are sometimes of great social importance (fundamental human rights matter to everyone), it is important that investigations of Internet governance focus on the relationship between technical infrastructure and Internet architecture and the impact of the Internet on broad policy questions. This idea can be summarized as a slogan: *focus on the nexus between Internet architecture and social policy.*

2.2. Analytic Framework: Architecture, Policy Analysis, and Models

How can we parse the problems of Internet governance? The approach advanced in this chapter is based on three central ideas: (*a*) the idea that the Internet is constituted by its architecture or code; (*b*) the idea that the problems of Internet regulation can be analysed by using the conventional tools of policy analysis, including but not limited to: (*i*) normative theory, (*ii*) economics, and (*iii*) social choice theory; and (*c*) the idea that the logical space for discussing Internet governance can be captured via a set of 'models' or ideal types for Internet regulation.

Each of these three ideas is controversial and deserves further comment. The first idea is that architecture or code matters. This idea is challenged by the counter-thesis that there are no unique issues of Internet governance, because such issues are no different for the Internet than they are for other policy contexts. This challenge is prominently associated with Judge Frank Easterbrook of the United States Court of Appeal for the Seventh Circuit and formerly a prominent member of the law faculty of the University of Chicago. In an essay entitled 'The Law of the Horse', Easterbrook famously wrote:

[T]he best way to learn the law applicable to specialized endeavors is to study general rules. Lots of cases deal with sales of horses; others deal with people kicked by horses; still more deal with the licensing and racing of horses, or with the care veterinarians give to horses, or with prizes at horse shows. Any effort to collect these strands into a course on 'The Law of the Horse' is doomed to be shallow and to miss unifying principles. Teaching 100 percent of the cases on people kicked by horses will not convey the law of torts very well. Far better for most students—better, even, for those who plan to go into the horse trade—to take courses in property, torts, commercial transactions, and the like, adding to the diet of horse cases a smattering of transactions in cucumbers, cats, coal, and cribs. Only by putting the law of the horse in the context of broader rules about commercial endeavors could one really understand the law about horses.

Now you can see the meaning of my title. When asked to talk about 'Property in Cyberspace,' my immediate reaction was, 'Isn't this just the law of the horse?' I don't know much about cyberspace; what I do know will be outdated in five years (if not five months!); and my predictions about the direction of change are worthless, making any effort to tailor the law to the subject futile. And if I did know something about computer networks, all I could do in discussing 'Property in Cyberspace' would be to isolate the subject from the rest of the law of intellectual property, making the assessment weaker.[8]

Analogously, one might object to the very idea of an essay on 'Internet Governance'. Internet Governance, it might be argued, should receive the same attention as 'Ranch Governance' or less flatteringly, 'Stable Governance'. There is waste that needs to be shovelled, but it does not rise to the level of academic interest.

The premise of this chapter and the book in which it appears is that the Internet does pose distinct and important problems—the analysis of which is strengthened rather than weakened by paying close attention to the nature of the Internet and the interactions between Internet architecture and Internet regulation. This is brought out by a simple point that draws on Easterbrook's analogy between Internet law and the law of the horse. Horses are commodities—the law regulates property rights in horses, contracts involving horses, and even races involving horses. But the law does not regulate the internal operation of horses and the physiology of horses does not significantly differ from that of other animals. If the law were to attempt to regulate horse physiology directly or if horse physiology were radically different from that of other animals in a way that affected the question whether horses could be property, there would indeed be 'a law of the horse'. When it comes to the Internet, there are policy questions about architecture and architecture does impact upon other policy questions—as becomes evident in the discussion that follows. For this reason, the Easterbrookian thesis that a focus on Internet governance will make policy analysis worse rather than better is mistaken.

Yet Easterbrook was not entirely wrong. The second idea upon which this chapter is premised is that Internet policy can be analysed using the conventional tools of policy analysis. This idea is challenged by

---

[8] Frank H. Easterbrook, 'Cyberspace and the Law of the Horse', *University of Chicago Legal Forum*, 1996, vol. 11, 207, 207–8. Contrast, for example, Lawrence Lessig, 'The Law of the Horse: What Cyberlaw Might Teach', *Harvard Law Review*, 1999, vol. 113, 501–46.

the counter-thesis that Internet governance should be driven exclusively or primarily by considerations of network engineering. This idea is not clearly articulated in the Internet-governance literature, because that literature is almost always the product of what might be called Internet outsiders—those who are not focused on the technical problems of Internet architecture and design. From the vantage point of a network engineer, it might look as though the fundamental problem of Internet governance is to prevent economists, policy analysts, and lawyers from interfering with good network engineering. That is, good Internet governance institutions should empower network engineers and computer scientists to make design decisions on the basis of the functional imperatives of the Internet itself. At a very high level of abstraction, that means that the chief aim of Internet governance is to produce an efficient global network of networks: everyone should be able to connect irrespective of hardware or operating system; the network should be neutral with respect to content of information that is transported, and should accomplish these goals efficiently (minimizing lag and maximizing throughput). Concomitantly, politicians, executives, economists, and policy analysts who are ignorant of network architecture are likely to make bad decisions on such matters—accidentally imposing huge costs as the unintended consequences of some short-term external policy goal.

There is, of course, something to the idea that the imperatives of network design should play an important role in shaping Internet governance institutions. That notion will be explored in some detail in this chapter. Yet from the fact that architecture is relevant to Internet governance, it does not follow that architecture should be the sole or exclusive factor in Internet governance. The Internet is not simply a congeries of research projects; it is increasingly becoming the most important medium for communication of ideas and information. The architecture of the Internet has consequences going beyond the realm of values that are relevant to network engineers. For example, the Internet facilitates anonymous encrypted communication that can be either impossible or extremely difficult to intercept or prohibit.[9] This information may be innocuous or it may be illegal sharing of copyrighted audio or video files; communications may be innocent and personal or they may be part of a terrorist plot. To the extent that Internet architecture facilitates

[9] See, for example, Chris Nicoll, 'Concealing and Revealing Identity on the Internet', in C. Nicoll, J. E. J. Prins, and M. J. M. van Dellen (eds.), *Digital Anonymity and the Law* (The Hague: T. M. C. Asser Press, 2003), 99–119; Ed Felten, 'Zfone Encrypts VoIP Calls', Freedom to Tinker, 23 May 2006, <http://www.freedom-to-tinker.com/?p=1019>, last accessed 30 April 2008.

or impedes regulation of content, Internet governance will have consequences that transcend engineering imperatives.

In addition, Internet governance deals with decisions about resource allocation. Domain names and IP numbers are economically scarce resources; economists have relevant things to say about how such resources can best be distributed or traded. Internet architecture may have effects on innovation in applications: economists may have things to say about the value of such innovation and the question whether network neutrality will or will not have harmful consequences for the rate of innovation.

Similarly, the institutions of Internet governance implicate questions of institutional design and normative theory. For example, if an Internet governance institution were structured so as to require consensus among interested stakeholders before policy decisions could be made, public choice theory would predict hold-out problems and rent-seeking behaviour. Even if the participants in the process have technical backgrounds, governments and firms are unlikely to allow Internet governance to operate without a consideration of their interests when the stakes are high.

The third idea is that the complex problems of Internet governance can usefully be analysed by reference to *ideal types* or *models* of Internet governance. This idea is challenged by the counter-thesis that each problem of Internet governance is best understood contextually on the basis of particular problems and tailored solutions. The best answer to this challenge is the most straightforward one: simply present the models and demonstrate that they can do interesting work. The next part of this chapter introduces five models: (*a*) the model of spontaneous ordering; (*b*) the model of transnational and international governance institutions; (*c*) the model of code; (*d*) the model of national regulation; and (*e*) the model of market-based ordering. The models do not reflect the positions of particular analysts, nor do they have exact analogues in existing institutions. Rather, these models are ideal types: we take a set of ideas about Internet governance and construct a model that is consistent with the logical implication of the ideas. Actual policy proposals and institutions inevitably reflect a mix of ideas and therefore are hybrids of the simplified models.

In sum, the framework of the chapter is based on the thesis that Internet governance is best understood by examining models of Internet governance in relationship to the interaction between Internet architecture and conventional policy analysis.

2.3. Five Models of Internet Governance

The fundamental subject of Internet governance is institutional—what institutions, if any, shall govern the Internet and how shall they be organized. Even a quick survey of existing Internet governance mechanisms reveals a complex set of institutions. At the surface level, there are a variety of institutions that are specifically targeted at Internet governance—the IETF, ICANN, and various other organizations. In addition, governments play a role. All national governments assert the power to regulate the physical infrastructure of the Internet and the activities of end users and content providers that take place within national boundaries. Further, the architecture of the Internet or its 'code' can be seen as a kind of Internet governance institution, because architecture may influence the feasibility and cost of various regulatory alternatives. Moreover, even after the 'dotcom' bust, it is apparent that the Internet is regulated by the market, and current controversies over network neutrality provide further evidence that market forces can impinge on the fundamentals of network design.[10] Although some have argued that the best (or even inherent) design for Internet governance is 'spontaneous ordering' or a separate realm called 'cyberspace', the best view is that Internet governance is a hybrid of various models.

The sections that follow explore five models of Internet governance:

- The model of cyberspace and spontaneous ordering which is premised on the idea that the Internet is a self-governing realm of individual liberty, beyond the reach of government control.

- The model of transnational institutions and international organizations which is based on the notion that Internet governance inherently transcends national borders and hence that the most appropriate institutions are transnational quasi-private cooperatives or international organizations based on treaty arrangements between national governments.

- The model of code and Internet architecture which is based on the notion that many regulatory decisions are made by the communications protocols and other software that determine how the Internet operates.

- The model of national governments and law which is based on the idea that as the Internet grows in importance fundamental regulatory

---

[10] See further Section 2.10.

decisions will be made by national governments through legal regulation.

- The model of market regulation and economics which assumes that market forces drive the fundamental decisions about the nature of the Internet.

2.4. Cyberspace and Spontaneous Ordering

Early thinking about the Internet is strongly associated with a romantic conception of cyberspace as a separate realm outside of physical space and the reach of either national governments or market forces. For example, David Post and David Johnson famously wrote:

Many of the jurisdictional and substantive quandaries raised by border-crossing electronic communications could be resolved by one simple principle: conceiving of Cyberspace as a distinct 'place' for purposes of legal analysis by recognizing a legally significant border between Cyberspace and the 'real world'. Using this new approach, we would no longer ask the unanswerable question 'where' in the geographical world a Net-based transaction occurred. Instead, the more salient questions become: What procedures are best suited to the often unique characteristics of this new place and the expectations of those who are engaged in various activities there? What mechanisms exist or need to be developed to determine the content of those rules and the mechanisms by which they can enforced? Answers to these questions will permit the development of rules better suited to the new phenomena in question, more likely to be made by those who understand and participate in those phenomena, and more likely to be enforced by means that the new global communications media make available and effective.[11]

Johnson and Post imagined that cyberspace could not and should not be regulated by national governments:

Governments cannot stop electronic communications from coming across their borders, even if they want to do so. Nor can they credibly claim a right to regulate the Net based on supposed local harms caused by activities that originate outside their borders and that travel electronically to many different nations. One nation's legal institutions should not monopolize rule-making for the entire Net. Even so, established authorities will likely continue to claim that they must analyze and regulate the new online phenomena in terms of some physical locations. After all, they argue, the people engaged in online communications still inhabit the material world, and local legal authorities must have authority to remedy the problems

---

[11] David R. Johnson and David G. Post, 'Law and Borders—The Rise of Law in Cyberspace', *Stanford Law Review*, 1996, vol. 48, 1367, 1378–9.

created in the physical world by those acting on the Net. The rise of responsible law-making institutions within Cyberspace, however, will weigh heavily against arguments that describe the Net as 'lawless' and thus connect regulation of online trade to physical jurisdictions. As noted, sysops, acting alone or collectively, have the power to banish those who commit wrongful acts online. Thus, for online activities that minimally affect the vital interests of sovereigns, the self-regulating structures of Cyberspace seem better suited to dealing with the Net's legal issues.[12]

When Johnson and Post were writing in the mid-1990s, this utopian vision of cyberspace as a separate realm beyond the reach of national governments may have seemed credible. Although they wrote only a little over 10 years ago, neither governments nor markets had fully digested the importance of the Internet and traces of a frontier atmosphere characterized by consensual transactions between individuals were still prominent. Certainly, the legal and economic environment of 2008, when this chapter was finalized, is different. It is now difficult to conceive of cyberspace as a sort of 'independent country'. Governments and large multinational firms now have pervasive presences in cyberspace.[13]

Nonetheless, there is a kernel of important truth in the model of cyberspace and spontaneous ordering. The architecture of the Internet is resistant to purely national control. Because the Internet is a global network of networks capable of transmitting any information that can be digitalized, it would be costly for any national government to attempt to comprehensively monitor all of the content on the Internet inside its national boundaries. Data on the Internet cannot be intercepted with the same relative ease as telephone calls can be monitored. On the Internet, data are broken into packets which may travel various routes to their final destination; the telephone system is line switched, meaning that a telephone call can be intercepted at any point in the telephone network. Routing on the Internet is very flexible. If a government tries to block one computer or server, data can be rerouted via what is called a 'proxy server'.[14]

We are all familiar with the consequences of the high cost of government regulation of the Internet. Content that once could be forbidden is now available. For example, local and state governments in the United States could effectively limit access to pornography before the Internet; after the Internet, the costs of such regulation would be astronomically

---

[12] David R. Johnson and David G. Post, 'Law and Borders—The Rise of Law in Cyberspace', *Stanford Law Review*, 1996, vol. 48, 1390–1.

[13] See further Chapter 3 (Section 3.3).

[14] Further on proxy servers, see <http://en.wikipedia.org/wiki/Proxy_server>.

high. Although China is able to make access to some content relatively difficult and expensive, sophisticated Internet users in China are able to circumvent, at least in part, the so-called 'great firewall'.[15] The Internet may not be a separate, self-governing, libertarian utopia, but it is still a realm that hampers government regulation.

2.5. Transnational Institutions and International Organizations

Closely related to the idea that cyberspace is an independent realm outside the control of national governments is the notion that the Internet should be governed by special transnational institutions that are outside the control of national governments and instead answer to the 'Internet community' or the 'community of network engineers'. In direct competition with this model is a rival that accepts the premise that the Internet is inherently international in character, but rejects the premise that it should be outside the control of national governments. This rival view would replace special transnational institutions—like ICANN or the IETF—with international organizations on the model of the International Telecommunications Union (ITU) or the World Intellectual Property Organization (WIPO).[16] Although we are examining these two ideas in tandem, they represent opposing tendencies—we are really dealing with two models here and not one. The core idea that both models share is that Internet governance requires institutional structures that cross national boundaries. The central disagreement between the two models is over the role of national governments: ICANN and the IETF are not international organizations created by treaties; WIPO and the ITU are agencies of the United Nations. So far, Internet governance institutions have followed the model of special transnational institutions, although there has been considerable pressure to move towards an international organizations model.[17]

ICANN can serve as a case study of the model of special transnational institutions. As elaborated in Chapters 3 and 5, ICANN has an organizational structure that is almost baroque in its complexity. This is partly a function of ICANN's institutional history. It will be recalled from Chapter 1 that ICANN replaced a predecessor organization, the IANA, which was essentially run by one individual, Jon Postel—himself an important Internet pioneer. In the Internet's early history, Internet governance by

---

[15] See further Section 2.7 of this chapter and references cited therein.
[16] For details of these organizations, see Chapter 3.   [17] See further Chapter 6.

personal authority was both possible and efficient—there was no need for an international bureaucracy for what was a cooperative research project governed by consensual decision-making of network engineers. By the time Postel was replaced by ICANN, the reality had changed and the Domain Name System implicated the interests of millions of users, multinational corporations, and national governments. Concomitantly, ICANN's complex organizational structure reflects the broad constellation of interests presently affected by domain name policy. Registries and registrars for the gTLDs have a direct economic stake in domain name policy, as do the operators of the ccTLDs. Because of the phenomenon of cybersquatting, the owners of trademarks also have a significant economic stake. Internet Service Providers (ISPs) and network administrators also have interests that are affected by ICANN.

Despite the complexity of its structure, at its heart ICANN is a non-profit corporation with a self-selecting and self-perpetuating board of directors. In economic terms, ICANN is a firm. It is certainly not a government or a treaty-based international organization. Admittedly, it has a special relationship with the US Department of Commerce. When ICANN was founded, responsibility within the US Government for the Internet had been transferred to the Department of Commerce (DOC); hence, that agency was involved in the process that led to the creation of ICANN in 1998. The precise legal nature of the relationship between DOC and ICANN is murky,[18] but whatever that relationship may be, ICANN is far from being a mere arm of DOC or the US government more generally.

The bylaws of ICANN contain a statement of core values that give pride of place to ensuring the 'operational stability, reliability, security, and global interoperability of the Internet'[19] —technical imperatives that reflect the corporation's origins in the community of network engineers. There is an emphasis too on making 'well-informed decisions based on expert advice'—another indicator that ICANN is attempting to preserve the ideal of cooperation between engineers in the face of pressure to both democratize policymaking and to allow for the operation of competitive market mechanisms.

Despite the nods to democratic participation and competition, ICANN is best understood as an attempt to institutionalize and preserve the autonomy of an engineering-based approach to Internet governance in face of pressures to cede control to either national governments or

---

[18] See further Chapter 3 (Section 3.2.8) and references cited therein.
[19] The statement of core values is fully set out in Chapter 3 (Section 3.2.8).

market mechanisms. Two fundamental facts confirm this hypothesis. First, ICANN has remained as an independent, non-governmental organization despite efforts by international organizations such as the ITU to establish influence over the Domain Name System.[20] Second, the corporation has for a long time resisted market approaches to the creation of new top-level domains. That is, ICANN represents a distinct model of Internet governance.

The model of international organizations has never established substantial authority to engage in Internet governance. The ITU and other suborganizations of the United Nations are interested in various aspects of Internet policy: for example, Internationalized Domain Names (which allow use of non-Roman character sets) have received attention from the UN Asia-Pacific Development Information Programme.[21] Yet to date, the role of international organizations in Internet governance has been limited to input and has not included formal authority.[22]

2.6. Code and Internet Architecture

The fundamental idea behind the model of code and Internet architecture can be called the *code thesis*.[23] The code thesis is the claim that the nature of Internet or cyberspace is determined by the code—the software and hardware that implements the Internet.[24] Unlike natural environments and processes, *how* the Internet runs or cyberspace operates is dependent on the code that implements it. This is a point at which the model of code and Internet architecture departs from the model of cyberspace and spontaneous ordering. The latter model—at least in simple forms—assumes that cyberspace has an inherent nature, and that regulation of the Internet must respond to that nature. The contrast between the two models is reflected in their different attitudes towards the question whether the Internet can be regulated by national governments. The model of cyberspace and spontaneous ordering is based on the premise that the Internet cannot be regulated by national governments, because,

---

[20] International Telecommunications Union, *ITU and its Activities Related to Internet-Protocol (IP) Networks: Version 1.1* (April 2004), especially Section 3.2, <http://www.itu.int/osg/spu/ip/itu-and-activities-related-to-ip-networks-version-1.pdf>, last accessed 30 April 2008.

[21] 'Internationalized Domain Names', APDIP e-note 9/2006, <http://www.apdip.net/apdipenote/9.pdf>, last accessed 30 April 2008.

[22] See further Chapters 3 and 6.

[23] Lawrence Lessig, *Code, and Other Laws of Cyberspace* (New York: Basic Books, 1999).

[24] Ibid. 6.

as a global network of networks, activity on the Internet can originate in any physical location, anywhere in the world.[25] The model of code and Internet architecture can concede that there is a large measure of truth in this claim, but supplements that concession with the claim that the Internet has this property because of the code or software that makes physical location irrelevant. That code could have been different or it could change in the future.

In this sense, code is the prime regulator in cyberspace—in Larry Lessig's felicitous phrasing, 'the Code is Law'.[26] The core of Lessig's point is that software or code has regulative effects on human behaviour. In this sense, Internet architecture is like the architecture of buildings and cities. Just as the architecture of a building enables and encourages humans to move and congregate in certain ways, so the architecture of the Internet enables some activities by users and regulators while discouraging others.

What then is the architecture of the Internet? More pointedly, which feature or features of Internet architecture are responsible for the distinctive and valuable functionality that the Internet provides? Lessig suggests that the answer to these questions can be captured in large part by a single principle; he has argued that the primary characteristic of the Internet architecture that enables innovation is *the end-to-end principle*.[27] As Lessig explains, the end-to-end principle says to keep intelligence in a network at the ends or in the applications, leaving the network itself to be relative simple. In short, the principle calls for 'stupid network' and 'smart applications'. The network simply forwards or routes the data packets and does not—and cannot by architecture—discriminate or differentiate traffic generated by different applications. The software at the transport and Internet protocol layers simply does not include code that would allow the Internet to associate data packets with application file types.[28] Thus, the Internet does not 'know' whether a given packet of data is a webpage (utilizing HTTP), a social science article downloaded from the Social Science Research Network[29] (utilizing FTP), an email message (utilizing Simple Message Transfer Protocol, SMTP), or an MP3 file being shared by use of, say, the peer-to-peer file-sharing program KaZaa. Nor

---

[25] See, for example, Justin Hughes, 'The Internet and the Persistence of Law', *Boston College Law Review*, 2003, vol. 44, 359, 365 *et seq.*

[26] Lessig, *Code*, 6.   [27] Ibid. 34.

[28] However, other software, for example, in the form of 'packet sniffers'—can examine the content of packets on a network. See further <http://www.webopedia.com/TERM/s/sniffer.html>. An example is Sniff'em, see <http://www.sniff-em.com/>, last accessed 30 April 2008.

[29] See <http://www.ssrn.com>.

does the Internet 'know' when email is being used to send a large file as an attachment. As a consequence, the Internet cannot coordinate the routing of packets so that they all arrive at a destination computer at the same time. Ninety-five per cent of the packets may arrive in the first minute, and the remaining five per cent, travelling by a different route on the Internet, might arrive minutes later. The Internet cannot decide that delivery of files that contain academic articles is a high priority for an academic institution and delivery of MP3 files for students is a low priority.

This lack of awareness illustrates what is sometimes called the 'stupidity' of the Internet. Alternatively, we can call this characteristic of the Internet *transparency*. The Internet is *transparent* to applications. The transparent, non-discriminatory nature of the Internet, Lessig has argued, is what has enabled the explosion of innovation and creativity on the Internet.[30] Since the network is non-discriminatory or transparent to applications and the intelligence is implemented at the ends by the applications, the innovation or creative activity is placed in the hands of the application creators. Thus, innovation is decentralized and the opportunity to devise new applications is available to millions of creative individuals with Internet access.

The economic significance of transparency is that it dramatically lowers the investment required to produce a given innovation. Given a transparent Internet, an innovator need only invest in innovation at the application layer. If the Internet were opaque, then new applications would also require investment in changes at lower layers (the transport, IP, link, or physical layers).

Moreover, transparency reduces the cost of innovation to consumers. Given a transparent Internet, a consumer need only invest in an application itself in order to make use of it. If the Internet were opaque, consumers would be required to invest in changes to their network infrastructure in order to utilize an innovative application. Because networks are complex and used by multiple users, network reconfiguration may be relatively expensive. Because the Internet is even more complex and used by hundreds of millions of servers, reconfiguration of the whole Internet to enable a new application would involve a very large investment.

This point about transparency and adoption costs leads to another important concept, *networking effects*. The economic value of some

---

[30] See Lessig, *Code*.

innovations depends on networking effects.[31] The value of an application like SMTP (email) is a function, in part, of the number of adopters; the more users of email, the more valuable it is.[32] For some applications, there may be a tipping point, at which the number of adopters reaches critical mass resulting in a discontinuous and large increase in value from networking effects or from similar phenomena with respect to awareness of (or belief in) networking effects. Once this tipping point is reached, the application becomes sufficiently valuable to broaden its appeal from early adopters to ordinary users. Reducing the cost of adoption for consumers increases the likelihood that these networking-effect gains will be realized. If adoption costs are too high for early adopters, the tipping point may never be reached. For this reason, transparency may be required to enable innovations that would be efficient even given the large costs associated with reconfiguring the Internet. Without transparency, the benefits of the innovation would never become apparent and hence the investments would never be made.

The economics of Internet innovation are illustrated by development of the World Wide Web by Tim Berners-Lee.[33] The core idea of the Web is the hypertext link, by clicking here, on this word, you go there, to that word. By clicking here, on this link, you go there to that webpage. Although Berners-Lee developed this idea independently, a similar idea had arisen previously, on several occasions—and before the rise of the Internet.[34] What the transparency of the Internet enabled was the implementation of Berners-Lee's Hyper Text Transfer Protocol (HTTP) and Hyper Text Markup Language (HTML) applications without any need for cooperation from or modification of the communications system on which they were implemented. That is, the transparent nature of the Internet dramatically lowered the investment that Berners-Lee and others had to make in order to produce the Web.

The World Wide Web sits on top of the Internet. From the application user's point of view, the Internet is simply invisible—except, of course, when network congestion calls it to our attention. If the architecture of the Internet had been opaque, then the counterfactual equivalent of TCP/IP would have required modification for HTTP/HTML to run on the Internet. And if that had been the case, there is good reason to believe

---

[31] See generally Oz Shy, *The Economics of Network Industries* (Cambridge: Cambridge University Press, 2001).

[32] For the purposes of illustration, we set aside the possibility that there may be a point at which additional users of email actually reduce its utility by creating sorting problems and encouraging spam.

[33] See Chapter 1 (Section 1.12).   [34] See Chapter 1 (Section 1.2).

that there would never have been a World Wide Web. The networking effects that transformed the World Wide Web from a merely great idea into an enormously useful communications tool would never have begun cascading if the platform on which the Web runs had not already been widely accessible. Berners-Lee faced real obstacles in getting HTTP/HTML accepted, even though he was giving these away and they could be run for free (at least from the point of view of short-run marginal costs).[35] Had Berners-Lee been required to convince managers of the Internet to expend resources to enable the Internet to run HTTP/HTML, we have every reason to believe that he would have failed. Indeed, he might have been unable to convince his own employers to allow him to make the necessary modifications in the network at CERN for the experimental work that developed HTTP/HTML.

The economics of Internet transparency and networking effects are very powerful. HTTP/HTML enabled what we now think of as 'the Internet revolution'. But the 'dotcom' boom and bust, eBay and Amazon.com, homepages and browsing—the cyberspace phenomena that have become the furniture of our day-to-day ordinary existence—all of these are the product of one innovative application suite, HTTP/HTML. The peer-to-peer phenomenon (from Napster to KaZaa and beyond) is the product of a small number of innovative applications. Whatever the numbers, it is clear that the contribution of the Internet to global economic growth and development is substantial.

The model of code and Internet architecture can be interpreted in a second way that contemplates and reinforces the code thesis and the end-to-end principle. Transparency is not a direct result of the end-to-end principle, but rather is a built-in characteristic of the layered architecture of the Internet. That is, it is *layers* that are the key, central characteristic of the Internet architecture. The end-to-end principle emerged from the layers model as an articulation and abstraction of implicit ideas inherent in the layers model.

What are the layers of the Internet? Viewed as a system of communication between users, the six layers that constitute the Internet are as follows:

- the Content Layer—the symbols and images that are communicated;
- the Application Layer—the programs that use the Internet (e.g. the Web);
- the Transport Layer—TCP, which breaks the data into packets;

[35] See further Berners-Lee, *Weaving the Web*, especially chapters 2–5.

- the Internet Protocol Layer—IP, which handles the flow of data over the network;
- the Link Layer—the interface between users' computers and the physical layer;
- the Physical Layer—the copper wire, optical cable, satellite links, etc.

The layers are organized in a vertical hierarchy. When information is communicated via the Internet, the information flows down from the content layer (the 'highest' level) through the application, transport, IP, and link layers to the physical layer (the 'lowest' level), across the physical layer in packets, and then flows back up through the same layers in reverse order. More specifically, communication on the Internet requires that content be digitalized by an application, and that the digital information be broken into packets by the transport layer and addressed by the Internet protocol layer so that it can be passed on by the link layer to the physical layer. Having reached the bottom layer, information then moves horizontally. The physical layer transmits the individual data packets by copper, fibre, and/or radio by various waypoints to an endpoint or destination on the network. Once at its destination, the information then ascends vertically through the layers to be interpreted by an application as content. In a nutshell, the fundamental architecture of the Internet is layered.

What is the relationship of end-to-end and layered architecture? The end-to-end principle derives from pioneering work in the theory of network design by Jerome Saltzer, David Reed, and David Clark. As they put it, end-to-end is an argument (or a class of arguments) that says:

The function in question can completely and correctly be implemented only with the knowledge and help of the application standing at the end points of the communication system. Therefore, providing that questioned function as a feature of the communication system itself is not possible.[36]

Stated in a generalized form, the end-to-end argument counsels against low-level function implementation.[37] What does this mean? Avoiding low-level function implementation means that a functionality desired by an application should be implemented at the level of the application rather than at a lower level. The version of end-to-end quoted above is a statement of the end-to-end principle for the engineering of the Internet and the software that uses the Internet.

---

[36] Jerome H. Saltzer, David P. Reed, and David D. Clark, 'End-to-end arguments in system design', *ACM Transactions on Computer Systems*, 1984, vol. 2, 277, 278.
[37] Ibid.

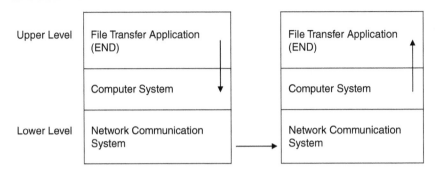

Figure 2.1. Vertical hierarchy in layered architecture

For example, the functionality of ensuring data integrity for a file transfer application is better implemented at the application level than at the network communication level. Even if the network delivered data without corruption, the reasoning goes, the file transfer application still needs to do the data checking because the data corruption could happen before the data reach the network—due to a bad disk, for example.

The simple example of error checking illustrates two general features of the end-to-end argument—vertical hierarchy and information mismatch. Each of these two features must be explicated and clarified in order to illuminate the meaning and significance of the end-to-end principle in relation to the layers model.

The end-to-end argument presupposes some sort of vertical hierarchy— that is, it assumes lower and upper levels. In the above example, the file transfer application is at an upper level with respect to the network communication system, which, in turn, lies at a lower level with respect to the application. The vertical hierarchy in the above example is illustrated in Figure 2.1.

The fundamental insight of the end-to-end principle is that any given functionality should be implemented at a level where it is needed—the 'end' point. Thus, an essential task of understanding and applying the end-to-end principle is identifying and understanding the relevant levels. Where is the 'end'? 'End' with respect to what? In the context of Internet architecture, the relevant vertical hierarchy implicit in the end-to-end argument is the layers of the TCP/IP protocol.

In general, a network protocol is a set of rules and conventions by which computers can communicate with each other.[38] Since a computer

---

[38] Andrew S. Tanenbaum, *Computer Networks* (Upper Saddle River, New Jersey: Prentice-Hall, 1996, 3rd edn.), 17.

network is nothing but a set of computers connected with each other, the network architecture is determined by the architecture of the network protocol.[39] The Transmission Control Protocol/Internet Protocol (TCP/IP) suite is the network communication protocol for the Internet. Thus, the architecture of the Internet as a network is determined by the architecture of the TCP/IP protocol.

The fundamental goal of the initial Internet architecture was to create a network of networks by interconnecting various computer network systems already in existence at the time.[40] In order to meet this goal, TCP/IP was designed to be software-only protocol, independent of any particular computer and network hardware. That is, TCP/IP is 'pure code'. It is *the* code of the Internet that determines the architecture of the Internet. In a significant sense, then, TCP/IP is the most important institution of Internet governance.

2.7. National Governments and Law

The model of national regulation and law is premised on the idea that the importance of the Internet entails that it should be subject to regulation on the same basis and for the same reasons that other human activities are regulated. And, of course, Internet-related activity is subject to regulation. Examples abound. Publication on the web is subject to laws on defamation. Contracts made on the web are enforceable. Internet fraud is subject to criminal sanction. Peer-to-peer sharing of files with copyrighted materials subjects users to civil and/or criminal liability. It is important not to lose sight of the basic reality that most Internet regulation is regulation by national governments of Internet-related activities. That regulation establishes the conditions for Internet-related markets and enables the background conditions that enable other modalities of Internet regulation. In this sense, the model of national governments and law is triumphant— even if its presence is taken for granted as part of the background.

The more difficult questions of Internet regulation concerning the application of national law arise in two paradigmatic contexts. The first context is the attempt to subject Internet architecture to national regulation. The second context is the attempt to censor open-access content.

[39] Andrew S. Tanenbaum, *Computer Networks* (Upper Saddle River, New Jersey: Prentice-Hall, 1996, 3rd edn.), 18.
[40] David D. Clark, 'The Design Philosophy of the DARPA Internet Protocols', *Computer Communication Review*, August 1988, vol. 18, 106–14.

The two contexts are sometimes related—as the regulation of architecture may be a means to the regulation of content. In both contexts, national regulation creates substantial costs that caution against the extension of national law.

The first context where caution is appropriate is the direct legal regulation of Internet architecture. Interestingly, no national government has made a serious attempt to try to change the fundamental architecture of the Internet's code. Arguably, any such attempt would be doomed to failure, because no one nation state has the regulatory clout to force a worldwide change in Internet architecture, and a successful change at the national level would result in the fragmentation of the Internet. However, the People's Republic of China has instituted policies that aim at creating the functional equivalent of fundamental architectural changes.

China's Internet regulations give the Chinese government a monopoly over all Internet connections going in and out of the country.[41] The regulations designate the Ministry of Information Industry (MII) as gatekeeper to the Internet, and access to the global Internet by networks (ISPs) is restricted exclusively to a handful of channels—the national backbones—provided or sanctioned by the MII. Under the 'Computer Information Network and Internet Security, Protection and Management Regulations', access to certain objectionable materials over the Internet is prohibited in China. The list of prohibited materials includes those (*a*) subversive of state power or the socialist system; (*b*) damaging to national unity; (*c*) inciting discrimination between nationalities; (*d*) disturbing to social order; (*e*) propagating feudal superstition; (*f*) related to pornography, gambling, or violence; (*g*) insulting or libellous; and (*h*) violating the Constitution or other laws. Pursuant to these regulations, a variety of international media outlets are blocked.

Blocking of websites is delegated to the ISPs, with the Public Security Bureau (PSB) sending out a list of websites to be blocked from users in China. The ISPs are required by law to follow the directions from the PSB, and essentially operate as agents for the government. Technically, the ISPs in China are required to block all traffic from or to specific IP addresses handed down by the government. Since the Chinese government has a

---

[41] The ensuing description of Chinese regulation builds principally on the following sources: OpenNet Initiative Study, 'Internet Filtering in China 2004–2005', <http://www.opennetinitiative.net/studies/china/>, last accessed 30 April 2008; Philip Sohmen, 'Taming the Dragon: China's Efforts to Regulate the Internet', *Stanford Journal of East Asian Affairs*, 2001, vol. 1, 17–26; Ronald J. Deibert, John G. Palfrey, Rafal Rohozinski, and Jonathan Zittrain (eds.), *Access Denied: The Practice and Policy of Global Internet Filtering* (Cambridge, Massachusetts: MIT Press, 2008), 263–71.

monopoly over the physical connection to the global Internet, and all ISPs that connect to the government sanctioned backbones are required to be licensed and thus required to follow the government orders, the government can completely block all objectionable contents from all of China, at least theoretically. It is like building an electronic Great Wall around China—hence the oft-used epithet 'Great Firewall'.[42]

However, uses of circumventing technologies—such as the peer-to-peer applications connected to anonymizing proxy servers outside China— make it difficult to completely block access based on the IP address of the true or ultimate destination. Nevertheless, in contrast to physical access control, China is deadly serious about enforcement of its IP layer regulation. First, rather than entirely relying on the ISPs to faithfully block banned sites, the Chinese authorities monitor and filter all Internet traffic going through China's eight primary gateways to the global Internet. Presumably, the packets from the banned IP addresses are dropped at these backbone gateways. At the other end of the ISPs, installation of site-blocking software is required on all end-user computers with public access, such as those in Internet cafés. In 2002, for instance, Shanghai police closed down almost 200 Internet cafés in the city during a week-long sweep for not blocking sites as required under the law.[43] Similarly, Chinese authorities reportedly shut down 17,000 Internet bars that failed to install the site-blocking software.[44] Although closing down the service and confiscating the computers is directed at the physical establishment, it should properly be regarded as a part of IP layer regulation, as the nature of action is enforcement of the regulations at the IP layer—that is, blocking access to sites at specific IP addresses. Of course, the ultimate goal of the regulation is to control social or political unrest by restricting flow of information in and out of China.

China's regulation of the Internet illustrates the conflict between the model of national regulation and law and the model of code and Internet architecture. The Internet is not designed to facilitate national regulation—for example, the IP number system is not designed to create a hierarchical IP address space that is rigidly associated with national boundaries. Nor is the system designed to allow for the identification of

---

[42] See, for example, Jonathan Watts, 'Behind the Great Firewall', *The Guardian*, 9 February 2008, <http://www.guardian.co.uk/technology/2008/feb/09/internet.china>, last accessed 30 April 2008; James Fallows, 'The Connection Has Been Reset', *Atlantic Monthly*, March 2008, <http://www.theatlantic.com/doc/200803/chinese-firewall>, last accessed 30 April 2008.

[43] 'Shanghai Cracks Down on Net Cafes', *Reuters*, 6 May 2002, <http://www.wired.com/news/politics/0,1283,52330,00.html>, last accessed 30 April 2008.

[44] Ibid.

content on the basis IP numbers. To the Internet, all IP addresses look alike so far as geography and content is concerned. As a result, China's attempts to regulate content are costly and, at least with respect to sophisticated Internet users, ineffective.

The attempt to regulate Internet content at the national level is costly, because most of the materials on the blocked websites would be beneficial or desirable to millions of users within China, and would have been matters of little or no concern even to the government. The regulation clearly impairs the overall transparency of the Internet significantly by preventing access to popular Internet services from a very large region for a very large number of people. China's attempt to regulate the Internet is ineffective because the Internet's fundamental architecture facilitates circumvention of the Great Firewall: sophisticated users can use proxy servers or a virtual private network (VPN) to evade the blocking of particular IP addresses.[45]

The second context for caution is the legal regulation of access to content by end users. In the case of China, this strategy would have been unavailing, because China lacked sufficient de facto power to influence content providers at an acceptable cost. Internet content providers outside of China did not have sufficient assets subject to Chinese control to give the Chinese government the means to coerce compliance with Chinese law restricting content. But when the government that wants to control content does have sufficient de facto power, the outcome may be different. This possibility is illustrated by the French Yahoo! case.

The case arose in early 2000 as a consequence of Yahoo!'s auction site, which is accessible from its French portal.[46] Among the items offered for sale on Yahoo!'s auction site is war memorabilia, including—at least back in 2000—items connected to the Nazi party. A French court attempted to prevent Yahoo! from auctioning Nazi items to or from France. That is, it was attempting to control the content delivered by the Internet to users who accessed the Internet from within French territory.

The French action resulted from suits filed by two French organizations, La Ligue Contre Le Racisme Et L'Antisemitisme (League Against Racism and Antisemitism, LICRA) and L'Union Des Étudiants Juifs De France (French Union of Jewish Students). These organizations brought a legal

---

[45] See, for example, Fallows, 'The Connection Has Been Reset'.

[46] For further detail on the case and its background, see, for example, Jack Goldsmith and Tim Wu, *Who Controls the Internet? Illusions of a Borderless World* (Oxford/New York: Oxford University Press, 2006), chapter 1.

action against Yahoo! in the Tribunal de Grande Instance de Paris (the 'French Court'). The French petitioners claimed that the sale of Nazi-related goods through Yahoo!'s auction site that is accessible in France violated Section R645-1 of the French Criminal Code, which prohibits exhibition of Nazi propaganda and artefacts for sale.[47] Because any French citizen is able to access the Nazi-related materials on the web site, the French Court found that Yahoo!'s auction site violates the French law, and entered an order requiring Yahoo! to block French citizens' access to the areas of Yahoo!'s auction site that offer for sale any Nazi-related materials.[48]

Yahoo! asked the French Court to reconsider its order, claiming that it was technologically impossible to selectively block French citizens from its auction site. Relying on expert testimony, however, the French Court found that blocking access from French citizens is technologically feasible. The panel of experts, including Vinton Cerf—one of the central designers of the Internet[49]—testified that some 70 per cent of the IP addresses of French users or users in French territory could be correctly identified to be located within the French territory.[50] By combining the IP address method with voluntary identification or registration, the experts opined that Yahoo! can filter French users with a success rate approaching 90 per cent. The French Court thus denied Yahoo!'s request and reaffirmed its earlier order.[51]

In response to the French Court's ruling, Yahoo! filed a complaint against the French organizations in United States District Court for the Northern District of California, seeking a declaratory judgment that the French Court's orders are neither cognizable nor enforceable under the laws of the United States. The defendants immediately moved to dismiss on the basis that the district court lacked personal jurisdiction over them.

---

[47] Indeed, it would seem that the auctioning of Nazi material also contravened the rules posted by Yahoo! at that time for the operation of its auction site—thus weakening the legitimacy of Yahoo!'s initial stance. See further Joel R. Reidenberg, 'Yahoo and Democracy on the Internet', *Jurimetrics Journal*, 2002, vol. 42, 261, 265–6.

[48] *LICRA v. Yahoo! Inc.*, T.G.I. (Tribunal de Grande Instance) Paris, 22 May 2000, No. 00/05308; unofficial English translation at <http://www.lapres.net/yahen.html>, last accessed 30 April 2008.

[49] See Chapter 1 (Section 1.6).

[50] 'Experts testify in French Yahoo! Case over Nazi Memorabilia', CNN, 6 November 2000, <http://www.cnn.com/2000/TECH/computing/11/06/france.yahoo.trial.ap>, last accessed 30 April 2008.

[51] *LICRA v. Yahoo! Inc.*, T.G.I. Paris, 20 November 2000, No. 00/05308; English translation at <http://www.cdt.org/speech/international/20001120yahoofrance.pdf>, last accessed 30 April 2008.

That motion was denied.[52] Yahoo! then moved for summary judgment on its declaratory judgment claim.

When considering the case on its merits, the District Court first noted that the case was not about the right of France or any other nation to determine its own law and social policies.[53] 'A basic function of a sovereign state is to determine by law what forms of speech and conduct are acceptable within its borders,' said the Court.[54] The issue was, according to the Court, 'whether it is consistent with the Constitution and laws of the United States for another nation to regulate speech by a US resident within the United States on the basis that such speech can be accessed by Internet users in that nation.'[55]

The conflict between the French and American judgments in the French Yahoo! case illustrates the inherent difficulty of national regulation of content on the Internet. Because the Internet is a global network of networks, the only way to ensure that content does not cross national boundaries is to eliminate the content altogether—meaning that the law of one nation will affect the availability of content throughout the world. The United States District Court in the French Yahoo! case based its decision on the principle that US law should trump the law of France in this situation. The District Court reasoned that 'although France has the sovereign right to regulate what speech is permissible in France, this Court may not enforce a foreign order that violates the protections of the United States Constitution by chilling protected speech that occurs... within our borders'.[56] Accordingly, Yahoo!'s motion for summary judgment was granted.

The French Yahoo! case exemplifies the central difficulty with the model of national regulation. That model assumes that the Internet can be regulated in accordance with the principle that each sovereign has power over its own territory. Taking the experts' opinion at its face value, it is possible to identify the geographical location of the computers on the Internet on the basis of their IP addresses with about 70 per cent accuracy. Thus, the blocking ordered by the French court would block about 70 per cent of the users from France, as well as many outside the country. The real problem, however, is what the figure 70 per cent represents. First of all, the experts themselves emphasized that 'there is no evidence to suggest

---

[52] *Yahoo!, Inc. v. La Ligue Contre Le Racisme Et L'Antisemitisme*, 145 F.Supp.2d 1168 (2001).

[53] Ibid. 1186.

[54] Ibid. Hence, at least one court in the United States should have no problem with China's regulation of the Internet.

[55] Ibid.   [56] Ibid. 1192.

that the same will apply in the future.'[57] In other words, the figure has no predictive value. The 70 per cent is a statistical figure estimated from the accidental history of how IP addresses were allocated around the world.[58] Moreover, it is a figure that was specific to France. It is not based on architecture or design constraints of the Internet. And there is nothing in the architecture of the Internet to prevent reassignment or reallocation of blocks of IP addresses to a different region or country. Thus, the 70 per cent given by the experts is not a stable figure that can be a basis for lasting regulation or policy. Therefore, any territorial blocking based on IP addresses is inherently over-inclusive and under-inclusive. How severe the problem is may be anyone's guess at a particular point in time.

The second problem is that IP address-based blocking can be easily circumvented by readily available technologies such as anonymizers. With such technology, users connect to a site through another server that hides the true origin of the user, and determination of the geographical location of the user based on IP address is consequently made impossible.[59] Thus, the anonymizers can render the regulation ordered by the French Court entirely under-inclusive where it really counts. That is, those users in France who insist on purchasing the Nazi-related materials on the Yahoo! site will easily circumvent the IP-based blocking, and the regulation would have very little impact.

There are technologies that can be used to 'dynamically discover' geographical location of the hosts based on their IP addresses.[60] But these technologies involve some sort of guessing game—for example, guessing physical distance by network response delay—that cannot guarantee a high rate of success.[61] In fact, under the current Internet architecture, any effort to map IP addresses to geographical location is fundamentally bound to be an inexact science, although rough and ready identification may be possible.[62] This is because allocation and distribution of IP

---

[57] *LICRA v. Yahoo! Inc.*, T.G.I. Paris, 20 November 2000, No. 00/05308 (English translation) at 9, <http://www.cdt.org/speech/international/20001120yahoofrance.pdf>, last accessed 30 April 2008.

[58] Further on the IP address allocation scheme, see Chapter 5 (Section 5.1).

[59] *LICRA v. Yahoo! Inc.*, T.G.I. Paris, Nov. 20, 2000, No. 00/05308 (English translation) at 9.

[60] See, for example, Venkata N. Padmanabhan and Lakshminarayanan Subramanian, 'An Investigation of Geographic Mapping Techniques for Internet Hosts', *Proceedings of ACM SIGCOMM 2001*, 2001, August, 173–85, <http://www.acm.org/sigs/sigcomm/sigcomm2001/ p14-pabmanabhan.pdf>, last accessed 30 April 2008. 'ACM SIGCOMM' stands for Association for Computing Machinery Special Interest Group on Data Communication.

[61] Ibid. 178.

[62] See also Dan Jerker B. Svantesson, 'Geo-Location Technologies and Other Means of Placing Borders on the 'Borderless' Internet', *John Marshall Journal of Computer & Information Law*, 2004, vol. XXIII, 101–39, 111–21; Dan Jerker B. Svantesson, ' "Imagine there's no

addresses are fundamentally activities above the TCP/IP layers—addresses are assigned without any *architectural* constraints or mandates—and information about them is simply not communicated to the IP layer. Thus, all efforts to map IP addresses to geographical location have the inherent problems of being over-inclusive and under-inclusive.

National regulation of the Internet does work in a variety of contexts, particularly when all of the parties to the regulated activity are within the physical territory of a particular nation state. But national regulation of the Internet is inherently costly and ineffective when the object of regulation is either the architecture of the Internet or content that originates outside of national boundaries. Thus, the model of national regulation by law cannot provide a complete solution to the problems of Internet governance.

2.8. The Market and Economics

If national regulation does not represent a complete solution to the problems of Internet governance, what about the market? By describing the problems of Internet governance as problems of regulation, an implicit assumption has been made—that market mechanisms do not provide a solution that obviates the need for government intervention or the creation of special transnational institutions. The model of the market and economics is premised on the idea that this implicit assumption is false. Rather than view Internet governance as a regulatory problem, the model attempts to redescribe the underlying phenomena in economic terms, as markets for products and services.

The economic approach to Internet governance can be illustrated by returning to ICANN and its regulation of the Domain Name System (DNS). There is much to be learned by stepping back and looking at the DNS as an ordinary service, provided by an ordinary organization, subject to the familiar laws of supply and demand. How can the provision of that service be organized so as to provide the greatest benefit of the public? How can the DNS be put to its highest and best use? As elaborated in Chapter 5 (Section 5.1), at the heart of the DNS is the root directory— the part of the system that allows the creation and utilization of top-level domains, like. com, .edu, and .org.

countries... " '—Geo-identification, the law and the not so borderless Internet', *Journal of Internet Law*, 2007, vol. 10, no. 9, 1, 18–21.

Root service is a scarce resource in the *economic sense*. The term 'scarce' can be used in a different sense, which we call the *engineering sense*. It is important to contrast and compare these two different senses of scarcity. When network engineers or network administrators approach the question of scarcity of domain names, they bring a particular perspective to the table. Does my name server have sufficient capacity to provide name service for everyone who is on my network? Is the set of allowable names large enough, so that I can give a name to everyone who makes a request? Thus, the network administrator for Widgets, Inc., would ask whether her name server can support all the third-level domains (3LDs) that are in use or likely to be in use. Perhaps, she needs to support www.widgets.com, ftp.widgets.com, and network.widgets.com. From her point of view, there is no scarcity. Even if she needed to add hundreds or thousands of 3LDs to her zone file, her name server could handle the work. No matter how many requests for 3LDs she gets, she will not run out of character strings. From her point of view, there is no scarcity in the SLD name server system or in the 3LD name space.

We can look at scarcity in the root in exactly the same way that our hypothetical engineer looks at scarcity in Widget's SLD. From the network engineer or network administrator's perspective, the root is not a scarce resource. There are currently less than 300 top-level domains (TLDs). This number does not even come close to taxing the capacity of the root server system. Moreover, if a very large number of new gTLDs did begin to tax the capacity of the system, it could simply be re-engineered. The theoretical capacity of the name space is vast.[63] From the engineering perspective, the root is not a scarce resource.

There is, however, an economic sense of the word scarcity that differs from the engineering sense. Economic scarcity exists whenever something is costly, even if it is abundant. A network engineer might say that there is no scarcity of capacity on an Ethernet network if the engineer has planned for sufficient resources (optical fibre, etc.) to meet anticipated demand into the foreseeable future. The same engineer might say that storage space on the email server is scarce, if the server is reaching its physical limit. To the economist, both resources are scarce. The various components that produce capacity on an Ethernet network all have costs. The optical fibre that created practical abundance is not free.

The root is a scarce resource in the economic sense for two distinct and independent reasons. First, the root server system itself is economically

---

[63] See further Chapter 5 (Section 5.1).

scarce. Second, the name space is economically scarce. If either of these propositions is true, then root service is a scarce resource from the economic point of view.

The root server system is scarce in the economic sense, because root service is not free. To provide root service, there must be root servers (computers that provide root service to the Internet). The root servers (i.e. the computers) are not free.[64] The software that runs the root servers is not free—it took human labour to create that software. The root servers must be maintained, and the labour that does the maintenance is not free. Root service is scarce in the economic sense.

This same point can be made by examining the capacity of the root server system. The precise capacity of the root server system is not documented and probably the upper limit has not been tested. Assume that a conservative upper limit on the current capacity of the system is from 1,000 to 10,000 TLDs. There is demand for TLDs, and the supply is, at least temporarily, limited by the capacity of the root system. It follows from the definition of economic scarcity, that TLDs are scarce and, therefore, if TLDs were sold, they will command a price.

So far this discussion has assumed a static root server system, but the hardware and software providing root service are not fixed in stone; therefore, the potential upper limit on the supply of TLDs is not inherently static. Even if the existing root server system can only support thousands of TLDs, a new and improved root server system might be able to support millions or even billions of TLDs. But this does not change the fact that root service is a scarce resource in the economic sense. Upgrading the root server system would be costly, and this fact suffices to establish the conclusion that root service is scarce in the economic sense.

There is another reason why the root is a scarce resource. The root name space is itself scarce. Names are simply strings of characters. If there were no upper limit on the length of a name string, then the name space as a logical construct would be infinite. Even if the limit were 10, the number of logically possible names would be in the quadrillions—so many that there are no conceivable circumstances under which the supply would be exhausted.[65] Nonetheless, the name space is a scarce economic resource. The economic scarcity of the root flows from the differential value of

---

[64] Of course, the owners or operators of the root servers may donate them to the system, but this does not make them free in the economic sense. Someone pays for the root servers. They do not appear out of the ether.

[65] The number of strings is $37^{10} + 37^9 + \cdots + 37^1 = 4,942,156,160,540,570$ (roughly 5 quadrillion). That would currently allow nearly a million domain names per person on Earth.

different names. For example, .com is more valuable than .kjd-7xx9-a, and this is true despite the fact that either string will do equally well at the job of connecting an end user to a server on the net.

There are two reasons to believe that different names have different values. The first reason is that the market prices different names differently—as elaborated in Chapter 5. The second reason is that different names have different useful characteristics; another way of putting this second point is to say that different names have different functional utilities.

Consider the first point. Experience in secondary SLD markets demonstrates that different names have different economic values. And there is little reason to doubt that the same would apply for TLDs if there were a market. Imagine, for example that ICANN conducted an auction for the following two TLD strings: '.sex' and '.8ki3—d'. It is obvious that the former TLD string would command a relatively high price,[66] and the other string would either attract no bids or bids at a much lower level.[67]

There is a good reason why the market prices different strings differently. Not all names are created equal. Due to their semantic and typographical properties, some names are more useful than others. For example, some names are more memorable than others. Strings that are memorable, such as .biz or .web, are more valuable than strings that are difficult to remember.

From the standpoint of economics, a good place to begin an analysis of root allocation and the creation of TLDs is the question, 'Should root service be provided by the market?' One reason for answering such a question in the negative is that the good or service in question is a 'public good' in the sense of a good that ought to be provided by government or a public entity. National defence and clean air are usually considered public goods. Conversely, if root service is a 'private good', without significant negative externalities (or social costs), then well-established and uncontroversial economic theory suggests that it can best be provided by markets.[68]

---

[66] In US litigation in 2003, a federal judge valued the use of sex.com over a five-year period at US$65 million: see *Kremen v. Cohen*, No. 01-15899 (9th Cir. 3 January 2003).

[67] Of course, there are imaginable scenarios in which the meaningless string would attract a high price. For example, if someone devised a use for a TLD that required that the string almost never be entered by accident, and if only one new TLD would be allowed into the root, an arbitrary, meaningless string might command a high price. But this example merely confirms the principal point, that different TLD name strings will command different prices in a market.

[68] Paul Samuelson, 'Pure Theory of Public Expenditure', *The Review of Economics and Statistics*, 1954, vol. 36, no. 4, 387–9.

The phrase 'public good' is ambiguous. In one sense, the public good is simply whatever is in the interest of the public as a whole; in this sense, 'public good' is a synonym for 'common weal'. Economists use the phrase 'public good' in a more restricted and technical sense. A given good or service is a 'pure public good' if and only if it meets the following two criteria: (*a*) non-rival consumption and (*b*) non-excludability. By 'non-rival consumption', economists mean that consumption of the good by one individual does not limit the availability of the good to any other individual. By 'non-excludability', economists mean that the providers of the good or service are unable to exclude individuals from access to the good.[69]

Is root service a public good? In the domain name policy literature, statements are sometimes made suggesting that the answer to this question is yes. For example, the operating principles of the Government Advisory Committee to ICANN state that 'the Internet naming and addressing system is a public resource that must be managed in the interests of the global Internet community'.[70] Because the notion of a 'public resource' is not defined, it is difficult to discern what this statement means.

Root service is clearly not a public good in the economic sense. Although root service might look like it is unlimited and free from a user's perspective, the same is not true from the perspective of a provider or proprietor of root service. First, root service to the proprietors of TLD registries is rivalrous. If the root points to a name server (or system of parallel name servers) operated by Verisign to provide name service for the .com TLD, then it cannot also point to a name server (or system) operated by a different registry for the .com TLD. For name service to work, each domain name must resolve to a unique IP address. This in turn requires that each second-level domain must be identified by a unique (or coordinated set of) first-level domain name server(s). If Verisign operates the name server for .com, then no one else can operate that same name server for a given root. Hence, root service, as well as other names services, is rivalrous in the economic sense.

Second, root service to the proprietors of TLD registries is excludable. Any given TLD can be either included or excluded from the root. Thus, the operator of the root can sell root service to TLD registries. If the

---

[69] See Dennis C. Mueller, *Public Choice II* (Cambridge: Cambridge University Press, 1989), 11; Mark Blaug, *Economic Theory in Retrospect* (Cambridge: Cambridge University Press, 1996, 5th edn.), 580.

[70] See Governmental Advisory Committee Operating Principles (adopted 25 May 1999), <http://www.icann.org/committees/gac/operating-principles-25may99.htm>.

proprietor of a given TLD registry refuses to pay, then the operator of the root can simply eliminate the TLD from the root or point to a name server operated by a rival registry proprietor. Hence, root service is excludable in the economic sense. By extension, all levels of name service are similarly excludable.

What are the implications of the conclusion that root service is a private and not a public good? At this stage, we will set aside the question whether there can be competition for root service. Given that root service is a private good, it could be provided efficiently by profit-seeking entities, such as for-profit corporations.

Private firms' sale of root service could be accomplished through a variety of pricing mechanisms. As discussed above, it would be difficult to sell root service directly to users and therefore root service providers would be more likely to sell root service to the proprietors of TLDs. Root service would be one of the factors (costs) of operating a TLD, and hence would be incorporated into the price the TLD operators charge to reg-istrants of SLDs, assuming the TLD proprietor was in the SLD business.[71] What price would be charged? If there were competition in the market for root service, the price would equal the costs of root service (including, of course, the cost of capital in the form of interest to lenders and dividends or share price appreciation for equity holders). Given that the cost of providing root service is relatively low,[72] the price would be low.

Why should private goods be provided by markets? At a fundamental level, the answer to this question lies in the Pareto Principle:[73] given the possibility of improving the welfare of one individual without harm-ing anyone, the Pareto Principle requires that we take the action that results in the improvement. A market transaction, where individual X and individual Y voluntarily exchange some good or service for payment, is required by the Pareto Principle, unless the transaction results in an externality—that is, a cost or harm to some third party. Markets both

---

[71] Some TLD operators might not sell SLDs. For example, if .ibm were a TLD, then Interna-tional Business Machines might use .ibm for its own purposes and not offer any other entities registrations in .ibm. In that case, the cost of .ibm would be passed on to the purchasers of IBM products.

[72] ICANN has provided the IANA functions for the entire Internet for only a few million dollars per year. See, for example, ICANN, *Proposed Fiscal Year 2004–2005 Budget* (17 May 2004), 7; available at <http://www.icann.org/financials/proposed-budget-14may04.pdf>, last accessed 30 April 2008.

[73] There are actually two Pareto Principles, Strong Pareto and Weak Pareto. Strong Pareto requires actions that improve the welfare of every person. Weak Pareto requires actions that improve the welfare of at least one person but do not make any person worse off. See, for example, Howard F. Chang, 'A Liberal Theory of Social Welfare: Fairness, Utility, and the Pareto Principle', *Yale Law Journal*, 2000, vol. 110, 173, 176–7.

allow Pareto-efficient transactions and give incentives for all such transactions to take place. In a market, the purchaser who derives the greatest benefit from a good or service will be willing to pay the highest price. For this reason, markets put resources to their highest and best use.

In the context of domain name policy, the point is that a market will allow the root to be put to its highest and best economic use. Unless a particular TLD would create a negative externality—a harm to the root itself or Internet users—the Pareto Principle says that TLD should be created. This is the economic version of what has been called *Cerf's Principle*: a string should enter the root if it will do no harm.[74] Economists would extend this principle: a TLD string or slot should be freely exchangeable, unless its exchangeability would harm some third party.

The idea that name service could be viewed as a private good does not imply the further conclusion that name service should be free of government regulation on the basis of social costs (or 'externalities' in the economic sense). For example, the string of characters that make up a name could make a false and injurious statement, triggering liability for defamation. Because domain names can communicate brief messages, they can become the vehicle for the creation of social costs similar to those created by other communications media. In this regard, domain names might be viewed as similar to text messages—but with the important additional feature that domain names are 'texted' to the whole world instead of a particular recipient.

The most important example of social costs associated with domain name registrations is 'cybersquatting'—the registration of a domain name that infringes a trademark for the sole purpose of extracting a payment for transfer of the domain name. If the root were to be auctioned, this would create the opportunity for 'root cybersquatting'.

Of course, if a new TLD were used to sell a product or service in a manner that infringed a trademark, the operator of the TLD would be subject to civil liability as would anyone who used any communications medium. That a new medium of communication creates new opportunities for trademark infringement is hardly an argument for treating the medium as

---

[74] The principle is named after Vinton Cerf. It is a corollary of Karl Auerbach's 'First Law of the Internet,' which states: 'Every person shall be free to use the Internet in any way that is privately beneficial without being publicly detrimental. The burden of demonstrating public detriment shall be on those who wish to prevent the private use. Such a demonstration shall require clear and convincing evidence of public detriment. The public detriment must be of such degree and extent as to justify the suppression of the private activity.' See Karl Auerbach, 'First Law of the Internet' (27 March 2003), <http://www.icannwatch.org/comments.pl?sid=1242&cid=11389>, last accessed 30 April 2008.

a public good. If that were the case, webpages should be treated as public goods, since any webpage used to sell a good or service can potentially be used for trademark infringement.

Cybersquatting differs from ordinary trademark infringement because cybersquatters do not use domain names to sell products or services. The purpose of cybersquatting is to extract a payment from the owner of the trademark. From the point of view of the economic model of Internet governance, the question is whether cybersquatting is inefficient or—to use slightly different terminology—whether cybersquatting creates a dead weight loss.

Economic analysis of this question can begin with the Coase Theorem— named for the Nobel Prize winning economist Ronald Coase.[75] Coase observed that in the absence of transaction costs, the assignment of entitlements does not affect the efficiency of outcomes. As applied to the problem of cybersquatting, the idea is very simple. If cybersquatters and trademark owners could bargain with zero costs, then domain names which had their highest and best use as the property of the trademark owner would all be sold to the trademark owners. Of course, there would be a distributional effect (a transfer from trademark owners to cybersquatters), but this does not result in economic inefficiency.

In the real world, however, the transfer of trademarked domain names from cybersquatters to copyright owners would result in positive transaction costs. Trademarked domain names are not commodities that have standard prices. Would the root name '.ibm' be worth a thousand euros or a million euros? It is not difficult to imagine that the negotiations to determine the answer to that question would consume considerable resources. Given positive transaction costs, the allocation of the original entitlement can be demonstrated to affect the efficiency of the outcome. In the case of domain names, this suggests that the right to register a trademarked name should be allocated to the trademark owner. That result could be accomplished by regulations enacted by national governments or it could be instituted unilaterally by the proprietor of the Domain Name System in order to avoid the cost and trouble that could result if the registration of trademarked domain names involves the operator of the name system in litigation.

If we assume that the problem of harmful domain names can be handled by a combination of market forces and government regulation, the

---

[75] Ronald H. Coase, 'The Problem of Social Cost', *Journal of Law and Economics*, 1960, vol. 3, 1–44.

economic model faces another important question: is the provision of root service a natural monopoly? From the technological point of view, there is no barrier to the creation of alternative roots. ICANN could operate one root system, and one or more other entities could operate competing roots. As elaborated in Chapter 5 (Section 5.1), alternative root services do exist but these provide service to only a tiny fraction of Internet users. Why? The following paragraphs argue that the economics of root service strongly favour a single root. The argument does not depend on technical considerations. Even assuming that multiple roots were technically feasible, the marketplace would result in a single root (or perhaps a dominant root, with a tiny fraction of purchased domain names residing in alternative roots). This conclusion is based on two factors: (*a*) the economic notion of networking effects; and (*b*) the cost structure of root service providers. These two factors would inevitably lead a system that began with competing alternative roots to evolve into a system with a single root. The same factors prevent a system with a single root from evolving into a system with multiple roots.

First, consider 'networking effects' or 'networking externalities'—terms here being used in a technical economic sense.[76] The value of root service increases with the number of users of the service. A single root with many users is more valuable than a single root with few users. Given any arbitrary number of users, root service is more valuable if all of the users patronize the same root, and as a consequence, root service is less valuable if the same users divide their patronage among two or more competing roots. Second, consider the cost structure of root service providers. Much of the cost of operating a root is fixed. Although a root with more customers in theory requires more server capacity, given the distributed nature of the DNS, the marginal costs of serving additional customers are relatively small as a share of total costs. Given these two factors (networking effects and a high ratio of fixed to marginal costs), rational TLD proprietors will choose to purchase root service from the market leader. This is because the market leader provides a more valuable service at a lower cost. ISPs will point towards the market leader's root server, because the market leader's root service is more valuable to the ISP's customers than is the root service provided by other root service providers. Both the networking and cost effects become more and more pronounced as the market share of the market leader becomes larger and larger. For this reason we would expect the market to lead to a single

[76] See, for example, Shy, *Economics of Network Industries*, 1–6.

firm providing root service, that is, root service will be provided by a monopolist.

The way that networking effects operate with respect to root service can be illustrated by performing a thought experiment. Imagine that the root became fragmented. If there were many competing roots, and many competing sets of TLDs, then different users would reach different destinations by entering the same domain name. ICANN's root presumably would result in www.amazon.com being resolved to the IP Address of the e-commerce retailer in Seattle, Washington. An alternate root might result in the same domain name being resolved to a tour operator in Brazil. Different Internet Service Providers (ISPs) would point requests for root service to different root servers. As a result, individuals would get different results for the same domain name when they moved from one ISP (at home) to another (at work or at an Internet café). As fragmentation increases, the value of domain names decreases.[77] If I am an Internet user, I am less likely to invest in memorizing or memorializing 'www.amazon.com' if it does not reliably get me to the website I am seeking. If I am a website proprietor, I am less likely to invest in publicizing a domain name, if users will frequently be directed to another proprietor's website when they enter the string of characters that I am advertising.

Profit-maximizing firms with monopolies will (in the absence of price regulation) extract monopoly rents. That is, they will charge rents that exceed their costs. Unless the monopolist can successfully engage in price discrimination, monopoly rents will be inefficient. The monopoly rent raises the price of the monopoly good, and as a result, some consumers of the good who would have paid the market price will not consume the good. In the case of domain names, however, price discrimination is a real possibility.[78] For example, the monopoly proprietor of the root could auction TLDs.[79] If a firm wished to become the proprietor of the .biz TLD,

---

[77] This conclusion would hold even if ISPs or third-party vendors provided a service that aggregated alternate roots, giving users a menu of the alternate destinations for a given domain name. The extra step, choosing among the alternative resolutions, increases the time required (and hence the cost) of the aggregated alternative root services.

[78] In fact, price discrimination already occurs with so-called premium domain names being sold for higher prices than 'standard' names. The former category of names is typically easy to remember and intuitively associated with potential e-commerce business models. See, for example, 'Premium .TV domain names', <http://www.totalregistrations.com/services/twstvpop.html>, last accessed 30 April 2008.

[79] As already happens. See, for example, 'Dot-mobi domains go to highest bidders', *The Register*, 11 October 2007, <http://www.theregister.co.uk/2007/10/11/dotmobi_domain_auction/>, last accessed 30 April 2008.

the monopolist could auction .biz. In cases where no bidder possesses monopsony power,[80] the auction price should provide a monopoly rent to the holder of the root-service monopoly and also ensure that the TLD goes to its highest and best economic use.

There are, moreover, limits on the rent that a monopoly proprietor of the root could charge. Most obviously, the monopolist could not charge a rent in excess of the value of the TLD to potential purchasers. There are additional limits. At bottom, the Internet is a communications system, and as such, it competes with other systems. If the proprietor of a root charged too much for root service, end users and information providers would use alternative communications systems—for example, telephone, broadcast, and direct mail.

So far, we have assumed that the proprietor of the root is a profit-maximizing firm and will charge monopoly rents. Does ICANN seek to maximize profit? An adequate account of the institutional economics of non-profit corporations is far beyond the scope of this chapter. Nonetheless, it is fairly clear that ICANN does not maximize profits in the way that for-profit firms do. That is, ICANN does not seek to maximize its revenues from root service. Indeed, ICANN continues to provide root service to ccTLD operators who refuse to pay ICANN any fee at all. ICANN, as a non-profit corporation, operates the root in the public interest. As a non-profit corporation organized under the laws of the State of California, it must have a 'public or charitable purpose'.[81]

The obligation to act in the public interest is, however, abstract and vague. This is true both as a matter of political philosophy and as a matter of law. As a matter of political philosophy, the nature of the public interest is, at the very least, contested. That is, whatever the ultimate resolution of philosophical debates about what counts as the public interest, as a practical matter this is a question of which we are unlikely to see a strong social consensus in a modern pluralist democracy.[82] The lack of consensus on the nature of the public interest is even more evident in the international context: the Internet affects diverse cultures with different value systems. As a matter of law, the obligation to act in the public interest underdetermines ICANN's actions. Undoubtedly, ICANN could

---

[80] There may well be cases in which one bidder will possess monopsony power. For example, the owner of a trademark may have a legal monopoly over use of the mark. For this reason, it may be that the proprietor of a TLD name that is identical or substantially similar to a trademark may have a legal right to exclude others from acting as proprietors of their TLD.

[81] Californian Corporate Code § 5111.

[82] Cf. John Rawls, *Political Liberalism* (New York: Columbia University Press, 1993).

85

make DNS policy in a variety of ways without endangering its status under Californian law, but there is one thing that ICANN cannot do given its legal status. ICANN cannot operate the DNS so as to maximize its own profits or so as to confer a private benefit on the various stakeholders that participate in ICANN operations.

What are the lessons of the economics of root service for the market model of Internet governance? It seems that the implications are mixed. On the one hand, economic analysis of the root suggests that ICANN's decision-making process regarding root expansion may have been—at least up until very recently—fundamentally flawed. Prior to June 2008, ICANN pursued a relatively restrictive policy on root expansion, resulting in artificial scarcity of TLDs and an inefficient allocation of those TLDs that have been created. However, this situation should change with ICANN's decision, announced in June 2008, to radically liberalize its policy.[83] On the other hand, networking externalities and the resulting monopoly suggest that competitive solutions may not be available for some services that are provided by Internet governance institutions. Thus, the basic premise of ICANN's creation—that name service should be provided in the public interest—may be valid, while ICANN's actual policy decisions prior to June 2008 may have been contrary to the public interest.

2.9. Hybrid Models

So which is the best model of Internet governance? The argument of this chapter has been that no single model provides the solution to all the problems that Internet regulation can address. Nonetheless, the analysis does suggest some tentative conclusions that can help to order thinking about making Internet governance policy.

First, a broad range of issues that involve the Internet can be resolved without recourse to any special institutions or principles of Internet governance. In a wide variety of circumstances, markets work perfectly well. When government is needed, many problems can be solved at the national level through regular lawmaking processes. In other words, the model of national regulation and the market model should be the first recourse of policymakers. It is only when markets and national

---

[83] See further Chapter 5 (Section 5.1.2).

governments both fail that special Internet governance institutions are required.

Second, not all of the remaining issues of Internet regulation require solutions. In some cases, the best policy is to leave the Internet alone. For example, the Internet frustrates government policies that seek to inhibit freedom of speech and liberty of conscience. To use the old metaphor, this is a feature, not a bug. Although the romantic idea of the cyberspace as a self-governing realm of spontaneous ordering and inherent freedom is exaggerated, it does contain an important kernel of truth. There are advantages to those features of Internet architecture that frustrate national regulation. There should be no general presumption in favour of a system of either national or international regulation that would transform the Internet to facilitate legal control of content along national lines.

Third, there are great virtues to the existing system for Internet governance in the narrow sense—that is, the system for the regulation of and by code and architecture. That system has produced the transparent Internet that serves as an engine of innovation and open communication. The model of transnational governance institutions that supports the existing architecture for reasons of network engineering serves as an institutional bulwark for the preservation of these features of the Internet. The alternatives, national or international regulation, seem likely to degrade rather than enhance these desirable characteristics.

Fourth, the virtues of the current system do not entail the conclusion that improvements cannot be made. On the one hand, national regulation can become more sensitive to the value of preserving the Internet's architecture: in particular, national regulation should respect the end-to-end principle and the layered design of the TCP/IP. On the other hand, transnational Internet governance institutions can become more sensitive to the economics of Internet regulation and the possibility that an engineering perspective may lead to decisions that waste Internet as a resource.

These four conclusions lead naturally to a fifth. The best models of Internet governance are hybrids that incorporate some elements from all five models. Internet governance is a complex task requiring a complex set of regulatory mechanisms. As a result, the optimal system of governance is a combination of regulation by transnational institutions, respect for the architecture that creates transparency, national regulation, and markets.

2.10. Internet Governance and the Future of the Internet: The Case of Network Neutrality

How will evolving models of Internet governance affect the future of the Internet? Current controversies over 'network neutrality' provide a case study for the complex ways in which modalities of Internet governance interact with substantive policy concerns.[84] Analysis of the issue might start with the model of Code. The architecture of the Internet is neutral among applications. TCP/IP is insensitive to the particular application; all packets are treated equally and no particular application or user is favoured over any other. As noted above, a variety of arguments can be made for network neutrality, importantly including the claim that the transparency of the Internet facilitates innovation.

The economic model of Internet governance might be used to generate a different set of insights. Network service providers can argue that they should be free to innovate in the provision of Internet service to firms and individuals. By discriminating against some services, such as peer-to-peer file sharing or streaming video, they may be able to provide a more responsive network environment. Consumers may prefer to purchase network services from a provider who discriminates against some packets in order to favour others. On the surface, at least, the economic model suggests that competition between service providers will provide the best answer to the question whether a neutral network or a discriminatory network is more valuable to consumers. Consumers who prefer a neutral network would patronize neutral ISPs; consumers who prefer a discriminatory network would buy broadband service from ISPs that discriminate against applications that 'hog' bandwidth.

This simple answer to the network neutrality question is based on the assumption that there is efficient competition between providers of broadband service. There are questions about the competitiveness of the market for broadband services. Phone companies that provide DSL service[85] or cable television providers might have monopoly power—at least with respect to some consumers. Some consumers may not have

---

[84] See generally, Christopher S. Yoo, 'Network Neutrality and the Economics of Congestion', *Georgetown Law Journal*, 2006, vol. 94, 1847–1908; Christopher S. Yoo, 'Beyond Network Neutrality', *Harvard Journal of Law & Technology*, 2005, vol. 19, no. 1, <http://jolt.law.harvard.edu/articles/pdf/v19/19HarvJLTech001.pdf>; Zittrain, *The Future of the Internet*, 178–85; Thomas M. Lenard and Randolph J. May (eds.), *Net Neutrality or Net Neutering: Should Broadband Internet Services Be Regulated?* (New York: Springer Publishing, 2006); Barbara van Schewick, 'Towards an Economic Framework for Network Neutrality Regulation', *Journal of Telecommunications and High Technology Law*, 2007, vol. 5, 329–83.

[85] Digital Subscriber Line, that is, transmission of digital data over a telephone network.

a choice: DSL service is not available at all geographic locations. Even consumers who could theoretically choose between DSL and cable may face high switching costs and difficulty obtaining information about the network neutrality policies of their providers.

Some advocates of network neutrality argue that if broadband providers have monopoly power, they may attempt to leverage that power. For example, a cable provider might discriminate against Internet video in order to advantage their own streaming or 'on demand' video products. Standard economic models predict that this will not occur. Although the models themselves are technical, their core insight is easy to understand. The monopolist broadband providers can extract their full monopoly rent in the price they charge for broadband service. Once they are charging the full monopoly price, the attempt to extract even more by discriminating in favour of their own video products will simply result in less demand for their broadband services.[86] Other economists have challenged the conventional wisdom, arguing that increased profits in the market for the complimentary product (in this case, video) can exceed the loss in monopoly rents in the primary market (in this case, broadband services).[87] Most recently, Barbara van Schewick has demonstrated that monopolists in the provision of broadband services can have an incentive to discriminate against applications in a variety of circumstances. For example, if AOL had a monopoly position in the provision of instant messaging services and was a local monopolist in the provision of broadband service, it might have an incentive to exclude rival instant messaging services from its broadband network in order to preserve its monopoly in instant messaging. The Federal Communications Commission in the United States considered a similar argument when it approved AOL's merger with Time-Warner on the condition that the combined firm not exclude competitors' instant messaging services from their networks.[88] Van Schewick also demonstrates that even if the market for broadband services is competitive, broadband service providers may have incentives to engage in inefficient discrimination among applications.[89]

---

[86] See, for example, Robert H. Bork, *The Antitrust Paradox: A Policy at War with Itself* (New York: Free Press, 1993, 2nd edn.), 372–5; Richard A. Posner, *Antitrust Law* (Chicago: University of Chicago Press, 2001, 2nd edn.), 198–9.

[87] See Michael D. Whinston, 'Tying, Foreclosure, and Exclusion', *American Economic Review*, 1990, vol. 80, 840, 850–2.

[88] Barbara van Schewick, 'Towards an Economic Framework for Net Neutrality Regulation', 352.

[89] Ibid. 377.

Even if we assume a competitive market and that broadband service providers will only discriminate against applications in response to consumer demand, such discrimination may generate social costs. As noted above in connection with the code model of Internet governance, network neutrality facilitates innovation at the application level. Neither consumers nor network service providers fully internalize these costs. An individual consumer's decision to patronize a discriminatory broadband provider will have a negligible effect on the benefits of application innovation to that consumer. Similarly, even a major broadband service provider will only absorb a small fraction of the total social costs of innovation that is discouraged by its discriminatory network. The magnitude of these costs is impossible to estimate in advance. Future application innovations may create economic value on the same order of magnitude as HTML created by enabling the World Wide Web, but it is also possible that there simply are no more 'killer applications' in the future of the Internet whether or not network neutrality is maintained.

The resolution of the economic arguments for and against broadband neutrality is beyond the scope of this chapter. The important point is that the economic model does not guarantee efficient results. This suggests that the network neutrality issue requires the engagement of another modality of Internet governance. The most obvious possibility is the model of national government regulation. In the United States, for example, the federal Congress has considered network neutrality legislation that would prohibit network service providers from discriminating among applications.[90]

Of course, government regulation of network neutrality at the national level would need to be coordinated in order to preserve the value of transparent global Internet.

Because regulation at the national level may be inadequate, it might be argued that the best solution to the network neutrality problem is provided by the model of transnational institutions and international organizations. As a practical matter, however, an international solution seems remote at best. None of the existing transnational governance institutions (such as IETF or ICANN) would conceive of network neutrality

---

[90] See Declan McCullagh and Anne Broache, 'Republicans Defeat Net Neutrality Proposal', *CNET News.com*, 5 April 2006, <http://news.com.com/2100-1028_3-6058223.html>, last accessed 30 April 2008. For an overview of US government actions and statements of officials concerning network neutrality, see John Windhausen, Jr., 'Good Fences Make Bad Broadband: Preserving an Open Internet through Net Neutrality', (Public Knowledge White Paper, 6 February 2006), <http://static.publicknowledge.org/pdf/pk-net-neutrality-whitep-20060206.pdf>.

regulation as within their respective mandate. No existing treaty-based international organization has jurisdiction over the Internet, and no such organization would view domestic network neutrality as an appropriate topic for international regulation. Thus, an international solution to the network neutrality problem would likely require a new treaty regime, and any new treaty regime faces enormous political obstacles. Because the costs of a loss of global Internet transparency are 'invisible' and difficult to estimate, the prospects for an international agreement that guarantees the future transparency of the global Internet seem dim at best.

What lessons for the future of Internet governance can be learned from the example of network neutrality? None of the models of Internet governance guarantees optimal policy. Transparency and neutrality were built into the TCP/IP, but the model of code requires the voluntary cooperation of all the key players to preserve neutrality between applications. In the early days of the Internet, when the key players were research institutions and cooperating government entities, there was some hope that the transparency built into the code could be preserved. This vision of Internet governance was extended to the earliest transnational Internet governance institutions—the IETF and IANA—but as the global Internet became economically important, giant corporations and national governments replaced universities and researchers in key roles. As a result, bottom–up, consensus-based decision-making that focuses on network engineering is no longer as feasible. Market forces and the interests that drive government regulation are sure to have a major role in shaping the future of the Internet. For this reason, the role of independent institutions and researchers that assess Internet policy and provide input into the decision-making processes of national regulators and transnational Internet governance institutions may be more important than ever. Multidisciplinary research that approaches problems of Internet regulation and governance from the perspectives of network engineering, law, economics, and social choice theory may offer the best hope for an Internet future that avoids catastrophic unintended consequences.

3

Governors of Internet

Lee A. Bygrave and Terje Michaelsen

3.1. Overview of Internet Governance Structure

There is no single governor of the Internet. Governance is rather wrought by a mélange of various bodies—private and public, old and new. Viewed from afar, the governance structure resulting from these bodies' inter-action appears relatively flat, open, sprawling, ad hoc, and amorphous. Lines of responsibility are blurred, as are lines of competence and funding. Many of the lines straddle if not eviscerate traditional organizational boundaries. All in all, it is a governance structure reflecting both the Internet itself and its history of development.

Concomitantly, the governance structure is relatively unencumbered by dirigiste ideology. While tentacles of government control are increasingly visible, private sector bodies have usually been permitted—and, indeed, often encouraged—to play the lead role in design and management of the Internet. Governments have acted more as facilitative partners of these bodies than as heavy-handed regulators—at least in Western, liberal democracies. To a large extent, then, governance has been exercised by cooperative networks rather than decree.

Just as there is no single governor of the Internet, there is no single Treaty that specifically lays down the ground rules for how the Internet is to be governed. This is not to say that governance of the Internet falls outside the ambit of international or national laws. Yet the mortar and brick for many of the central elements of the governance structure are provided outside a treaty framework, and often without a direct basis in legislation. Contracts and quasi-contractual instruments—typically the tools of private law—play a relatively dominant role. Moreover, disputes tend not to be resolved by recourse to litigation in courts of law but by the use of various extra-judicial mechanisms (i.e. systems for 'alternative dispute resolution' or 'ADR').

A governance structure without a direct basis in treaties, where legislation in many respects plays second fiddle to contract, and where ADR is preferred to court litigation, is far from unique to the Internet. Nonetheless, numerous aspects of Internet governance are unusual, if not unique. In the congeries of Internet governors there exists a host of novel organizational creatures with rather special modes of operation. This subset of governors deals primarily with so-called Critical Internet Resources—in other words, the core architecture and infrastructure for Internet communication, particularly management of the Domain Name System, root servers, and IP addresses. The main bodies making up this governor subset are the Internet Society (ISOC), the Internet Architecture Board (IAB), the Internet Engineering Task Force (IETF), the World Wide Web Consortium (W3C), the Internet Assigned Numbers Authority (IANA), and the Internet Corporation for Assigned Names and Numbers (ICANN).

These bodies are described in more detail in Section 3.2. They and their individual members constitute the first generation of Internet governors. The reference to 'individual members' underlines the fact that governance in this first generation has been exercised under the relatively strong influence of individual persons. These persons have been able, alone and together, to make their mark over and above the organizations to which they have been attached. Prominent examples include Jon Postel, Vinton Cerf, and Tim Berners-Lee. They are persons who gained authority as governors and 'policy entrepreneurs' through a combination of technological prowess, strong charisma, considerable political insight, and high dedication to public service ideals.[1] Internet governance was particularly 'personal' in the above sense from the 1970s through to the late 1990s. In more recent years, relatively faceless organizations have increasingly taken over.

The first generation of Internet governors has governance of Internet architecture and infrastructure (or elements of it) as their chief remit. They variously exercise governorship in three broad, overlapping capacities:

---

[1] See further, for example, the description of the 'cult of Jon Postel' in Goldsmith and Wu, *Who Controls the Internet?*, 33–5.

1. As designers, creators, and fine-tuners of core protocols and applications for Internet communication (e.g. IP, TCP, HTTP).

2. As guardians of these protocols/applications and their inherent design principles (e.g. 'end-to-end').

3. As developers and guardians of the *decisional* principles upon which adoption, etc., of the communications architecture is based (e.g. 'rough consensus and running code').

In all three capacities, it is tempting to see these bodies as engineers or architects rather than politicians. Likewise, it is tempting to see them as primarily concerned with technical issues rather than issues of public policy. Yet as shown in this and other chapters, the line between the two types of issues is porous. The ostensibly technical decisions of the engineers have frequently an inherent public policy dimension or serve as catalysts for discussion on matters of public policy. One cannot, for example, properly understand much of the World Summit on the Information Society without recourse to some of the decisions taken by Internet engineers.[2]

The principal development in the overall governance structure for the Internet since the late 1990s is the entry of a host of new governors. They include national governments, intergovernmental organizations, business groups, consumer groups, and civil society groups. Indeed, the numbers of actual and potential Internet governors, together with the breadth of their constituencies, are now so large that it is tempting to describe the resulting governance structure as, in effect, governance by the world.

Unlike the first generation of Internet governors, the bulk of the new governors have traditionally not had governance of the Internet as their primary remit. Certainly some of them have long had a hand in Internet governance—the case particularly with the US government—though this has been typically in a monitoring or facilitative role. Many of them still do not have Internet governance as their chief concern but they are increasingly making conscious efforts to make their influence felt in the field. In doing so, they are infusing discourse on Internet governance with new policy agendas. And with these new agendas come new lines of tension and cleavage.

The impact of these actors—chiefly national governments—is explored at greater length in Section 3.3 of this chapter and in Chapter 6.

[2] Further on the World Summit on the Information Society, see Chapter 6.

3.2. The First Generation of Internet Governors

3.2.1. *Internet Society*

The Internet Society (ISOC) was formed in 1992, with Vinton Cerf as founding president. The primary motivation for its establishment was to provide an organizational umbrella for Internet standards development. Part and parcel of this rationale was a need to protect the individual persons involved in standards development from lawsuits. Prior to the founding of ISOC, it was difficult to pin legal responsibility on any particular organization for the standards created; hence, individuals became increasingly worried about being held personally liable for harm resulting from their standards decisions.[3] In addition, the issue of funding was rearing its head as DARPA and other US government bodies began to wind down their financial support for Internet standards development.

The Internet Society is formally registered as a non-profit corporation in Washington, DC, with offices in Geneva, Switzerland, and Reston, Virginia. According to its articles of incorporation (clause 3), the Society's main objects include

... to facilitate and support the technical evolution of the Internet as a research and education infrastructure, and to stimulate the involvement of the scientific community, industry, government and others in the evolution of the Internet.... [4]

An important purpose of the Society is to fund the work of the Internet Engineering Task Force (IETF)—the main workhorse in Internet standards development.[5] The Society also provides the IETF with insurance to cover liability for potential damage incurred by the IETF standards development process. Further, ISOC funds the position of Request-for-Comments (RFC) Editor and retains copyright in all published RFCs.[6]

Membership of ISOC falls into two main categories—organizational and individual—with each category breaking down into several sub-categories for which different membership fees apply.[7] There are currently more than 150 organizational members and 28,000 individual members spread in over 90 chapters around the globe. Membership is open to any person

---

[3] Mueller, *Ruling the Root*, 94.

[4] See <http://www.isoc.org/isoc/general/trustees/incorp.shtml>.

[5] See further Section 3.2.3 and Chapter 4 (Section 4.1).

[6] The RFC Editor manages (i.e. edits, publishes, and maintains a registry of) RFCs. Jon Postel originally carried out this task. It is now carried out by the Information Sciences Institute at the University of Southern California, where Postel worked.

[7] See generally ISOC By-Laws, Article V at <http://www.isoc.org/isoc/general/trustees/bylaws.shtml>.

or organization. It is cheapest for 'bona fide full-time students' (US$25 p.a.) and most expensive (US$10,000 p.a.) for 'regular' organizational members. At the same time, programmes are in place to allow donation by organizational members of considerably larger amounts of money to ISOC which the members concerned are able to earmark for designated purposes, such as sponsoring training workshops in developing countries.

ISOC is governed by a Board of Trustees that may consist of up to 20 persons. The Society's daily operations are taken care of by a staff of just over 30 persons. Board members are elected through a complex process for three-year terms by various constituencies—organizational members, chapters, and the Internet Architecture Board (described in Section 3.2.2).[8] Under the By-Laws, individual members have voting rights too, though these rights are currently suspended. The Board of Trustees itself may also appoint a small number of Trustees over and above the constituency-based Trustees.

Membership-fee payments and sponsor donations are a significant but not the sole means by which ISOC funds its activities. A considerable amount of revenue is generated through the operations of the Public Interest Registry (PIR), the organization that allocates domain names under the .org TLD. The Registry was established by ISOC in 2002 to bid for the authority to allocate names under the .org domain, upon expiration of Verisign's authority to do so. The bid was successful. Although PIR is a non-profit organization, it is able to charge a small amount for each domain name it allocates—currently just under US$7. These fees generated revenue of US$6.1 million for ISOC's 2006 budget and were projected to generate revenue of US$9.7 million for the 2007 budget.[9]

3.2.2. Internet Architecture Board

The Internet Architecture Board (IAB) was formed in 1992 as a sort of 'council of elders' presiding over development of Internet standards. Its precursors comprise a long list of bodies that morphed from one to the other over the preceding 20 years.[10]

---

[8] See further <http://www.isoc.org/isoc/general/trustees/select.shtml>.

[9] See further '2007 Budget', <http://www.isoc.org/isoc/general/trustees/agenda-nov-06.shtml>, last visited 20 June 2008.

[10] These include the Internet Configuration Control Board (formed in 1979 by Vinton Cerf); which was replaced by the Internet Advisory Board (in 1984); which then became the Internet Activities Board (in 1986) before morphing into the current IAB (in 1992). See further 'A Brief History of the Internet Advisory/Activities/Architecture Board', <http://www.iab.org/about/history.html>.

Formally, the IAB is chartered both as a committee of the IETF and as an advisory body of ISOC.[11] Its main tasks are to oversee and coordinate IETF activity, applying a long-term perspective. As part of this remit, the IAB approves new IETF working groups; appoints members of the Internet Engineering Steering Group (IESG—see further Section 3.2.4); appoints the chair of the Internet Research Task Force (IRTF—see further Section 3.2.5); approves appointment of the RFC Editor; and serves as appeal board for complaints alleging improper execution of the standards development process.

The IAB consists of 13 full members one of which functions as chair of the IETF and IESG.[12] The members serve one-year renewable terms. They serve as individuals, not as representatives of other bodies, and are not to owe any fiduciary duty of loyalty or care to IAB, IETF, IRTF, or IESG. They are selected for appointment by a Nomination Committee ('NomCom') on the basis of a complex procedure.[13] The ISOC Board of Trustees formally approves their appointment. The IAB, however, selects its own chair, who may appoint an honorary Executive Director to manage internal IAB operations.

3.2.3. *Internet Engineering Task Force*

The Internet Engineering Task Force (IETF) was established in 1986. As indicated above, it is the main workhorse in Internet standards development. Its basic mission is, in short, 'to make the Internet work better'.[14] As part of this mission, it produces a range of technical and engineering documents (protocol standards, best current practices, etc.) that are published in the RFC series. These documents typically identify pressing operational and technical problems in the Internet and propose solutions to these by standards specification.

An example of the sort of problems that the IETF typically works with is the availability and number of IP addresses. The IP currently most in use (IPv4) supports in total approximately 4 billion IP addresses. Although

---

[11] RFC 2850: Charter of the Internet Architecture Board (author: B. Carpenter) (May 2000), <http://www.ietf.org/rfc/rfc2850.txt>.

[12] In addition, there are several ex officio and liaison members who have no standing to participate in IAB decisions. For instance, the IRTF chair is an ex officio member.

[13] See RFC 3777: IAB and IESG Selection, Confirmation, and Recall Process: Operation of the Nominating and Recall Committees (author: J. Galvin) (June 2004), <http://www.ietf.org/rfc/rfc3777.txt>. The NomCom procedure is described in Chapter 4 (Section 4.1.3).

[14] RFC 3935: A Mission Statement for the IETF (author: H. Alvestrand) (October 2004), <http://www.ietf.org/rfc/rfc3935.txt>.

huge, this number is unlikely to be sufficient in the future as increasing numbers of devices and users link to the Internet. Thus, the IETF has developed a new IP version (IPv6)[15] which provides a massively bigger pool of addresses, thus permitting a much larger number of devices to have their own IP address.[16]

The IETF is not incorporated; nor does it operate with an elected board. It has an open and free international membership composed primarily of network engineers, designers, operators, vendors, and researchers. In principle, anyone can participate in its face-to-face meetings (held three times per year) and/or its email lists.

The bulk of decisions are made bottom–up and by 'rough consensus', with emphasis on openness, fairness, and inclusiveness. Provision is also made for dispute resolution procedures in which the IAB or ISOC Board of Trustees act as final arbiters.[17]

The main work of the IETF is carried out in working groups devoted to specific sets of issues. There are currently over 120 such groups. Each group zones to one of eight subject areas ('applications', 'routing', 'security', 'transport', etc.).[18] For each area there is an Area Director to manage and coordinate group efforts. Each working group appoints its own chairperson who acts as formal contact point between the group and the relevant Area Director.

The process for development of standards within the aegis of the IETF is termed the 'Internet Standards Process'. The basic elements of that process are set out in RFC 2026,[19] though the latter is under revision and has been amended several times.[20]

A standard in this context is essentially

the specification of a protocol, system behaviour or procedure that has a unique identifier, and where the IETF has agreed that 'if you want to do this thing, this is the description of how to do it'.[21]

---

[15] RFC 2460: Internet Protocol Version 6 (IPv6) (authors: S. Deering and R. Hinden) (December 1998), <http://www.ietf.org/rfc/rfc2460.txt>.

[16] Deployment of IPv6, though, has been slower than many expected, partly because the address pool offered by IPv4 is still some way from depletion. That in turn is due partly to the application of Network Address Translators allowing networks of devices to share the same address. See further <http://en.wikipedia.org/wiki/Network_address_translation>.

[17] See further Chapter 4 (section 4.1.3).

[18] See further <http://www.ietf.org/html.charters/wg-dir.html>.

[19] RFC 2026: The Internet Standards Process—Revision 3 (author: S. Bradner) (October 1996), <http://www.ietf.org/rfc/rfc2026.txt>.

[20] For an overview of the state of play (as of April 2008), see B. Carpenter, 'The IETF Process: An Informal Guide' (14 April 2008), <http://www.ietf.org/IESG/content/procdocs.html>, last accessed 20 June 2008.

[21] RFC 3935, section 2.

Adherence to a standard is voluntary:

[the standard] does not imply any attempt by the IETF to mandate its use, or any attempt to police its usage—only that 'if you say that you are doing this according to this standard, do it this way'.[22]

There are two main categories of standards: Technical Specifications and Applicability Statements. The latter describe how and under what circumstances the former work. Some standards may be further categorized in terms of their 'maturity level'. There are three such levels: (*a*) Proposed Standard; (*b*) Draft Standard; (*c*) Full or Internet Standard. Advancement from the one level to the next takes place according to a procedure called 'standard track' and requires successful operational experience with the specification according to certain criteria.[23] However, as noted in Chapter 4 (Section 4.1.3), most specifications never advance beyond level 1. Further, not all documents/specifications published by the IETF are on the standard track.[24]

The origins, organizational mechanics, and achievements of the IETF are described more fully in Chapter 4 (Section 4.1).

3.2.4. *Internet Engineering Steering Group*

The IESG manages and oversees the technical operations of the IETF. It can be seen as essentially the IETF's executive body. Its charter has never been formally established but its current responsibilities are documented in RFC 3710 (informational only) as follows:

The Internet Engineering Steering Group (IESG) is the group responsible for the direct operation of the IETF and for ensuring the quality of work produced by the IETF. The IESG charters and terminates working groups, selects their chairs, monitors their progress and coordinates efforts between them. The IESG performs technical review and approval of working group documents and candidates for the IETF standards track, and reviews other candidates for publication in the RFC series. It also administers IETF logistics, including operation of the Internet-Draft document series and the IETF meeting event.[25]

---

[22] Ibid.   [23] Set out in RFC 2026, section 4.1.
[24] The case with 'informational' and 'experimental' RFCs, along with 'Best Current Practice' (BCP) RFCs. See further RFC 2026, section 4.2.
[25] RFC 3710: An IESG Charter (author: H. Alvestrand) (February 2004), <http://www.ietf. org/rfc/rfc3710.txt>.

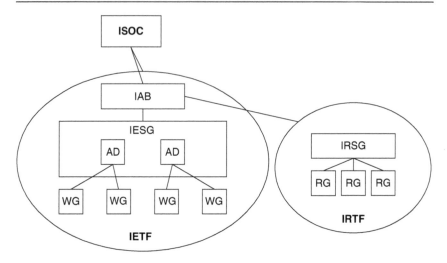

Figure 3.1. Organizational chart for IETF and associated bodies

The IESG consists of the IETF Chairperson and Area Directors, with the Chairperson of the IAB and the IETF Executive Director[26] as ex officio members. IESG members are selected through the same 'NomCom' process that applies for IAB membership.[27]

3.2.5. *Internet Research Task Force*

The Internet Research Task Force (IRTF) is affiliated with the IETF but formally separate from it. The latter attends to relatively short-term engineering and standards issues, whereas the former focuses on long-term research issues.[28] The IRTF is made up of several Research Groups (RGs) with small, stable membership. There are currently 12 such groups. Examples include the Anti-Spam RG, Crypto Forum RG, and Internet Congestion Control RG.

The IRTF is managed by the Internet Research Steering Group (IRSG). The latter is composed of the IETF Chairperson, chairs of the various research groups, and ad hoc 'members-at-large'.

---

[26] The person charged with running the IETF Secretariat.
[27] See further Chapter 4 (Section 4.1.3).
[28] See further <http://www.irtf.org/>. See too RFC 2014: IRTF Research Group Guidelines and Procedures (authors: A. Weinrib and J. Postel) (October 1996), <http://www.ietf.org/rfc/rfc2014.txt>.

3.2.6. *World Wide Web Consortium*

Tim Berner-Lee established the World Wide Web Consortium (W3C) in 1994 at the Massachusetts Institute of Technology (MIT). Establishment occurred in collaboration with CERN—the European Organization for Nuclear Research where Berners-Lee had developed the WWW[29]—and with support from DARPA and the EU Commission.

The W3C mission is, in short, 'to lead the Web to its full potential'.[30] The Consortium carries out this mission mainly by developing standards (termed 'Recommendations') for the web. So far, it has issued over 100 Recommendations.[31] Prominent examples are XML (Extensible Markup Language), CSS (Cascading Style Sheets), and P3P (Platform for Privacy Preferences).

The Consortium is unincorporated. It relies on three host institutions for facilities and infrastructure: MIT (Computer Science and Artificial Intelligence Laboratory), the University of Keio in Japan, and the European Research Consortium in Informatics and Mathematics (ERCIM) in France. As host institutions, these are not W3C members; however, all legal acts of W3C are really acts of one or more of them. In addition, the Consortium has 15 regional offices around the world. These are also often located within larger research institutions.

At present, W3C has approximately 400 member organizations. Membership is open in principle to any organization on payment of a fee. There is no class of membership tailored to individual persons, although these may join as 'affiliated members'. Membership fees are fixed according to the annual revenues, type, and location of headquarters of the member organization. Thus, a company based in Bangladesh will typically pay less than a US company.

Consortium activity and policy are determined through the complex interaction of several organizational subunits of W3C. The role, competence, and procedural rules for the respective bodies are set out in the 'W3C Process Document', which is binding on Consortium members by way of contract.[32]

Management of the Consortium lies primarily with the 'W3C Team'. This is composed of more than 60 researchers and engineers (most

---

[29] See Chapter 1 (Section 1.12).
[30] See W3C Process Document (version of 14 October 2005), section 2, <http://www.w3.org/ 2005/10/Process-20051014/>, last accessed 20 June 2008.
[31] For an up-to-date overview, see <http://www.w3.org/TR/>, last accessed 20 June 2008.
[32] The latest version is dated 14 October 2005, available at <http://www.w3.org/2005/10/Process-20051014/>, last accessed 20 June 2008.

employed at host institutions), led by the Director of W3C (Berners-Lee) with the aid of a Chief Operating Officer and Management Team. The Director is not elected. In effect, Berners-Lee holds the office in perpetuity. There is also a 10-member Advisory Board to advise the W3C Team. The Board has no binding decision-making powers. Its chair is appointed by the Team; the other nine members are elected by an Advisory Committee. The latter is composed of one representative from every member organization. It provides advice to the Team primarily through the Advisory Board.

Additionally, there is a Technical Architecture Group whose main task is to document, clarify, and build consensus on Web architecture principles. It is made up of eight persons and the W3C Director (who also chairs the Group). Three of these persons are appointed by the W3C Team and five by the Advisory Committee.

The 'nitty-gritty' of standards development is undertaken by Working Groups. The process of adopting W3C Recommendations parallels the 'standard track' for the Internet Standards Process within the IETF. There are some differences, though. For instance, the W3C procedure operates with four rather than three maturity levels: (*a*) Working Draft; (*b*) Candidate Recommendation; (*c*) Proposed Recommendation; (*d*) W3C Recommendation. Moreover, although W3C rules place much emphasis on procedural fairness, the fact that work done within Working Groups may be kept confidential makes for less transparency than under IETF processes. Further, as the W3C Director (Berners-Lee) has final say in disputes, more power attaches to one particular (and non-elected) person than is the case with dispute resolution in the aegis of the IETF.

The origins, organizational mechanics, and achievements of the W3C are described in more detail in Chapter 4 (Section 4.2).

3.2.7. *Internet Assigned Numbers Authority*

The function of the Internet Assigned Numbers Authority (IANA) has been to manage various unique codes, numbering systems, and other parameters which are crucial for Internet communication. In particular, it has been responsible for allocating IP addresses and managing the data in the root name servers that are integral to the DNS.[33]

The work of IANA was initially conducted under the aegis of the Information Sciences Institute (ISI) of the University of Southern California as a research project funded by DARPA. In essence, that work was carried

---

[33] See further <http://www.iana.org/>.

out by one person, Jon Postel, aided by a small band of ISI colleagues. In 1988, when DARPA entered into a new research contract with ISI, Postel began to call his management of protocol standards a function of the 'Internet Assigned Numbers Authority'.[34] The IANA function was claimed to be exercised on behalf of the Internet Activities Board,[35] which was subsequently represented within the technical community as the primary source of authority for IANA.[36] After its establishment in 1992, ISOC was also named as a source of authority.[37] In this way, IANA took on a life and de facto authority of its own. However, the contract between DARPA and ISI made no reference to IANA and the precise legal status of the latter remained unclear, at least for the duration of the contract. The situation is perhaps most accurately summed up in an influential US government report issued in June 1998:

IANA has functioned as a government contractor, albeit with considerable latitude, for some time now. Moreover, IANA is not formally organized or constituted. It describes a function more than an entity... [38]

When the contract between DARPA and ISI expired in 1999, the US government transferred the IANA functions to the Internet Corporation for Assigned Names and Numbers (ICANN). These functions are now carried out by ICANN under a renewable contract with the US Department of Commerce. The contract and related agreements for address and number management are described in Chapter 5 (Section 5.1.3).

3.2.8. *Internet Corporation for Assigned Names and Numbers*

The Internet Corporation for Assigned Names and Numbers is a non-profit public benefit corporation registered in California. It was incorporated in September 1998. The background to its emergence is a fascinating yet complex story that cannot be retold here in depth.[39] It suffices to

---

[34] The first official mention of IANA is in RFC 1083: IAB Official Protocol Standards (author: Jon Postel) (December 1988), section 7.2, <http://www.ietf.org/rfc/rfc1083.txt>.

[35] Ibid.   [36] See Mueller, *Ruling the Root*, 93 and references cited therein.

[37] See RFC 1700: Assigned Numbers (authors: J. Postel and J Reynolds) (October 1994), Introduction, <http://www.ietf.org/rfc/rfc1700.txt>.

[38] National Telecommunications and Information Administration (NTIA—a branch of the US Department of Commerce), 'Management of Internet Names and Addresses', *Federal Register*, 1998, vol. 63, no. 111, 31,741–51, <http://www.ntia.doc.gov/ntiahome/domainname/6_5_98dns.htm>. In discourse on Internet governance, the report is commonly referred to as simply the 'White Paper'.

[39] The story is ably told in Mueller, *Ruling the Root*, chapters 5–9; and, in more condensed form, in David Lindsay, *International Domain Name Law* (Oxford/Portland, Oregon: Hart Publishing, 2007), [2.4]–[2.11].

say that its creation was in response to a call from the US Department of Commerce for a new corporate entity ('NewCo') to assume primary responsibility for managing uniquely assigned parameters on the Internet.[40] Behind the call was perception on the part of the US government that the management regime then in place suffered from significant flaws.[41]

Among identified flaws was the ad hoc, relatively informal, and US-centric nature of the regime. The government also expressed concern about the lack of competition in the registration of domain names. At the time, one actor dominated the market for registration services—Network Solutions, Inc. (NSI). This had been given monopoly registration powers for the generic Top-Level Domains .com, .net, and .org under a contract with the National Science Foundation. Moreover, the mechanisms for resolving conflicts between trademark holders and domain name holders were considered expensive and cumbersome. The government's proposed solution to these problems was to create a new management system spearheaded by a New Corporation (NewCo). The latter was to be a non-profit, privately led organization with firm roots in the Internet community.

Four groups answered the government's call to form the NewCo. The winning bid was made by ICANN, which had been hastily created with the central involvement of Jon Postel.[42]

The mission and organizational principles of ICANN are laid down in its Bylaws.[43] Particularly illuminating is its statement of core values, which are set out as 11 goals. These marry technical imperatives with ideals of democracy, cooperation, and due process, balanced by reliance on market mechanisms to stimulate a healthy degree of competition:

1. Preserving and enhancing the operational stability, reliability, security, and global interoperability of the Internet.

2. Respecting the creativity, innovation, and flow of information made possible by the Internet by limiting ICANN's activities to those matters within ICANN's mission requiring or significantly benefiting from global coordination.

[40] NTIA, 'Management of Internet Names and Addresses' ('White Paper').

[41] Ibid. See too the Green Paper that preceded the White Paper: NTIA, 'Improvement of Technical Management of Internet Names and Addresses', *Federal Register*, 1998, vol. 63, no. 34, 8825–33, <http://www.ntia.doc.gov/ntiahome/domainname/022098fedreg.htm>.

[42] Postel was formally designated ICANN's Chief Technology Officer but died less than a month after its incorporation.

[43] Bylaws (as amended effective 15 February 2008), Article I, <http://www.icann.org/general/bylaws.htm>. See too ICANN's Articles of Incorporation (as revised 21 November 1998), particularly Articles 3 and 4, <http://www.icann.org/general/articles.htm>.

3. To the extent feasible and appropriate, delegating coordination functions to or recognizing the policy role of other responsible entities that reflect the interests of affected parties.

4. Seeking and supporting broad, informed participation reflecting the functional, geographic, and cultural diversity of the Internet at all levels of policy development and decision-making.

5. Where feasible and appropriate, depending on market mechanisms to promote and sustain a competitive environment.

6. Introducing and promoting competition in the registration of domain names where practicable and beneficial in the public interest.

7. Employing open and transparent policy development mechanisms that (a) promote well-informed decisions based on expert advice and (b) ensure that those entities most affected can assist in the policy development process.

8. Making decisions by applying documented policies neutrally and objectively, with integrity and fairness.

9. Acting with a speed that is responsive to the needs of the Internet while, as part of the decision-making process, obtaining informed input from those entities most affected.

10. Remaining accountable to the Internet community through mechanisms that enhance ICANN's effectiveness.

11. While remaining rooted in the private sector, recognizing that governments and public authorities are responsible for public policy and duly taking into account governments' or public authorities' recommendations.[44]

To fulfil ICANN's mission, a web of contracts and more informal agreements has been spun between the corporation and the bodies with which it deals.[45] These agreements are described in Chapter 5 (Sections 5.1.3 and 5.1.4). For present purposes, the most important agreement to note is the renewable Memorandum of Understanding (MOU) between ICANN and the US Department of Commerce (DOC). The MOU—referred to as the 'Joint Project Agreement' (JPA)—was first entered into on 25 November 1998 with an initial expiry date of 30 September 2000.[46] It constitutes the basic legal foundation for ICANN's role in Internet governance generally.

The MOU charters ICANN with five tasks which are to be carried out jointly with and under the supervision of DOC:

---

[44] Bylaws, Article I(2).
[45] For a full list, see <http://www.icann.org/general/agreements.htm>.
[46] Available at <http://www.icann.org/general/icann-mou-25nov98.htm>.

1. Establishment of policy for and direction of the allocation of IP number blocks;
2. Oversight of the operation of the authoritative root server system[47];
3. Oversight of the policy for determining the circumstances under which new top-level domains would be added to the root system;
4. Coordination of the assignment of other Internet technical parameters as needed to maintain universal connectivity on the Internet; and
5. Other activities necessary to coordinate the specified DNS management functions, as agreed by the Parties.

The MOU has since been renewed and amended several times. The latest version of the JPA was entered into in September 2006 and will expire in September 2009.[48] The overall result of the successive changes has been a gradual increase in ICANN's autonomy in organizing its internal affairs, though DOC continues to have a supervisory role.[49] Believing it has met the JPA objectives, ICANN requested in January 2008 that the agreement be discontinued and the US government relinquish all official control over the corporation and DNS.[50] At the time of writing this chapter, the official US response to the request was not known.

ICANN has, to say the least, an intricate and multiplex organizational structure. Its electoral and other decision-making processes are equally so. This reflects the multiplicity of stakeholders in ICANN's field of responsibility—some of which have considerable political and/or economic clout—together with ICANN's commitment to basing its decisions on broad consensus. In essence, ICANN is run by a Board of Directors with the help of several Supporting Organizations and Advisory Committees. ICANN as such has no individual or organizational members. Rather, participation in ICANN's work occurs primarily through work in the Supporting Organizations and Advisory Committees. The criteria for participation in these vary from strict professional requirements to open at-large participation. In the following paragraphs, we give a brief outline of the main bodies and their responsibilities (Figure 3.2).

The Board of Directors consists of 15 voting members ('directors') and 6 non-voting liaisons. The directors are elected in a complicated process, involving a number of advisory bodies, committees, and at-large consultations. Formally, it is the Board that decides ICANN policy. However, much of that policy is initiated and developed by the ICANN constituencies,

---

[47] The root server system is explained in Chapter 5 (Section 5.1.2).

[48] Available at <http://www.icann.org/general/JPA-29sep06.pdf>.

[49] See further Lindsay, *International Domain Name Law*, [2.13]–[2.17].

[50] Letter of 9 January 2008 from the ICANN Board of Directors to the NTIA, <http://www.icann.org/correspondence/dengate-thrush-to-sene-09jan08.pdf>, last accessed 20 June 2008.

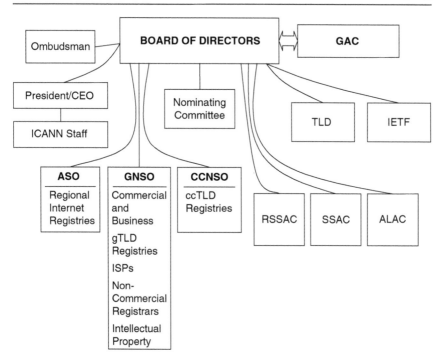

Figure 3.2. ICANN's organizational structure

usually within the framework of the Supporting Organizations that are specifically charged with initiating Policy Development Processes (PDP). If a policy proposal has emerged through a PDP with broad agreement from the constituencies concerned, the Board's decision will usually be either to adopt or to reject the proposal, not to develop the policy further on its own.

The Address Supporting Organization (ASO) advises the Board on policy issues relating to the operation, assignment, and management of Internet addresses. The ASO is established under an MOU with the Number Resource Organization,[51] which is the umbrella organization of the Regional Internet Registries.

The Generic Names Supporting Organization (GNSO) is responsible for developing and recommending to the Board substantive policies relating to gTLDs. It has several self-organized constituencies, namely, commercial and business users of the Internet, gTLD registries, registrars, ISPs,

[51] ICANN Address Supporting Organization (ASO) MOU (adopted 21 October 2004), available at <http://aso.icann.org/docs/aso-mou2004.html>.

non-commercial users of the Internet, and 'Intellectual Property Interests'. The organization supports ICANN in, inter alia, creating process documents on the expansion of the root with new gTLDs, and developing policy for operation of WHOIS services.

Policy development is typically a bottom–up, consensus-based process. Thus, if an issue arises that requires a policy decision of ICANN on the generic domain name scheme, the GNSO decides whether a PDP is to be initiated. If it is initiated, a task force or—more recently—a working group is created and a time-line adopted. The policy proposal is developed and put forward to the GNSO based on the greatest possible consensus among the constituencies. The GNSO also seeks, in turn, to find a consensus decision, which then is handed over to the Board. As mentioned above, the Board will usually decide simply whether to adopt or reject the proposal, not develop the policy further by itself.

The Country-Code Names Supporting Organization (ccNSO) has a similar set of functions to GNSO but with respect to global policy matters related to country-code top-level domains. It consists of ccTLD managers who have agreed to participate in it.

An especially significant player is the Governmental Advisory Committee (GAC). One of the main objections to the ICANN regime has been the central role played by the US government in its development. GAC is envisaged as an important instrument for providing more international input into DNS management and policy. It is charged with providing advice to the Board 'on the activities of ICANN as they relate to concerns of governments, particularly matters where there may be an interaction between ICANN's policies and various laws and international agreements or where they may affect public policy issues'.[52]

Membership of GAC is open to all national governments. It is also open, by invitation, to distinct economies, multinational governmental organizations, and treaty organizations. As its name indicates, GAC is an advisory body only, but the purchase of its influence on the Board has increased over the years both formally and informally. Indeed, some commentators have claimed that GAC has gained something akin to veto power in its field.[53] The current version of ICANN's bylaws provide that GAC advice 'shall be duly taken into account [by the Board], both in the

---

[52] ICANN Bylaws, Article XI, section 2(1)(a).

[53] See, for example, Wolfgang Kleinwächter, 'Beyond ICANN vs. ITU', in D. MacLean (ed.), *Internet Governance: A Grand Collaboration. An Edited Collection of Papers Contributed to the United Nations ICT Task Force Global Forum on Internet Governance, New York, March 25–26, 2004* (New York: United Nations ICT Task Force, 2004), 45.

formulation and adoption of policies'.[54] Moreover, if the Board decides not to follow that advice it must inform GAC of the reasons for its decision. The two bodies shall then 'try, in good faith and in a timely and efficient manner, to find a mutually acceptable solution'.[55] In the event that such a solution cannot be found, the Board must again state why it has decided not to follow GAC's advice, and such statement 'will be without prejudice to the rights or obligations of Governmental Advisory Committee members with regard to public policy issues falling within their responsibilities'.[56] GAC is the only Advisory Committee formally accorded this level of influence.

GAC is represented with one non-voting liaison to the Board, and also in a number of Supporting Organizations and committees, including the important Nominating Committee (described below). According to GAC Operating Principles,[57] GAC gives advice to the ICANN board upon reached consensus. The nature of GAC as a voice for every country disallows majority actions. If consensus is not reached, all views must be conveyed by the GAC Chair to the ICANN Board.

The Security and Stability Advisory Committee (SSAC) consists of representatives appointed by the Board. It is responsible for advising the Board on 'matters relating to the security and integrity of the Internet's naming and address allocation systems'.[58] Members of SSAC include technical experts like the Internet Systems Consortium (described in Section 3.2.9).

Advice on the operation of the DNS root name servers is provided by the Root Server System Advisory Committee (RSSAC). The RSSAC is made up by the operators of root servers and other members as appointed by the Board.

The At-Large Advisory Committee (ALAC) represents the individual Internet users. The members of ALAC are elected according to complex election procedures aimed at reflecting the geographical and social diversity of Internet users. The so-called At-Large structures form Regional At-Large Organizations (RALOs). There is one RALO in each geographic region (Africa, Asia Pacific, Europe, Latin America, and North America). The ALAC comments on a wide spectrum of ICANN work, including proposed Internationalized Domain Names (IDNs), new gTLDs, and

---

[54] Bylaws, Article XI, Section 2(1)(j).   [55] Ibid.

[56] Bylaws, Article XI, Section 2(1)(k).

[57] Governmental Advisory Committee Operating Principles (as amended, Mar del Plata, April 2005), especially Principle 47, <http://gac.icann.org/web/home/GAC_Operating_Principles.pdf>.

[58] Bylaws, Article XI, Section 2(2)(a). See also Security Committee Charter (adopted 14 March 2002), <http://icann.org/committees/security/charter-14mar02.htm>.

corporate ICANN actions. The main responsibilities of ALAC are to function as a communication hub between ICANN and individual Internet users, and to analyse the community impact of proposed ICANN decisions. ALAC has five voting members in the NOMCOM (described directly below), as well as a non-voting liaison to the ICANN Board.[59]

An important administrative committee is the Nominating Committee (NOMCOM) that is currently charged with selecting 8 of the 15 Board members.[60] It does not select the President (who is elected by the Board itself) or those directors selected by the Supporting Organizations (these select two Board members each—six in total). In carrying out its selection, NOMCOM must seek to ensure that the ICANN Board displays diversity in geography, culture, skills, experience, and perspective.[61] The criteria for NOMCOM membership together with the NOMCOM election process are extremely involute.[62] In the words of one commentator, 'everyone seems to elect everyone else in an Ourubus Worm of interlocking Supporting Organizations, Nominating Committee, and Board'.[63]

In November 2004, ICANN set up the office of Ombudsman in order to provide an independent internal evaluation of complaints by members of the ICANN community who believe that the ICANN staff, Board, or an ICANN constituency has treated them unfairly. The Ombudsman has no power to set aside or amend decisions made by the bodies subject to complaint; the Ombudsman may merely mediate and make recommendations.[64]

In addition to the bodies mentioned above are numerous past and present committees, task forces, and other groups providing advice related to specific matters. One such group is the Technical Liaison Group (TLG) which acts as a bridge between the Board and appropriate sources of technical advice relevant to ICANN. The TLG consists of four organizations: W3C, IAB, the European Telecommunications Standards Institute (ETSI), and the Telecommunications Standardization Sector of the International Telecommunications Union (ITU-T).

Funding of ICANN derives mainly from registrar and registry fees in the gTLD market. Under ICANN's proposed budget for the fiscal year 2008–9 these fees are projected to generate revenue of approximately

---

[59] Bylaws, Article XI, Section 2.4.   [60] Bylaws, Article VII.
[61] Bylaws, Article VII, Section 5.   [62] Bylaws, Article VII, Section 2.
[63] Lawrence Solum, 'Blogging from Brazil 7', <http://lsolum.blogspot.com/2003_03_01_lsolum_archive.html#200053016>, last accessed 20 June 2008.
[64] See further <http://www.icann.org/ombudsman/>.

US$60 million.[65] At the registrar level, there is first a transactional fee (currently US$0.25 per transaction) paid to ICANN for each registration, renewal, or transfer of a gTLD name. Secondly, each registrar pays accreditation fees to ICANN pursuant to their accreditation agreement with the latter.[66] Registrar-derived fees (both transactional and accreditational) account for just over 50 per cent of ICANN's total revenue. The remaining revenue derives largely from registry fees, with Verisign contributing the bulk.[67]

ICANN is seeking more income from ccTLD managers. There are currently no agreements between ccTLD managers and ICANN on funding. However, a handful of ccTLD managers have made voluntary contributions to ICANN,[68] and a fee-structure is being negotiated in the ccNSO.

ICANN has attracted a significant amount of criticism. One category of criticism concerns its origins, though the criticism tends not to be directed so much at ICANN itself as at the US government's role in its conception. For example, a strong argument has been made out that the government conceived its NewCo outside the bounds of US constitutional and administrative law.[69]

Another category of criticism concerns ICANN's modus operandi. ICANN has been accused of opaque, slow, and arbitrary decision-making—particularly with regard to the issue of root extension—and of failing to give civil society groups adequate representation in its policy development.[70] These accusations were particularly trenchant during ICANN's early years of operation. A round of organizational reforms resulting in adoption of new Bylaws in December 2002 went a considerable way to meeting some of the criticism. Nevertheless, calls continue to be made for strengthening the influence of individual Internet users in determination of ICANN policy.[71]

---

[65] See 'Adopted FY09 Operating Plan and Budget' (25 June 2008), <http://www.icann.org/en/financials/adopted-opplan-budget-v3-fy09-25jun08-en.pdf>. Total expenditure is projected to amount to just over US$57 million.

[66] See Registrar Accreditation Agreement (17 May 2001), section 3.9, <http://www.icann.org/registrars/ra-agreement-17may01.htm>.

[67] See, for example, the fee structure established pursuant to section 7.2 of the .com Registry Agreement (1 March 2006) between ICANN and Verisign, <http://www.icann.org/tlds/agreements/verisign/registry-agmt-com-01mar06.htm>.

[68] For an overview, see <http://www.icann.org/en/maps/cctld-contributions-0708.htm>.

[69] See especially Michael Froomkin, 'Wrong Turn in Cyberspace: Using ICANN to Route around the APA and the Constitution', *Duke Law Journal*, 2000, vol. 50, 17–184.

[70] See, for example, Jonathan Weinberg, 'ICANN and the Problem of Legitimacy', *Duke Law Journal*, 2000, vol. 50, 187–260; Froomkin, 'Habermas@discourse.net', 749, 843–55.

[71] Annette Mühlberg, 'Users and Internet Governance—The Structure of ICANN's At-Large Advisory Committee (ALAC)', in Kleinwächter (ed.), *The Power of Ideas*, 249–53.

Another category of criticism attaches to ICANN's continued subjection to US government supervision.[72] Again, though, this criticism tends to be directed more at the US government than at ICANN, it undermines the transnational legitimacy of ICANN—as demonstrated in the debate during WSIS. Thus, although measures have been taken to strengthen ICANN's legitimacy in terms of the fairness of its internal organizational processes, its US-supervised authority remains controversial.

At the same time, it is important to note that considerable elements of ICANN's activity are rarely controversial. This is the case, for instance, with allocation of IP addresses—one of the 'IANA functions' exercised by ICANN.[73] That function is largely administrative with very little room for policy discretion.

Nonetheless, ICANN is not simply a technical coordination body able continuously to skirt around issues of public policy. Its very constitution requires it to take account of, and serve, the public interest. In doing this, ICANN must inevitably make value judgements based on more than narrow technocratic concerns. And certain issues it faces have an especially salient political, economic, and/or moral dimension.

One issue on point concerns the composition of the Board of Directors, particularly the extent to which civil society groups are to be represented on the Board.[74] Another issue on point concerns the recognition of new TLDs. How this issue is resolved has obvious economic, cultural, and political repercussions.[75] Moreover, it can intersect with content regulation, thereby bringing moral concerns into play.

The latter point is well illustrated by the controversy over the proposed introduction of a .xxx TLD in 2005. ICANN's proposal to permit this particular extension of the root was defeated by strong opposition on predominantly moral grounds from a variety of sources, including the US and Brazilian governments, and religious groups.[76] The announcement by ICANN in June 2008 to radically liberalize its policy for permitting new

---

[72] See, for example, Konstantinos Komaitis, 'ICANN: Guilty as Charged?', *The Journal of Information, Law and Technology*, 2003, Issue 1, <http://elj.warwick.ac.uk/jilt/03-1/komaitis.html>, last accessed 30 May 2008. See too the criticisms mounted during WSIS, as related in Chapter 6.

[73] See Section 3.2.7.

[74] Currently only 7 of the 21 Board members are elected from the civil society constituencies; most of the rest of the Board members come from the business sector.

[75] On the economic factors at play, see Chapter 2 (Section 2.8).

[76] See e.g. Declan McCullagh, 'Bush Administration Objects to .xxx Domains', *CNET News*, 15 August 2005. <http://news.cnet.com/Bush-administration-objects-to.xxx-domains/2100-1028_3-5833764.html>, last accessed 30 June 2008.

TLDs is likely to open up for more of these types of conflict,[77] though ICANN claims that these disputes will not be resolved by itself but by an 'international arbitration body utilizing criteria drawing on provisions in a number of international treaties'.[78]

Controversy aside, in legal and organizational terms, ICANN is a fascinating experiment in creating an international organization outside a Treaty framework. Part of the fascination lies in the delicate balance of power struck between a non-profit corporation under Californian law and national government—both the US government acting through DOC and governments more generally acting through GAC. Part of the fascination lies too in how ICANN tries to embody a bottom–up decisional strategy, where initiatives may be begun on the lowest tier of the organization and thrashed out on their way upward.

Also fascinating is the way in which ICANN exercises formal power. A traditional international organization is based on a treaty, an agreement between sovereign states. Through the treaty, the states transfer parts of their sovereignty to the organization, and—to the extent specified by the treaty—the organization may make decisions based on the public authority transferred in this way with respect to the members of the treaty organization. How very different is the set-up of ICANN! As a private corporation in the jurisdiction of California, it does not have any public authority. It has to rely on private autonomy wielded through contracts and quasi-contractual instruments. Obviously, to construct and manage an international organization largely on the basis of private autonomy is not just a fascinating experiment but a daring one too.

3.2.9. *Other Standards Bodies*

Numerous bodies other than those described in the preceding sections also contribute to the development and deployment of network technologies. Most of these, however, do not have development of Internet-specific standards as their sole or principal remit. One exception is the Internet Systems Consortium (ISC), which acts as host for a number of important software systems basic to the functioning of the Internet.[79]

---

[77] See further ICANN's announcement on 26 June 2008; available at <http://www.icann.org/en/announcements/announcement-4-26jun08-en.htm>, last accessed 30 June 2008.

[78] Ibid. FAQ 4 ('Offensive names will be subject to an objection-based process based on public morality and order. This process will be conducted by an international arbitration body utilizing criteria drawing on provisions in a number of international treaties. ICANN will not be the decision-maker on these objections').

[79] See further <http://www.isc.org/index.pl>.

It was founded in 1994 to maintain the BIND code supporting DNS servers,[80] and is currently involved in several other open-source projects (e.g. NetBSD, XFree86, and kernel.org). As noted in Section 3.2.8, the Consortium participates in the ICANN SSAC.

Another notable body is the IEEE (Institute of Electrical and Electronics Engineers).[81] With regard to the Internet, IEEE's work has been chiefly important for facilitating the hook-up of devices to communications networks—that is, for broadening the Internet's reach—rather than development of core Internet standards. It is, for example, responsible for developing key standards for wireless networking, such as Ethernet (IEEE standard 802.3), Bluetooth (IEEE standard 802.15.1), and Wi-Fi (IEEE standard 802.11b).

The Telecommunications Standardization Sector of the International Telecommunications Union (ITU-T) has also developed standards important for facilitating hook-up of devices to the Internet. Additionally, it has developed standards with more central Internet applications but these have generally failed to gain significant purchase. One reason given for this is that the standards are complex, with hierarchical premises that tend to straight-jacket broad application.[82] The same has been said of the Internet-related standards developed by the International Organization for Standardization (ISO).[83] The outcome of the 'war of protocols' related in Chapter 1 (Section 1.9) is a case in point.

Nonetheless, the ITU has formal links to ICANN (both through GAC and the Technical Liaison Group, as noted in Section 3.2.8) and cooperates extensively with the IETF (e.g. with respect to ENUM—the process of mapping Internet addresses and telephone numbers). It has also made considerable efforts recently to engage on domain name issues, these efforts being formalized in, inter alia, several resolutions adopted at its 2006 Plenipotentiary Conference in Antalya.[84]

---

[80] BIND stands for 'Berkeley Internet Name Domain'. Further on BIND, see <http://en.wikipedia.org/wiki/BIND>.

[81] The IEEE, a non-profit organization formally incorporated in New York, is probably the world's largest technical professional body in terms of membership numbers. See further <http://www.ieee.org/>.

[82] See further, for example, Jeremy Malcolm, *Multi-Stakeholder Governance and the Internet Governance Forum* (Perth: Terminus Press, 2008), 57–61.

[83] Ibid. 62–4.

[84] See Resolution 101 (Internet Protocol (IP)-based networks); Resolution 102 (Management of Internet domain names and addresses); Resolution 133 (Role of administrations of Member States in the management of internationalized (multilingual) domain names).

3.3. Internet Government and Self-Governance

As noted in Section 3.1, the principal development in Internet governance during the past decade has been the emergence of a new congeries of governors. These comprise an immense array of actors. To describe each of them in detail is beyond the scope of this chapter. In the following, we focus on one set of them—national governments. We do so because governments, both alone and in concert, have potentially the greatest impact on the activities of the first generation of Internet governors and can thus shape development of Internet architecture. Moreover, their regulatory policies have potentially a direct impact on the activities of all Internet users.

The preceding sections have already touched upon some of that impact—primarily in relation to US government supervision of the Internet naming and numbering system. That supervision, together with supervision exercised by other national governments over ccTLD operators within their respective jurisdictions, is further elaborated in Chapter 5. Thus, we do not deal with such supervision in depth in this section. Neither do we attempt to comprehensively describe other aspects of the regulatory policies of specific national governments. Instead, we highlight various ways in which government regulatory policy generally, though particularly in the form of legislation, can affect development and use of the Internet. In doing so, we also highlight the shifting balance between regulatory intervention by government and self-regulatory ideals and practices of Internet users.

As noted in Chapter 2 (Section 2.4), during the 1980s and up until the mid-1990s, it was popular in some circles to deny and deride the application of traditional law to the transactional space created by the Internet—cyberspace. These claims reached their highpoint in hubris and rhetorical flourish in a 'Declaration of the Independence of Cyberspace', issued by John Perry Barlow in 1996.[85] In this Declaration, Barlow grandly proclaimed that cyberspace is and ought to be beyond the tentacles of government control. The opening paragraph reads:

Governments of the Industrial World, you weary giants of flesh and steel, I come from Cyberspace, the new home of Mind. On behalf of the future, I ask you of the past to leave us alone. You are not welcome among us. You have no sovereignty where we gather.

[85] See <http://homes.eff.org/~barlow/Declaration-Final.html>. Barlow was a co-founding member of the Electronic Frontiers Foundation (EFF).

Implicit in this declaration is the notion that the denizens of cyberspace could sensibly govern themselves. At the time of Barlow's declaration, this was an appealing notion. Many cyberspace denizens—then typically termed 'netizens'—tended to see themselves as caring and responsible people committed to promoting the generative, collaborative aspects of Internet communication without having economic profit as their main motivation. In the words of Michael Hauben, netizens are 'people who care about the Usenet and the bigger Net and work towards building the cooperative and collective nature which benefits the larger world'.[86] Among these people were—and are—many of the technologists who playe(d) key roles in the development of Internet architecture.

This is not to say that netizens envisage(d) doing without rules of any kind. Rules did emerge early on in the Internet world and were generally embraced, either in the form of procedural rules for standards development or in the form of rules concerned primarily with maintaining basic standards of politeness and courtesy in cyberspace. The latter set of rules tends to go under the name of 'netiquette' [derived from combining 'net(work)' and 'etiquette']. The first netiquette rules originated in text-based electronic forums from the pre-WWW era. RFC 1855 constitutes an early (and now somewhat dated) attempt to systematically collate and present these rules.[87] It sets out, for instance, a long list of rules for email communication, including the following:

- 'never send chain letters by electronic mail';
- 'be conservative in what you send and liberal in what you receive';
- 'use mixed case. UPPER CASE LOOKS AS IF YOU'RE SHOUTING';
- 'wait overnight to send emotional responses to messages'.

While it can be tempting to trivialize them, these rules play an important role in maintaining civility in cyberspace. Similar sets of rules are evolving for use in new virtual communities, such as Second Life,[88] and for the operation of numerous other platforms for online collaboration, such as

---

[86] Hauben and Hauben, *Netizens*, x (preface).

[87] RFC 1855: Netiquette Guidelines (author: S. Hambridge) (October 1995), <http://www.ietf.org/rfc/rfc1855.txt>. The guidelines were produced by an IETF Working Group—Responsible Use of the Network (RUN). For another early attempt at drafting netiquette, see Virginia Shea, *Netiquette* (San Rafael, California: Albion Books, 1994).

[88] For example, IBM has adopted a set of 11 netiquette guidelines to be observed by its employees when they spend time in Second Life and other publicly accessible virtual environments. See 'IBM Issues Employee Conduct Rules for Second Life', *InformationWeek*, 27 July 2007, <http://www.informationweek.com/news/internet/showArticle.jhtml?articleID = 201201541>, last accessed 20 June 2008.

wikis.[89] Their evolution makes us all potentially Internet governors in the limited sense that we each personally have the ability to help develop and manage ethical standards for online behaviour.

Netiquette and the like aside, another implication of Barlow's declaration is directly related to Internet governance in the more traditional sense. It is an implication that is potentially very threatening to governments because it concerns the issue of actual control of Internet architecture. While Barlow's declaration was not necessarily supported by the majority of members of the Internet standards community of the time, there were not long afterwards several attempts on their part to assert a right of self-governance with respect to control over critical Internet resources—in other words, to exercise control independently of the US government or any other national government. A salient case in point is the so-called gTLD-MOU initiative in 1997 led by ISOC. This initiative tried to place authority over the Internet naming and numbering system in the hands of a new international body that would itself be mainly under ISOC control.[90] The creation of IANA along with the subsequent attempts, through RFCs, to place IANA's source of authority in the IAB and ISOC are also relevant examples. In the words of Mueller, these attempts

reflected the technical community's growing conception of itself as an autonomous, self-governing social complex. Explicit claims on the right to manage name and address assignment were being made by an authority structure that existed solely in Internet RFCs and lacked any basis in formal law or state action.[91]

However, as related in Sections 3.2.7–3.2.8, the US government did not acquiesce to these claims. The Clinton administration effectively killed the 'gTLD-MOU' initiative, adamantly holding that the US government had ultimate authority over the Internet as it had funded development of the network under a series of contracts.[92] Shortly thereafter, it facilitated the transfer of IANA functions to a NewCo that operated under closer government supervision. Moreover, from the late 1990s, other national governments also began to assert greater control over the management of

---

[89] The most prominent being Wikipedia. For description and discussion of the self-regulatory regime for Wikipedia operations, see Zittrain, *The Future of the Internet*, chapter 6.

[90] See further Mueller, *Ruling the Root*, 142–62; Goldsmith and Wu, *Who Controls the Internet?*, 36–43; Andrew D. Murray, *The Regulation of Cyberspace: Control in the Online Environment* (Milton Park: Routledge, 2007), 103–5.

[91] Mueller, *Ruling the Root*, 93.

[92] Mueller, *Ruling the Root*, 142–62; Goldsmith and Wu, *Who Controls the Internet?*, 36–43; Murray, *The Regulation of Cyberspace*, 105.

the ccTLDs pertaining to their jurisdiction—treating these, in effect, as a national resource under their sovereignty.

Nevertheless, as noted in Chapter 2 (Section 2.7), national governments have never made any real attempt to alter basic Internet architecture. Generally, in the vehicle that is Internet development, governments (at least in the Western world) have usually sat in the passenger seat, albeit with their hand ready to pull the handbrake if they are threatened with being thrown out. They have been largely content to sit there, partly for reasons of expediency, but also because they have inclined to the view that the vehicle is driven well and carries enormously valuable goods that ought not to be damaged by heavy-handed intervention. This is manifest in the various policy documents issued by Western governments back in the early 1990s when the broad importance of the Internet for economic and social growth began to dawn on them.[93] Within the EU, for example, the influential 'Bangemann Report' issued by a task force headed by Martin Bangemann (then a member of the European Commission) pushed for the rapid implementation of a 'European Information Infrastructure' the main driving force for which would be the private sector and 'market forces'.[94] This was in harmony with the concurrent policy of the Clinton–Gore administration in the United States on the building of the 'Information Superhighway'.[95] It is a line that continues to inform government policy in many jurisdictions.

Up until at least the mid-1990s, many governments showed little specific concern for Internet and associated governance issues. As Leib writes, for example, with respect to the EU, '[u]ntil the second half of the 1990s, the Internet was almost an irrelevant issue in the plans of the European Union'.[96] There were, though, sporadic legislative forays to combat certain forms of net-related activity—typically the hosting and communication of offensive content. A prominent instance is the US

---

[93] See generally Stephen Saxby, *Public Policy and Legal Regulation of the Information Market in the Digital Network Environment*, CompLex 2/96 (Oslo: TANO, 1996), especially chapter 2.

[94] *Europe and the Global Information Society. Recommendations to the European Council* (Brussels, 26 May 1994), 30. The main conclusions of the report were endorsed by the European Commission in its communication, *Europe's Way to the Information Society. An Action Plan* [COM(94) 347 final, 19 July 1994].

[95] See especially Information Infrastructure Task Force, *The National Information Infrastructure: Agenda for Action* (Washington, DC, 15 September 1993), especially 8. See too 'A Framework for Global Electronic Commerce' (Washington, DC, 1 July 1997), <http://www.technology.gov/digeconomy/framewrk.htm>, last accessed 20 June 2008.

[96] Volker Leib, 'ICANN—EU can't: Internet governance and Europe's role in the formation of the Internet Corporation for Assigned Names and Numbers (ICANN)', *Telematics and Informatics*, 2002, vol. 19, 159, 161.

Communications Decency Act passed in 1996.[97] This initiative directly occasioned Barlow's 'Declaration of the Independence of Cyberspace'. Yet it is noteworthy that the Act was struck down in part by another branch of government—the judiciary—partly on the view that the Internet is a unique communications platform deserving of strong protection from government interference.[98]

Although Internet governance has until recently rarely figured prominently in their plans, governments have often made decisions with potential if not actual impact on Internet development and usage. There is a myriad of ways in which governments may shape, directly or indirectly, standards development.[99] An example of direct influence is legislation requiring information systems to be designed so as to avoid unnecessary collection of personal data.[100] An instance of a more indirect form of influence is legislation providing tax relief for certain industrial sectors (thus stimulating investment), or simply to *threaten* legislative intervention in a particular sector if the latter fails to tackle a specified problem itself. As noted below, such a threat has been instrumental in stimulating efforts by ISPs in some Western countries to block public access to illegal or otherwise offensive content.

Of course, the effect of these various strategies on actual standards development will vary, but they can bite. A case in point is the work of the W3C in developing its Platform for Internet Content Selection (PICS)— work that was catalysed by the preparations for, and enactment of, the US Communications Decency Act.[101] We see too that *relaxation* of a threat of regulatory intervention can also affect the self-governing regimes of the Internet community. Again the W3C's PICS specification is a case in point—once the anti-obscenity provisions of the US Communications Decency Act were struck down by the Supreme Court, interest in further development and use of PICS waned.[102] Another case in point is the fate of the Norwegian Net Tribunal (Nettnemnda). This was established in early 2001 with sponsorship from the Norwegian ICT industry, and was probably the first scheme in the world to offer both a set of 'Ethical rules

---

[97] Public Law No. 104–104 (1996).

[98] *American Civil Liberties Union v. Reno*, 521 U.S. 844, 851, 868–9 (1997) (per Justice Stephens).

[99] See further, for example, Jay P. Kesan and Rajiv C. Shah, 'Shaping Code', *Harvard Journal of Law & Technology*, 2005, vol. 18, 319–99.

[100] See, for example, Germany's Federal Data Protection Act of 1990 (*Bundesdatenschutzgesetz*, as amended in 2001) stipulating that '[t]he design and selection of data processing systems shall be oriented to the goal of collecting, processing or using no personal data or as little personal data as possible' (section 3a).

[101] See further Chapter 4 (Section 4.2.4).   [102] Ibid.

for the Internet' and a workable dispute resolution procedure. The scheme was largely an attempt by the local ICT industry to head off government intervention by showing that the industry itself could adequately regulate the field. Once government regulatory pressure was relaxed a couple of years later, the willingness to finance and sustain the scheme dissipated. The scheme is now operationally defunct.

Often, governments have become 'unwitting' Internet governors in the sense that they have stumbled into the role without thinking specifically about the realities of the Internet. They have typically done so when passing legislation prior to, or on the cusp of, the emergence of the Internet as a major tool for commerce and personal self-realization, and drafting the legislation broadly enough to apply to the digital world.

A case in point is the Data Protection Directive adopted by the EU in 1995.[103] The Directive was drafted with little, if any, conscious account taken of the Internet or digital environment more generally. Yet its provisions are generally applicable to the digital world. The problem is that they do not always apply with sensible results. An example is Article 4 of the Directive which provides for the law data protection of an EU state to apply outside the EU in certain circumstances—most notably where a data controller, based outside the EU, utilizes 'equipment' located in the state to process personal data for purposes other than merely transmitting the data through that state [Article 4(1)(c)]. Applied to the online world, implementation of the provision carries a distinct risk of regulatory overreaching in the sense that EU member states' data protection laws are given so broad a field of application that there is little realistic chance of enforcing them. This risk looms particularly large in the online environment where, for instance, routine use of cookies mechanisms by website operators in third countries may involve utilization of 'equipment' in an EU state (assuming that the cookies are properly to be classified as personal data). Is it, for instance, realistic to expect a website operator in India that puts cookies on the browser programs of website visitors from the EU to comply with EU member states' privacy norms? Is it realistic to expect such an operator to be even aware of this compliance duty?

---

[103] Directive 95/46/EC on the Protection of Individuals with Regard to the Processing of Personal Data and on the Free Movement of Such Data (O.J. L 281, 23 November 1995, 31–50); adopted 24 October 1995.

With this in mind, let us again return to Barlow's declaration. To claim, as he did, that cyberspace is beyond the reach of traditional laws is clearly facetious. The Internet and cyberspace have never been beyond the reach of the law. Of course, some laws have been drafted in a manner that makes their application to the Internet difficult, but much law is sufficiently technologically neutral in its formulation as to permit application to new forms of ICT—as the Data Protection Directive exemplifies. Hence, the basic question when assessing the applicability of laws to the Internet and cyberspace is usually not: do the laws apply? It is rather: *how* do they apply? The latter question breaks down into several other questions: Do the laws apply with sensible results? Do they achieve a desirable balancing of interests? Are the results unexpected or awkward? Do the laws give sensible guidance as to what Internet-related activity is permitted and what is not permitted? These are questions that governments in their legislative role ought now always to address.

Despite having sometimes been 'unwitting' Internet governors, governments—together with intergovernmental organizations like the Organization for Economic Cooperation and Development (OECD) and Council of Europe—are turning increasingly to deal directly and intentionally with certain aspects of Internet-related activity. Cybercrime and spam are two sets of activity being targeted, albeit with limited success.[104] More problematic is the increasingly systematic effort by governments to regulate public access to information on the World Wide Web for political, religious, and/or social reasons. This effort takes the form of establishing various filtering schemes that impose (or require others—typically ISPs and search engines—to impose) technical barriers to the flow of data from websites. These barriers are seldom incapable of circumvention for the technologically savvy net-user but they do make real and significant inroads into freedom of communication.[105] The imposition of such barriers is growing:

---

[104] For a critical overview of legislative efforts to counter cybercrime, see Bert-Jaap Koops and Susan W. Brenner (eds.), *Cybercrime and Jurisdiction—A Global Survey* (The Hague: T.M.C. Asser Press, 2006). For a critical overview of legislative efforts to counter spam, see Tania S. L. Cheng, 'Recent international attempts to can spam', *Computer Law & Security Report*, 2004, vol. 20, 472–9. For in-depth discussion of the effectiveness of EU anti-spam rules, see Dana Irina Cojocarasu, *Anti-Spam Legislation between Privacy and Commercial Interest: An Overview of the European Union Legislation Regarding the E-Mail Spam*, CompLex 1/06 (Oslo: Unipub, 2006).

[105] For an overview of the functionality and efficacy of the various filtering mechanisms, see Steven J. Murdoch and Ross Anderson, 'Tools and Technology of Internet Filtering', in Deibert et al. (eds.), *Access Denied*, chapter 3.

The emerging trend points to more filtering in more places, using more sophisticated techniques over time. This trend runs parallel to the trajectory of more people in more places using the Internet for more important functions of their lives.[106]

The trend is most salient in countries in the regions of Asia, the Middle East, and North Africa, though the intensity and extent of their respective censorship practices vary greatly. China and Iran are reported as having the most comprehensive filtering controls. The filtering regimes of, say, Singapore, Jordan, and Morocco are relatively light-touch.[107]

It would be wrong to characterize filtering of online content as exclusively a practice of governments on the margins of the Western, liberal, democratic sphere. Numerous countries in the centre of that sphere have also filtering schemes in place, though these tend to be voluntary initiatives targeted mainly at blocking public access to child pornography. They are voluntary in the sense that they are formally the initiative of private bodies (typically ISPs) rather than imposed through government decree. Nonetheless, they are often undertaken in close cooperation with police and other state agencies and with the implicit threat of legislative intervention in the absence of action. An example is Project Cleanfeed, launched in 2004 as a voluntary initiative of British Telecom in cooperation with the UK Home Office, but now embracing the bulk of UK-based ISPs.[108] Other countries, such as Canada, Italy, and the Scandinavian countries, have similar schemes in place.[109] Australia, already home to a relatively aggressive scheme targeting obscene material,[110] is planning to introduce an ISP-level blocking system too.[111]

Much of the Internet-specific policy developed by the EU is also directed at combating dissemination of harmful or illegal content on the Internet. The policy takes the form of an Action Plan the chief elements of which are sponsoring development of filtering tools and promoting

[106] Jonathan Zittrain and John Palfrey, 'Introduction', in Deibert et al. (eds.), *Access Denied*, p. 3.

[107] See generally Robert Faris and Nart Villeneuve, 'Measuring Global Internet Filtering', in Deibert et al. (eds.), *Access Denied*, chapter 1.

[108] See further Sangamitra Ramachander, 'Internet Filtering in Europe', in Deibert et al. (eds.), *Access Denied*, 188.

[109] Ibid. and references cited therein.

[110] For details, see Evan Croen, 'Internet Filtering in Australia and New Zealand', in Deibert et al. (eds.), *Access Denied*, 166–76.

[111] See Press release of 13 May 2008 by the Federal Minister for Broadband, Communications and the Digital Economy, Senator Stephen Conroy, <http://www.minister.dbcde.gov.au/media/media_releases/2008/033>, last accessed 30 May 2008.

voluntary schemes for monitoring and takedown of content by ISPs.[112] But the purchase of the Action Plan has been somewhat undercut by other concerns—notably, promotion of e-commerce and protection of freedom of expression. These concerns are manifest, for example, in a 2008 recommendation by the Council of Europe cautioning against the use of universal or general blocking software.[113] They are also manifest in the high threshold set by the E-Commerce Directive for imposing legal liability on ISPs for hosting or disseminating offensive content.[114] In effect, ISPs are exempt from liability if they act as a mere conduit or cache for transmission or storage of illegal content, in the absence of any knowledge on their part of the illegality of the material, or if they act quickly to remove the material once they do acquire such knowledge. Moreover, ISPs are not required to monitor content or otherwise actively look for indications of illegality. Exactly how far these exemptions reach continues to be the subject of much debate, particularly in the context of the national legal systems in which they are to be transposed.[115] Some commentators fear that the protections they provide for ISPs and, ultimately, the freedoms for those utilizing ISP services will be whittled away or circumvented through a combination of factors.[116] One factor is increased attempts to force ISPs to reveal the identities of those using their services.

This brings us to the issue of surveillance. For it is not just in their sponsoring of filtering schemes that governments are now making a significant impact on Internet usage. They may make an equally if not greater impact

[112] See Decision No. 276/1999/EC of the European Parliament and of the Council of 25 January 1999 adopting a multiannual Community action plan on promoting safer use of the Internet by combating illegal and harmful content on global networks (O.J. L 33, 6 February 1999, 1–11); Decision No. 1151/2003/EC of 16 June 2003 amending Decision No. 276/1999/EC adopting a multiannual Community action plan on promoting safer use of the Internet by combating illegal and harmful content on global networks (O.J. L 162, 1 July 2003, 1–4); Decision No. 854/2005/EC of 11 May 2005 establishing a multiannual Community Programme on promoting safer use of the Internet and new online technologies (O.J. L 149, 11 June 2005, 1–13).

[113] Recommendation CM/Rec(2008)6 of the Committee of Ministers to member states on measures to promote the respect for freedom of expression and information with regard to Internet filters (adopted 26 March 2008).

[114] See Directive 2000/31/EC of 8 June 2000 on certain legal aspects of Information Society services, in particular electronic commerce, in the Internal Market (O.J. L 178, 17 July 2000, 1–16), Articles 12–15.

[115] In the Norwegian context, see, for example, Jon Bing, *Ansvar for ytringer på nett—særlig om formidlerens ansvar* (Oslo: Universitetsforlaget, 2008), especially 207–40.

[116] See, for example, Lilian Edwards, 'The Problem of Intermediary Service Provider Liability', in Lilian Edwards (ed.), *The New Legal Framework for E-Commerce in Europe* (Oxford/Portland: Hart Publishing, 2005), 93, 129–36.

through their development of various surveillance schemes directed at electronic communication. Much of this development in recent years has been rationalized as part of the 'war on terror' but, in practice, the surveillance schemes often cast their net broadly. The schemes come in various forms. Some are directly engaged in monitoring electronic communication. A case in point is the 'DCS' programme (Digital Collection System; previously termed 'Carnivore') of the US Federal Bureau of Investigation and National Security Agency.[117] Another case in point is the so-called Echelon system reportedly operated by the signals intelligence agencies of the United States, UK, Australia, Canada, and New Zealand.[118]

Others do not engage directly in monitoring but ensure that certain elements of electronic communications data are logged and stored by the electronic communications service providers so that the data can subsequently be accessed by government authorities if necessary. An example is the scheme for retention of electronic communications traffic data currently being rolled out in Europe pursuant to Directive 2006/24/EC.[119] It requires EU member states to ensure that providers of public communications networks store such data for a minimum of 6 months and a maximum of 2 years.

The actual impact of surveillance and data retention schemes on Internet usage is difficult to gauge. Part of the difficulty lies in the fact that some such schemes are clouded in secrecy (the case, for example, with the so-called Echelon system), while others have yet to be fully rolled out (the case, for instance, with the EU's traffic data retention initiative). Yet they tend to arouse much public controversy and may arguably have a 'chilling effect' on people's online behaviour.

To sum up, the regulatory environment for the Internet is markedly different to the 1980s and early 1990s when the ideals of digital libertarianism flourished. Those ideals now have little purchase. Back then, it was glibly claimed that '[t]he Net interprets censorship as damage and routes

---

[117] Further on this and other surveillance measures by US security agencies, see, for example, S. Gorman, 'NSA's Domestic Spying Grows As Agency Sweeps Up Data', *Wall Street Journal*, 10 March 2008, A1, <http://online.wsj.com/public/article_print/SB120511973377523845.html>; T. Nabbali and M. Perry, 'Going for the throat: Carnivore in an Echelon World', *Computer Law & Security Report*, 2003, vol. 19, 456–67.

[118] See, for example, <http://en.wikipedia.org/wiki/ECHELON>.

[119] Directive 2006/24/EC of 15 March 2006 on the retention of data generated or processed in connection with the provision of publicly available electronic communications services or of public communications networks and amending Directive 2002/58/EC (O.J. L 105, 13 April 2006, 54–63).

around it'.[120] The recent emergence of comprehensive Internet-filtering systems undermines this claim. Back then, it was claimed that cyberspace was outside the reach of traditional law. That claim is wrong: cyberspace and the Internet have never been beyond the reach of the law, and present legislative initiatives are increasingly targeting central elements of the digital environment. Back then, governments were characterized as 'weary giants of flesh and steel'. With respect to the digital environment, governments presently show no signs of tiredness in their regulatory zeal.

[120] A statement attributed to John Gilmore, one of the co-founders of the EFF. See <http://www.toad.com/gnu>, last accessed 30 May 2008.

4

Development of core Internet standards: the work of IETF and W3C

Harald Alvestrand and Håkon Wium Lie

4.1. The Internet Engineering Task Force[1]

4.1.1. *Introduction*

The Internet Engineering Task Force (IETF) is the standards body that probably has the largest influence on the technologies used to build the Internet. Yet it has no formal authority over anything but its own publishing process, and aggressively disavows any responsibility for such tasks as verifying conformance or policing compliance with the technologies or even for evangelizing them. In order to understand how this situation came to be, and how it is able to work today, we have to examine both the history of the IETF and the mechanisms that it currently employs to create and maintain the standards within its scope of operations.

There are technological principles that powerfully influence the technology decisions of the IETF, for instance the 'end-to-end principle' and the principle that network congestion needs to be tackled in a cooperative manner. This chapter focuses, however, on the organizational mechanics of the IETF; the technological principles are well covered in other publications and in other chapters of this book.

---

[1] Section 4.1 is written by Harald Alvestrand.

4.1.2. A Brief History of IETF

The IETF was started formally on 16 January 1986 as a gathering of 21 people around a table in San Diego, United States. Before lunch they were the GADS (Gateway Algorithms and Data Structures) Task Force; after lunch they had reconstituted themselves as the Internet Engineering Task Force.[2] This group consisted solely of US government-funded researchers, but among the ideals and visions held by this little group, we can recognize many of the important characteristics that form the Internet today.

In 1986, there were a few trends that powerfully influenced the way people were thinking about networking. To begin with, IBM had a dominant position in computer networking for enterprises, through its SNA (System Network Architecture) family of products. This family of products was hugely successful, massively complex, and with specifications totally controlled by IBM. If one connected non-IBM equipment to an IBM infrastructure and the equipment did not work, this was 'not IBM's problem'.

Second, many governments around the world, led by the US government, were on a charge to replace this domination by IBM with an open, standardized alternative of equivalent functionality (and equal complexity). Governments aimed to ensure the adoption of this alternative by mandating it for government use—the famous 'GOSIP mandate'.[3]

Third, some researchers had cobbled together an infrastructure that was able to pass data around using rather simple protocols, which therefore could be implemented cheaply and quickly, and provided useful functionality even when just a few things were done right. They called the technology 'internetworking', and it powered a few academic networks and intra-company networks, both of which were largely built on the so-called workstation platforms from Sun and Silicon Graphics.

These researchers constituted the first participants in the IETF. Their experience with the other two methods of defining and implementing networking protocols listed above led to an IETF that espoused the following basic principles of network-building:

- Open specifications: everyone has to be able to see how the mechanisms that power the network function; all should be freely able

---

[2] See Proceedings of the 16–17 January 1986 DARPA Gateway Algorithms and Data Structures Task Force (prepared by Phillip Gross), <http://www3.ietf.org/proceedings/prior29/IETF01.pdf>.

[3] See Chapter 1 (Section 1.9).

to implement those specifications; and no implementation should enjoy a privileged status.

- Open development: all interested parties should be able to provide input into the protocol development, and no body or group of bodies should have a veto power to override serious technical objection—even if they were the majority of people present. This principle later manifested itself in the IETF slogan of 'rough consensus and running code'.

- No enforcement: if the standards work, people will build them; if the standards are right, people will follow them; if it turns out that people need to deviate from them in order to have working products, the standards need to change.

The last point could be seen as the ultimate quality control for the IETF itself—if it did not produce results that people thought useful, people would stop coming to the IETF and it would become irrelevant.

The IETF has changed vastly since its first meeting. Some highlights in this development include the opening up, later in 1986, of IETF membership to any interested persons; the 'Kobe/POISED revolution' in 1991–2 that created a leadership selected from the IETF community[4]; the founding of the Internet Society (ISOC) in 1992, which formed a legal umbrella for IETF work[5]; the end of US government subsidies for the IETF in 1997 and its subsequent self-funding through imposition of meeting fees; the growth of the Internet coupled with the growth of the IETF—hitherto peaking at the IETF's December 2001 meeting which attracted almost 3,000 participants; and the redesign of the administrative support structure for the IETF under ISOC's umbrella in 2005.[6]

Currently, the IETF's budget is some US$4 million a year. The money is contributed by the organizational members of the Internet Society and the meeting fees of the IETF participants. Nowadays approximately 1,300 people attend each of the three official IETF meetings held each year.

---

[4] See RFC 1640: The Process for Organization of Internet Standards Working Group (POISED) (author: S. Crocker) (June 1994), <http://www.ietf.org/rfc/rfc1640.txt>. On the background to this 'revolution', see, for example, Mueller, *Ruling the Root*, 95–7.

[5] See RFC 2031: IETF-ISOC relationship (author: E. Huizer) (October 1996), <http://www.ietf.org/rfc/rfc2031.txt>.

[6] Documented in RFC 4071: Structure of the IETF Administrative Support Activity (IASA) (editors: R. Austein and B. Weijnen) (April 2005), <http://www.ietf.org/rfc/rfc4071.txt>.

4.1.3. *IETF Mechanics*

The IETF mission statement (RFC 3935) states:

The goal of the IETF is to make the Internet work better. The mission of the IETF is to produce high quality, relevant technical and engineering documents that influence the way people design, use, and manage the Internet in such a way as to make the Internet work better. These documents include protocol standards, best current practices, and informational documents of various kinds.[7]

This mission statement plainly positions the IETF chiefly as a document-producing organization.

The main components of the IETF are as follows:

- the participants, who are in the IETF as individuals, representing nobody but themselves;
- the Working Groups (WG), which work on mailing lists, may meet at IETF meetings, and are open to any participant;
- the Areas, which are groups of working groups, each presided over by one or two Area Directors (AD);
- the Internet Engineering Steering Group (IESG), which consists of all the Area Directors;
- the Internet Architecture Board (IAB), which worries about the long-term issues affecting the Internet, and also carries out some oversight and appeal functions (elaborated below).

There are also organizations closely affiliated with the IETF. One of these is the Internet Research Task Force (IRTF), which charters groups that look at more long-term issues for the Internet, and is also supervised by the Internet Architecture Board. Another is the Internet Assigned Numbers Authority (IANA) which, through the agency of ICANN, maintains protocol parameter registries on behalf of the IETF.[8]

There is no formal requirement for qualification as an IETF member, but the people who participate tend to be networking professionals. Many

---

[7] RFC 3935: A Mission Statement for the IETF (author: H. Alvestrand) (October 2004), <http://www.ietf.org/rfc/rfc3935.txt>.

[8] This function is governed by an IETF-IANA MOU documented in RFC 2860: see Memorandum of Understanding Concerning the Technical Work of the Internet Assigned Numbers Authority [authors: B. Carpenter (IAB), F. Baker (IETF), M. Roberts (ICANN)] (June 2000), < http://www.ietf.org/rfc/rfc2860.txt>. That function is distinct from the management of the DNS root zone and IP address allocation. Further on the protocol registries, see <http://www.iana.org/protocols/>. Further on IANA's functions, see Chapter 3 (Section 3.2.7) and Chapter 5 (Section 5.1).

of them are employees of networking equipment companies, Internet service providers, or researchers in Internet technology.

The Internet Society, which is a non-profit organization devoted to the welfare of the Internet in a wider sense, takes no part in the standards process directly. Rather, it contributes to funding and serves as the organizational backstop for the IETF whenever a formally recognizable organization is required.

The progress of a specification in the IETF usually occurs along the following path:[9]

- Proposal: someone comes to the IESG and says 'I think a standard for X would be a good thing'. 'X' may at this stage be a specification, an implemented protocol, a rough set of notes, or just an opinion that some problem area needs addressing.

- Interest gauging: the IESG may ask around, look at mailing lists, and try to figure out whether there is sufficient interest in doing 'X' or something similar. In many cases, the IESG will also allow the proposer to hold a 'birds of a feather' session (BOF) at an IETF meeting to gauge if there is interest in pursuing the issue.

- Working group chartering: the IESG and the proposers work out a description of what the WG is expected to do and when it is supposed to have it done. This is approved by the IESG, and WG chairs are selected by the IESG.

- Working group process: the WG will attempt to write a series of internet-drafts (temporary documents) that describe the problem and the solution to it. These are then discussed on the mailing list, and possibly at meetings, until the WG chair is able to declare that there is rough consensus for the documents as written. This can take several revisions and sometimes years.

- Document approval: the WG chair passes the documents to the IESG, which will initiate an IETF-wide Last Call on the documents. Comments coming back may lead to revisions of the documents, or may cause the documents to be returned to the working group for

---

[9] The basic elements of the standards process are described in RFC 2026: The Internet Standards Process—Revision 3 (author: S. Bradner) (October 1996), <http://www.ietf.org/rfc/rfc2026.txt>. Some amendments and expansions are found in RFC 2418: IETF Working Group Guidelines and Procedures (author: S. Bradner) (September 1998), <http://www.ietf.org/rfc/rfc2418.txt>; RFC 3978: IETF Rights in Contributions (editor: S. Bradner) (March 2005), <http://www.ietf.org/rfc/rfc3978.txt>; and RFC 3979: Intellectual Property Rights in IETF Technology (editor: S. Bradner) (March 2005), <http://www.ietf.org/rfc/rfc3979.txt>.

more fundamental revision. If there are no significant comments or objections, the documents get approved by the IESG.

- Document publication: the IESG informs the RFC Editor that the documents (identified by their draft name) have been approved, and the RFC Editor publishes them in the RFC series.

After publication, the documents are fixed for all time. Their status may change, or new documents may be published containing a revised version of the protocol, but the RFC (identified by number) is stable.

Formally, a newly adopted IETF standard is called a 'Proposed Standard', and is expected to be elevated or updated based on experience, leading to a 'Draft Standard' and finally a 'Full Standard'. However, this procedure is followed so rarely that the phrase 'the Internet runs on Proposed Standards' is commonly heard in IETF circles.[10]

Decisions of IETF bodies are generally subject to appeal. A participant can appeal the decision of a WG chair to the AD, an AD decision (including a negative decision on an appeal) to the IESG, and an IESG decision to the IAB. The latter is the final authority on all matters of technology. However, an appeal may lie to the ISOC Board on a point of procedure—specifically, in the case where the appellant alleges that the IETF procedural rules are unfair. So far, such an appeal has never been mounted; complaints have tended to be of the form 'I think that the process was carried out in an unfair manner and reached a conclusion that is unsupportable based on the facts of the case', rather than challenging the rules of the process itself.

The IESG and IAB are selected through the 'Nomination Committee' (NomCom) process, which is unique to the IETF.[11] First, a NomCom chair is selected by the ISOC president. A call for volunteers is then sent out to the IETF community. Anyone who has attended three of the last five IETF meetings can volunteer. Among the volunteers, 10 people are selected at random by a publicly verifiable algorithm executed by the NomCom chair. The 10 selected members, plus liaisons from the IESG, IAB, and ISOC, form the NomCom. Each year, the NomCom selects half

---

[10] The somewhat more worrisome phrase 'the Internet runs on internet-drafts' refers to the common practice of vendors shipping products based on a snapshot of working group discussions, which then may undergo considerable change before being released as Proposed Standard. This is problematic for several reasons, but time-to-market considerations often trump considerations of process for the vendors.

[11] The details of the NomCom process are given in RFC 3777: IAB and IESG Selection, Confirmation, and Recall Process: Operation of the Nominating and Recall Committees (editor: J. Galvin) (June 2004), <http://www.ietf.org/rfc/rfc3777.txt>.

the members of the IESG and the IAB, in addition to some other roles. The only consideration given to companies in the whole process is a rule stating that no more than two NomCom members can be from the same company.

4.1.4. *IETF Working Principles*

The IETF mission statement (RFC 3935) expresses a number of 'cardinal principles' for the body's work:

Open process—any interested person can participate in the work, know what is being decided, and make his or her voice heard on the issue. Part of this principle is our commitment to making our documents, our WG mailing lists, our attendance lists, and our meeting minutes publicly available on the Internet.

Technical competence—the issues on which the IETF produces its documents are issues where the IETF has the competence needed to speak to them, and that the IETF is willing to listen to technically competent input from any source. Technical competence also means that we expect IETF output to be designed to sound network engineering principles—this is also often referred to as 'engineering quality'.

Volunteer core—our participants and our leadership are people who come to the IETF because they want to do work that furthers the IETF's mission of 'making the Internet work better'.

Rough consensus and running code—we make standards based on the combined engineering judgement of our participants and our real-world experience in implementing and deploying our specifications.

Protocol ownership—when the IETF takes ownership of a protocol or function, it accepts the responsibility for all aspects of the protocol, even though some aspects may rarely or never be seen on the Internet. Conversely, when the IETF is not responsible for a protocol or function, it does not attempt to exert control over it, even though it may at times touch or affect the Internet.

In this list, there are a number of tasks that are *not* included: the IETF does not touch conformance criteria, it does not specify or run conformance tests, it does not police its specifications or claims of conformance, and it does not arbitrate about protocol interpretations. The theory behind IETF protocols is that the documents should be clear enough to make it obvious what the 'right' way to do something is. If two reasonable people disagree about the interpretation of the protocol, the disagreement is seen as a fault in the protocol specification, and is reason for starting work on a revision of the document.

This is partly a reaction against the experience of the OSI standards process. In that process, conformance requirements figured prominently, and the people who had been through that experience discovered that the process was expensive, time-consuming, and often did not add much value. For instance, when the 'conformance-tested' products were connected together in the field, they often failed to communicate for reasons that the conformance tests had failed to anticipate. The tradition of the community making up the IETF was rather to stage 'interoperability events'. These were sessions in which vendors with various implementations would meet, connect their half-written code together, and when the connection did not work, sit down with the specification and try to revise it until it unambiguously described how to do a certain function. They then went back to their code and made it behave that way on the spot. Yet these events have been formally outside the IETF process—the IETF does not formally arrange them; it is IETF participants who choose to initiate them, and to report back to the IETF on the results.

4.1.5. IETF Standards in the Marketplace

Many IETF standards are being used heavily in the marketplace. The basic Internet standards—TCP, IP, BGP,[12] UDP,[13] DNS, SMTP, HTTP—form the basis of the Internet as we know it today. There are, however, thousands of other IETF standards published. Some of these have seen limited use while others have seen no commercial take-up at all. The imprimatur of 'IETF proposed standard' is definitely not a guarantee that a protocol will be heavily used on the Internet. And in some cases—such as the network management protocols SNMPv1 and SNMPv3, where the IETF community identified serious problems with the former and standardized and heavily promoted the latter—the market simply ignored the IETF and went on shipping (largely) SNMPv1-compliant products.

The first reason why people chose to adopt IETF standards was because the standards worked. They solved a problem effectively, and people could implement them and use them without 'jumping through hoops'. Furthermore, the lack of formal conformance requirements meant that it was possible to implement a protocol badly if that solved a particular problem. Many of the early implementations of IETF standards were flawed in significant ways but they interoperated for the common cases,

---

[12] Border Gateway Protocol is the basic Internet routing protocol.
[13] User Datagram Protocol is a protocol for sending short messages (datagrams) between networked computers.

and that served a useful purpose. Quality of implementation would only become a marketplace factor much later (if at all).

The open availability of the standards documents helped here too. When someone wondered whether an IETF standard would suit their purpose, they could simply download all the relevant standards and read them; there was no need to pay fees, join consortia, or sign nondisclosure agreements in order to get started.

There is one evolution which one would expect given classic economic theory, but which has not happened: one would expect to see 'tweaked' versions of IETF standards (such as TCP implementations with different time constants) that benefit the users of that implementation, but harm the overall community. The reason for this not happening is far from clear, but may involve a type of peer pressure. Everyone knows that what they do in these matters will be visible to others; the engineers blessing such an implementation as 'good' will be shunned by their peers, and their company will receive significantly bad publicity. An important factor here is that the society of Internet engineers is a *social* environment. The people who work on Internet systems know each other, and they care what their peers think of them.

Other forms of standards abuse have happened, however, such as the embrace-and-extend proliferation of extensions to LDAP (Lightweight Directory Access Protocol)[14] that is the Microsoft Active Directory.[15] Yet in these cases, it is rather hard to see the direct harm to the overall community, so this has generally not led to strong reactions, and is a perennial problem in the Internet context.

Large customers who see significant advantage in not being bound to a single supplier form the biggest countervailing force to this trend. If a large customer (of the size of General Motors, British Telecom, or the US federal government) insists to a vendor that interoperability should occur, interoperability is likely to occur. This allows the customer (in theory) to mix and match brands of equipment with impunity, and

---

[14] The LDAP is a mechanism for access to online directory functions, including user information.

[15] Embrace-and-extend refers to the practice of adopting a standard, thus allowing one's own product to enter a marketplace where conformance to that standard is a requirement, and then extending it with features that other implementations do not have, so that there is pressure on one's customers to push other users to adopt the same product, in order to get the benefits from these proprietary 'extensions'. This can lead to market dominance in an ostensibly standard-defined field, and is of great concern for those who think that open standards bring benefits to society.

has proved a great force towards keeping a healthy marketplace in communications technology. However, this strategy depends on there being existing standards to refer to. In areas like office systems, where Microsoft Windows is dominant, the lack of pre-existing standards makes it much harder for organizations to use this strategy.

Notably absent from this picture is laws and their enforcement, and the specific actions of governments. While the laws on monopolies and monopoly abuses are certainly important, and the buying power of governments is considerable, the most important 'enforcement' of IETF standards seems to be done by a combination of marketplace forces and social forces. The marketplace participants see self-interest in adherence to standards, and the people who do the engineering take pride in making and implementing those standards. This combination has been quite powerful so far.

4.1.6. IETF and Legal Issues

A commonly heard slogan in the IETF has been 'the IETF does not exist'. This slogan is, of course, not strictly true. The IETF is formally organized as an activity of the Internet Society (ISOC), which is a US not-for-profit organization. However, the IETF is far older than ISOC, and has carefully attempted to keep its distance from its 'corporate parent'. The Internet Society plays no role at all in the processing of standards; its only involvement in the selection of the leadership is the 'approval' of the NomCom's proposals for IAB members; and its only involvement in the making of the rules by which the IETF operates is a carefully worded statement that the ISOC Board of Directors observes that the IETF has changed its rules whenever that happens.[16]

Much of the IETF's procedure, where it touches on legal issues, has been focused on not making the IETF a party to any dispute. So far, this has worked very well. The IETF has been subpoenaed for material in multiple court cases involving standards and patents, but has never been named as a defendant in a court case.

One of the steps the IETF takes to make sure it stays out of legal trouble is never to speak to the validity of a patent. Where patents may be

---

[16] The last time this happened was in 2006—see ISOC resolution 06/36 which reads: 'RESOLVED, that the Board of Trustees accepts or confirms its acceptance of the IETF process documents current at this time, and accepts the responsibilities of ISOC as described in these documents.' Resolution 06/36 is available via <http://www.isoc.org/isoc/general/trustees/resltn-06.shtml>.

required to practise a standard, and the IETF seeks to figure out whether the terms under which licensing is offered are reasonable and non-discriminatory, the IETF seeks assurance from implementers that they have worked out the patent issues to their satisfaction, but does not ask for disclosure of specific terms, or verify the details of the agreements—the statement that the implementer does not have a problem is taken at face value. This means that if, for instance, an implementer claims that it has no problem because a license to the patent in question is not necessary, a patent-holder's fight would be with the claimant, not the IETF.

Another step is that the IETF never verifies the validity of an implementation. Again, the claim (usually by the implementer) that an implementation conforms fully to the standard is taken at face value.

Moreover, the IETF refuses to handle material that cannot be freely distributed, such as trade secrets. Anyone who contributes material to the IETF must agree that the contribution can be distributed to others. Further, the rules for openness, free availability of archives, and the record of who participated in discussions are critical for avoiding conflict with US antitrust laws. There is a specific exception in those laws for standards-making, and the IETF tries very hard to stay within that exception (while preserving its own unique nature).

4.1.7. IETF and Other Standards Bodies

The IETF is not alone in the world of IT standardization. There are several large standards organizations active, and literally hundreds of consortia and industry fora that try to produce specifications for some aspect of communication related to the Internet.

The IETF's favoured method of cooperation with standards bodies is 'shared people': anyone, including the people who are active in other standards bodies, are welcome to come to an IETF meeting or join an IETF mailing list, and talk about what they are doing and how they think it should affect the IETF's work. In return, the IETF expects them to listen, understand what the IETF is doing, and carry that information back to their respective organizations.

In several cases, the procedures of other standards bodies are based on the formal exchange of letters—so-called liaison statements—and the procedures require these to be exchanged within the context of a 'liaison agreement'. To satisfy these procedural restrictions, the IETF has entered into liaison agreements with several organizations, including the Institute of Electrical and Electronics Engineers (IEEE), some ISO subcommittees, and the ITU.[17]

In some cases, the IETF also has established liaisons that regularly touch base with the other bodies, in order to make sure the work of each body will fit harmoniously together with that of the other, or to discuss where work items that could belong in either group should be handled. This is the case, for instance, with the World Wide Web Consortium.

In the past, there have been instances where people tried actively to depict the relationship between the various bodies as competitive and conducive to the practice of 'forum-shopping'—that is, asking multiple standards bodies to consider a technology, with the intention of getting a specification standardized by the body that would make the least requests for modification or change control. This tendency has decreased some-what in later years, and most relationships are now better characterized by cooperation rather than competition. This does not mean that the organizations always see eye to eye on how technology should evolve. The IETF tends to focus on technical solutions that work well in multiple economic contexts, while the ITU, for instance, has tended to focus on technologies that work in economies dominated by 'carriers' that mediate interconnection between users. By contrast, the World Wide Web Consortium has tended to ignore the intermediaries and start off with the assumption that all parties to a communication are directly connected to each other.

A large problem for the IETF is that there are not very many people available to do this kind of liaison work—all technical work, including the liaison work, in the IETF is carried out by volunteers, not by paid staff. This means that the people doing liaison work have to be chosen from the set of people who are seen as technically competent, have the trust of the IETF, and are willing to spend volunteer time on IETF work— which is the same pool of people that provides the IETF with its active participants, document editors, and leadership. This is one reason why the IETF tries to keep the number of formal liaisons to a minimum.

The IETF also has working relationships with numerous bodies with which it has no formal agreement. For instance, there is no MoU governing the relationship between IETF and OASIS (home of the ODF

---

[17] Details of how the IETF handles liaison work are described in RFC 4052: IAB Processes for Management of IETF Liaison Relationships (editor: L. Daigle) (April 2005), <http://www.ietf.org/rfc/rfc4052.txt>; RFC 4053: Procedures for Handling Liaison Statements to and from the IETF (authors: S. Trowbridge, S. Bradner, F. Baker) (April 2005), <http://www.ietf.org/rfc/rfc4053.txt>; RFC 4691: Guidelines for Acting as an IETF Liaison to Another Organization (editor: L. Andersson) (October 2006), <http://www.ietf.org/rfc/rfc4691.txt>.

document format specification) or CableLabs (home of specifications for cable modems), but several people participate in both the IETF and in those other communities, and issues are worked out as needed. Formal liaison statements are usually signed because of the other organization's requirements, not the requirements of the IETF.

The IETF also has a relationship with ICANN, which is not a standards body. As noted above, ICANN runs the IANA protocol parameter registry for the IETF, and the IETF picks some representatives to sit on various ICANN bodies (Nomcom, Board liaison, etc.). The argument given for this representation is that ICANN has a need for the technical competence and knowledge of the underlying Internet standards which the IETF can provide. Moreover, the IETF leadership is in the optimal position to select the right people for these positions.

Taken together, these relationships form an important part of the reason for the significant impact that the IETF has on the Internet. The IEFT is not attempting to be 'all things to all people', or to address all conceivable problems that can be construed as Internet-related, but it does demand respect as the custodian of the suite of specifications that constitutes the current technical 'code of the Internet'. To a very large degree, it has been granted that respect, and its position in the universe of Internet-related standardization, seems unlikely to be challenged in the short run.

4.1.8. Conclusion

The IETF is a standardization body that works. This is despite it having no formal membership, no voting rules, and no explicit representation from companies, governments, or organizations. The enforcement of IETF standards is carried out by social networks and by the marketplace, not by formal requirements or policing. The result is something that has worked to build the Internet we have today. There is a good chance it will continue working.

4.2. The World Wide Web Consortium[18]

4.2.1. Introduction

The World Wide Web Consortium (most often referred to as W3C) is a non-commercial organization formed to 'lead the World Wide Web

---

[18] Section 4.2 is written by Håkon Wium Lie.

to its full potential by developing protocols and guidelines that ensure long-term growth for the Web'.[19] The Consortium was started in 1994 and at the time of writing (April 2008) has about 400 members, mostly companies in the computer industry, and around 70 staff members. As such, W3C is a major player in the world of Internet standards.

4.2.2. Background

In the history of computer technology, the period around 1990 will be remembered for three influential projects. All of them had open exchange of information as a goal, and they contributed technology as well as philosophy to the world of computing. In Finland, Linus Torvalds launched the Linux operating systems which took enabled open source software to form a complete, stable, operating system. In other parts of the world, experts on text encoding started collecting and classifying character sets from all written languages into a specification called Unicode. And, third, at CERN in Geneva, Tim Berners-Lee developed the 'World Wide Web' project into what we today commonly refer to as simply 'the web'.

The topic of this section is W3C, the organization that Berners-Lee subsequently formed to oversee the development of the technical specifications that describe how the web works. Linux and Unicode are mentioned to provide some context for the development of the web, and to name two of the components that helped build a successful web. Web servers running Linux provided a stable and inexpensive publishing platform for webpages around the world, and Unicode provided a way to write webpages in all languages. A third and essential component for the web was the Internet, which provided a deployed infrastructure onto which the web was built.

It is worth noting that neither Linux, Unicode, nor the Internet itself is under the control of W3C. Moreover, W3C does not control the web itself with its manifold sites and content. The scope of W3C is limited to developing and maintaining specifications and guidelines for the web, and to advocating their use. So far, W3C has issued around 80 'Recommendations' (which is the Consortium's term for a 'standard'). The next section discusses some of these.

---

[19] See <http://www.w3.org/Consortium/>.

4.2.3. *The Early Years*

The initial web, as described by Tim Berners-Lee, consisted of three specifications. Documents were written in HTML (HyperText Markup Language)
and transferred over the Internet by way of HTTP (HyperText Transfer
Protocol). Hypertext links were represented as URLs (Uniform Resource
Locators). In the first years of the web, specifications did not exist and
authors relied on web browsers to verify the correctness of documents.
One of the IETF mantras was used to defend forgiving web browsers:

I support Marc [Andreessen] completely in his decision to make Mosaic work as
best it can when it is given invalid HTML. The maxim is that one should be
conservative in what one does, liberal in what one expects.[20]

One important reason to form W3C was to have an organization that
would write and maintain formal specifications. Even if browsers would
accept invalid HTML (as the quoted message above argues for), there
should be a clear definition of what correct HTML is. And, as more authors
and software vendors were attracted to the web, new ideas for technical
development were proposed. Some considered the IETF to be the natural
place for discussing and standardizing web technologies. However, strong
interest from industry, along with MIT's tradition in creating industry
consortia, led to the forming of W3C.

The Consortium was formed at MIT in 1994.[21] To underline the importance of a *world-wide* web, two co-hosts in different parts of the world
joined in 1995 [the French National Institute for Research on Computer
Science and Control (INRIA)—later replaced by the European Research
Consortium for Informatics and Mathematics (ERCIM)] and 1996 (Keio
University in Japan). Members of the emerging web industry also signed
up quickly and, as a result, W3C was able to hire staff members and start
working groups. Representatives of governments, universities, and other
non-commercial organizations also joined, although in smaller numbers.
Formally, members sign agreements with the three host organizations, not
with W3C.

The Consortium was formed without a clearly defined plan of how it
would work and what the deliverables would be. This was not unexpected,
given the speed at which the web developed and the fact that it was a
consortium where members, in principle, would finance and decide on
activities. Two other organizations served as role models for the newly

---

[20] Tim Berners-Lee in a message sent to the www-talk mailing list on 20 August 1993.
[21] See further Berners-Lee, *Weaving the Web*, chapter 8.

created consortium. One was the X Consortium which was formed by MIT in 1998.[22] Its primary objective was to develop and maintain the source code for the X Window system. The other was the IETF, which mainly produced specifications and left it to others to produce the code that implemented the specifications. In the early years of W3C, there were efforts to create both code and specifications; if one could convince web users to use the same underlying software libraries that would implement the specifications correctly, interoperability would be enhanced. The lib-www library[23], the Arena browser[24], the Jigsaw server[25], and the Amaya editor[26] are examples of code projects at W3C. However, W3C would later focus primarily on producing specifications. This was in line with what leading members desired—both Netscape and Microsoft wanted control of their own source code.

4.2.4. W3C Recommendations

The first Recommendation issued by W3C (on 1 October 1996) was the Portable Network Graphics (PNG) image format. This format had been developed outside W3C but still received W3C endorsement. This was— along with recognition of the technical contribution of PNG—a polit- ical signal. The PNG format had been developed to avoid the patent- encumbered Graphics Interchange Format (GIF), and W3C herewith sig- nalled that software patents were disruptive to an open web.

The next Recommendation (published 31 October 1996) also sent a political message. The Platform for Internet Content Selection (PICS) specification allowed content to be described in machine-readable ways to support automatic content filtering. The purpose of publishing PICS as a W3C Recommendation was to show that the emerging web industry was responsible and that government control of the web was not necessary. PICS can be seen as a technical response to the US Communications Decency Act of 1996, parts of which were later overturned by the US Supreme Court.[27] Since then, PICS has seen little use.

Cascading Style Sheets (CSS) was the third and last Recommendation issued in 1996. CSS is now widely in use to describe colours, typography, and layout of webpages. The political message in CSS is that both web

---

[22] See further <http://en.wikipedia.org/wiki/X_Window_System>.
[23] See further <http://www.w3.org/Library/>.
[24] See further <http://www.w3.org/Arena/>.
[25] See further <http://www.w3.org/Jigsaw/>.
[26] See further <http://www.w3.org/Amaya/>.
[27] *American Civil Liberties Union v. Reno*, 521 U.S. 844 (1997).

authors and web users should be allowed to influence the presentation of web content.

As of April 2008, W3C has issued just over 100 Recommendations.[28] Among these are some notable acronyms with world-wide recognition. HTML was established as the dominant document format before W3C was formed, and W3C still maintains it. In recent years, the XHTML dialect has been promoted. The 'X' comes from XML (Extensible Markup Language) which also is a W3C Recommendation. The relative simplicity of XML (compared to its predecessor SGML), combined with eagerness to put data (as opposed to documents) on the web, led to a slew of W3C Recommendations starting with 'X' from around 1998. Examples include XLink, XForms, and XSL. Although XML only provides a syntactic layer in these specifications, the marketing benefits of attaching other specifications to XML have been substantial.

The overall influence of W3C Recommendations on the web is debatable. First, many of W3C's specifications are used incorrectly or not used at all. Almost all webpages claim to be HTML (which is a W3C Recommendation), but a vast majority of those documents are not written according to the HTML specification. The fact that there does not exist an official description of how HTML is used on the web is a shortcoming. Although XHTML has been widely promoted in recent years, only a small subset of web documents use this dialect. XML—and the formats built on top of it—are often used to store and exchange data in web servers, but little XML is exchanged between web servers and browsers. W3C has used a great deal of resources on developing and promoting other specifications (e.g. RDF[29] and P3P[30]), but so far they have seen little use.

Second, many of the specifications that are used on the web are not under the control of W3C. Most images on the web use the GIF or JPEG formats but these formats predate W3C. The programming language of choice on the web (JavaScript) is standardized by another organization, Ecma International [formerly ECMA (European Computer Manufacturers Association)]. RSS and Atom, two sets of popular formats for alerting users to new web content, were also developed outside W3C.

However, some W3C Recommendations are very successful. Although the use of XML on the web is limited, it has had profound influence on

---

[28] For an up-to-date overview, see <http://www.w3.org/TR/>.

[29] Resource Description Framework—a format for representing metadata about web resources. See further <http://www.w3.org/RDF/>.

[30] Platform for Privacy Preferences—a protocol enabling automated negotiation between websites and browsers over information collection practices. See further <http://www.w3.org/P3P/>.

opening up data formats. For example, the two most popular office packages (Microsoft Office and OpenOffice) both support XML-based formats, albeit different ones. Also, CSS and DOM (Document Object Model) are extensively used in contemporary web design.

Further, there are signs that W3C is paying more attention to the existing web rather than an ideal future web. In 2007, a new HTML working group was chartered with the task of defining and developing 'classic HTML'. If successful, the resulting HTML specification will become much more relevant to web designers.

4.2.5. Beyond Recommendations

Although W3C is focused on producing Recommendations, it also tries to improve the web through other means, including the following:

- Validators: W3C has developed several validators and made them available on the web. Users can upload documents to a validator to verify whether the document conforms with a specification or not. Currently, W3C offers validators for HTML and CSS.

- Accessibility: the Web Accessibility Initiative (WAI) is a W3C program to help make the web accessible to people with disabilities. WAI raises awareness of accessibility on the web and tries to lower barriers that make it difficult or impossible for many people with disabilities to use the web.

- Mailing lists: W3C serves as a home to many mailing lists and quite a few are open to the public. This allows anyone to take part in discussions on web technology.

- Legal issues: in one specific case, W3C stepped forward to try influencing a court to rule against a software patent.[31] Berners-Lee, the W3C director, has been outspoken against software patents in general. The W3C process, although not strictly patent-free, is also slanted against software patents.[32] Members have reacted differently to this policy; some have left W3C, others have aligned their internal patent policies with the W3C policy. In general, there seems to be agreement that W3C's stand on software patents has been beneficial both for the web and for W3C.

---

[31] See 'World Wide Web Consortium Presents US Patent Office with Evidence Invalidating Eolas Patent', <http://www.w3.org/2003/10/28-906-briefing>.

[32] The patent policy of W3C is available at <http://www.w3.org/Consortium/Patent-Policy-20040205/>. No specific policy exists for copyright or trademarks.

4.2.6. *W3C Today*

W3C has around 400 member organizations today. Members pay yearly fees based on their size and purpose. Commercial organizations pay more than non-commercial organizations, and big commercial organizations (measured by revenue) pay more than small commercial organizations. Also, fees are higher in high-income countries than in countries with lower incomes. The yearly fee ranges between EUR 65k to EUR 2k. Depending on their location, members pay fees in USD, EUR, or Yen. Due to unexpected currency fluctuations, European members pay around 60 per cent higher fees than American members.

Members have two main ways of influencing W3C. First, each member has a representative in the Advisory Committee (AC). The AC meets twice per year to discuss the state of the Web and how to best organize W3C. Second, members can participate in working groups. Working groups are established to produce W3C Recommendations and, by participating in such a group, members can influence the outcome of the group's efforts. In line with the IETF's mantra of 'rough consensus and running code', W3C puts high value on achieving consensus within working groups and demands two interoperable implementations in order for a specification to become a W3C Recommendation.

Working groups typically communicate through electronic mailing lists, weekly telephone conferences, and physical meetings which take place a few times per year. Once a year, all working groups convene at the Technical Plenary (TP) meeting to discuss within the group and to meet other groups. The week-long meeting includes one plenary day to address issues of common interest. As in all distributed organizations, physical meetings are also social events that allow people to meet and discuss issues in amicable surroundings.

All W3C members have access to the email archives of all Working Groups, but these are not publicly available. W3C has therefore been criticized for lack of transparency.[33] The recently chartered HTML Working Group has taken a more open approach by allowing anyone to join the group and by conducting all communication in public.

When consensus has formed around a 'Working Draft' (WD), the specification can progress through a 'Last Call' into a 'Candidate Recommendation'. At this stage, implementation experience is actively sought and a

---

[33] See, for example, the criticism by Jeffrey Zeldman at <http://www.zeldman.com/2006/07/17/an-angry-fix/>, last accessed 30 April 2008.

test suite is often created. If the results are deemed satisfactory, the specification can become a 'Proposed Recommendation'. This is the last chance for members to voice opposition to a specification before it is turned into a W3C Recommendation. The whole process is described in a separate 'W3C process' document. The process has increased in complexity over the years.[34] For example, Working Groups are now subject to a 'heartbeat' requirement entailing that they publish an updated specification (prior to it becoming a Recommendation) at least every three months.[35]

Formally, it is the W3C director who decides when a specification is moved from one stage to another through the W3C process. As such, the director has broad discretionary powers and members only have an advisory role.[36] Most often, the director favours those who want to advance a specification rather than those who oppose a specification. In other words, consensus is sought at the working group level but is not required among all W3C members.

When a specification becomes a W3C Recommendation, many working groups consider their mission completed. However, having the mark of approval from W3C is not always enough to win over implementors and users on the web. Some working groups therefore continue their work after a Recommendation has been issued. Documenting errata, developing test suites, resolving ambiguities, and promotion are among the tasks to be performed.

One factor that has inhibited acceptance of W3C Recommendations is that one vendor, Microsoft, dominates the web browser market. Due largely to its bundling with the Windows operating system, Microsoft's Internet Explorer (IE) was able to overtake Netscape's Navigator in the late 1990s—as noted in Chapter 1 (Section 1.13). Microsoft's dominant position has allowed it to accept or reject new specifications without having to consider the competition.

4.2.7. Summing Up

The web is an immensely successful medium that will live for a long time. It offers easy access to electronic information on a scale never seen before,

---

[34] In 2001, the HTML version of the W3C Process Document was 134k long. In 2005, the same document was 218k long. See further <http://www.w3.org/2005/10/Process-20051014/>.

[35] W3C Process Document (version of 14 October 2005) Clause 6.2.7, <http://www.w3.org/2005/10/Process-20051014/groups.html#three-month-rule>.

[36] This is one point where the W3C differs from the IETF.

and most of the data formats and protocols are open for anyone to use. Not all Recommendations issued by W3C have seen real use. However, W3C Recommendations describe some of the most widely used languages on the web, including CSS and DOM, and efforts are underway to describe HTML properly in a W3C Recommendation. W3C also deserves recognition for its role in establishing a patent policy that minimizes the damage of software patents on the web.

5

The naming game: governance of the Domain Name System

Lee A. Bygrave, Susan Schiavetta, Hilde Thunem,
Annebeth B. Lange, and Edward Phillips

5.1. Introduction to Domain Name System[1]

5.1.1. *Domain Names*

Domain names are essentially translations of IP numbers/addresses into a more semantic or meaningful form. Under IPv4, an IP address is a 32 bit string of 1s and 0s.[2] This string will be represented by four numbers from 0 to 255 separated by dots/periods—for example, 153.110.179.30. However, that IP number tells most people little or nothing; <telenor.no> is much more easily remembered and catchy. Thus, the main reason for domain names is mnemonics; that is, domain names make it easier for humans to remember identifiers.

Arguably, though, domain names have two other overlapping functions as well. The first is that they enhance categorization of information, thus making administration of networks more systematic and making it easier for people to find information. The second is stability: IP addresses can frequently change, whereas domain names will tend to be more stable reference points (assuming that the DNS can accommodate changes in the IP address level—which it can).

---

[1] Section 5.1 is written by Lee A. Bygrave.
[2] Under IPv6, which is currently being deployed (albeit slowly), the IP address space has been increased to 128 bits.

Unlike IP addresses, domain names are not essential to movement of data packets. The Internet could dispense with them altogether and still function. Yet it would not be as user-friendly.

Each domain name must be unique but need not be associated with just one single or consistent IP number. It must simply map onto a particular IP number or set of numbers which will give the result that the registrant of the domain name desires.

A domain name has two main parts arranged hierarchically from right to left: (*a*) a top-level domain (TLD) and (*b*) a second-level domain (SLD). It will commonly also have a third-level domain. The number of domains is usually between two and five.

The potential number of domain name strings is huge (though not unlimited). The name set currently operates with 37 characters (26 letters, 10 numerals, and the '-' (dash) symbol).[3] While domain names consisting of single characters are not permitted, there are 37^2 or 1,369 two-character combinations, 37^3 or 50,653 three-character combinations, and 37^4 or 1,874,161 four-character combinations. Obviously, the number of combinations will increase significantly if the character set is increased—a possibility that is currently being discussed and tested with respect to 'Internationalized Domain Names' (IDNs).[4]

There are two principal classes of top-level domains: (*a*) generic (gTLD) and (*b*) country code (ccTLD).[5] The first class covers the following TLDs such as: .com, .net, .org, .gov, .edu, .mil, .int, .info, and .biz. The second class covers TLDs such as .au, .no, .ru, and .uk.[6] The first class also covers TLDs that are set up for use by a particular community or industry (so-called sponsored TLDs). Examples are .cat (set up for use by the Catalan community in Spain) and .mobi (set up for users and producers of mobile telecommunications services). The generic TLDs may further be classified according to whether they are open to use by anyone; some are reserved for use only by specified groups/sectors. For example, .pro is restricted to licensed professional persons; .name is restricted to individual persons; and .gov is restricted to US government institutions.

---

[3] However, the dash symbol cannot form the initial or final character of a domain name. Note too that the 'dot' (or period) is used only to separate DN segments; it does not otherwise form a distinguishing element of a name.

[4] See further the overview of activity at <http://www.icann.org/topics/idn/>, last accessed 28 June 2008.

[5] Additionally, there is one TLD falling outside these categories: the address and routing parameter area domain .arpa. This enables retrieval of essential data records for core Internet infrastructure.

[6] For a complete list, see <http://www.iana.org/cctld/cctld-whois.htm>. With one exception (.uk), country code abbreviations are based on the list set down in ISO standard 3166-1.

Table 5.1. Current gTLDs

gTLD	Introduced	Purpose	Registry
.aero	2001	Air transport industry	Société Internationale de Télécommunications Aéronautiques SC
.asia	2006	Asian community	DotAsia Organization, Ltd.
.biz	2001	Business	NeuStar, Inc.
.cat	2005	Catalan linguistics and cultural community	Fundació puntCAT
.com	1995	Unrestricted	VeriSign, Inc.
.coop	2001	Cooperatives	DotCooperation, LLC
.edu	1995	US educational institutions	EDUCAUSE
.gov	2001	US government	US General Services Administration
.info	2001	Unrestricted	Afilias Ltd.
.int	1998	Organizations established by international treaties between governments	IANA
.jobs	2005	International community of human resource managers	Employ Media LLC
.mil	1995	US military	US DoD Network information Center
.mobi	2005	Mobile content providers and users community	mTLD Top Level Domain, Ltd.
.museum	2001	Museums	Museum Domain Management Association
.name	2001	Individuals	Global Name Registry, Ltd.
.net	1995	Unrestricted	VeriSign, Inc.
.org	1995	Unrestricted	Public Interest Registry (ISOC)
.pro	2002	Accountants, lawyers, other professionals	RegistryPro, Ltd.
.tel	2006	e-communications address/numbers information	Telnic, Ltd.
.travel	2005	Travel and tourism community	Tralliance Corporation

The number of TLDs is set to rise dramatically with the announcement by ICANN in late June 2008 that it will radically liberalize its policy for recognizing new TLDs.[7]

5.1.2. *The Domain Name System*

The Domain Name System (DNS) is essentially a system for mapping, allocating, and registering domain names. Basically, it translates domain names into numerical addresses so that computers can find each other.

---

[7] See <http://www.icann.org/en/announcements/announcement-4-26jun08-en.htm>.

Thus, it is analogous to a telephone number directory that maps the names of telephone subscribers onto telephone numbers.

The fundamental design goal of the DNS is to provide the same answers to the same queries issued from any place on the Internet. Accordingly, it ensures (*a*) that no two computers have the same domain name and (*b*) that all parts of the Internet know how to convert domain names into numerical IP addresses, so that packets of data can be sent to the right destination.

The core of the system is a distributed database holding information over which domain names map onto which IP numbers. The data files with this information are known as 'roots' and the servers with these files are called 'root servers' or 'root nameservers'. The servers are arranged hierarchically. The top root servers hold the master file of registrations in each TLD and provide information about which other computers are authoritative regarding the TLDs in the naming structure.

In terms of DNS management, it is important to note that the system is organized hierarchically, with administrative power devolving from TLDs to sub-domains. This hierarchical feature stands in contrast with much of the rest of Internet architecture. The addition of new TLDs may only be carried out by ICANN (under US government oversight). The addition of new second-level domains may only be carried out by administrators of TLDs, and only administrators of second-level domains may add new third-level domains.

It is also important to note that the DNS operates with a functional (and, to some extent, legal) distinction between two main classes of domain name manager. The first class is the registry, which operates a database for registration of domain names in the domain it administers. The second class is the registrar, which facilitates actual registration of domain names. In some cases, a registry will also operate as registrar—the case, for example, with the .no and .eu domains.

The principal DNS root is managed by ICANN and references to the DNS are normally to that particular root service. However, a handful of alternative root systems do exist. These operate independently of the ICANN regime, with separate root servers and TLDs. Examples are New.Net, UnifiedRoot, and .OpenNIC.[8] However, they have only a tiny share of the Internet user market due to the networking and cost factors outlined in Chapter 2 (Section 2.8).

---

[8] For an overview, see <http://en.wikipedia.org/wiki/Alternative_DNS_root>.

The main points of conflict and controversy with respect to operation of the DNS have largely arisen in two respects. The first relates to how domain names are allocated to persons/organizations. The second relates to which TLDs (and thereby domain names) are permitted. These are not the only points of conflict. Another point relates to the operation of WHOIS services;[9] yet another to control of root servers. However, the latter conflicts have not been as salient as the former two.

The conflict over domain name allocation and recognition is due primarily to the changing function of domain names. They have gone from being just easily remembered address identifiers to signifiers of broader identity and value (such as trademarks). At the same time, while they are not scarce resources technically, they are scarce resources in the economic sense. And some have come to assume extremely large economic value.[10] Indeed, in at least one jurisdiction, there has been some judicial recognition of domain names as a form of property.[11]

5.1.3. Governance of DNS: A Web of Contracts

Governance of the DNS is largely contractual, at least with respect to management of gTLDs. However, as related in Sections 5.4 and 5.5, some of the regimes for management of ccTLDs have a legislative footing.

As described in Chapter 3 (Section 3.2.7), management of names and numbers was originally carried out essentially by Jon Postel at ISI under the nomenclature of the IANA. The IANA functions were transferred to ICANN in 2000 pursuant to contract. That contract has been renewed and modified twice. The current contract, entered into in August 2006, was initially set to expire in September 2007 but has options to extend the term annually until September 2011.[12] Under this agreement, the IANA functions are specified to include the following:

- coordination of the assignment of technical protocol parameters;
- management of the root zone of the DNS; and
- allocation of Internet numbering resources.

While ultimate formal responsibility for distribution of IP addresses lies with IANA/ICANN, a network of supporting bodies helps to carry out this

[9] These are dealt with in Section 5.2.1.
[10] See further, for example, Anupam Chander, 'The New, New Property', *Texas Law Review*, 2003, vol. 81, 715–97.
[11] See particularly *Kremen v. Cohen & Network Solutions*, 337 F.3d 1024 (9th Cir. 2003).
[12] ICANN/US Government Contract for the IANA Function, 11 August 2006, <http://www.icann.org/general/iana-contract-14aug06.pdf>.

function. Chief among these bodies are the Regional Internet Registries (RIRs). There are five RIRs all of which are non-profit organizations:

- ARIN (American Registry for Internet Numbers);
- APNIC (Asia Pacific Network Information Centre);
- LACNIC (Latin American and Caribbean IP Address Regional Registry);
- RIPE NCC (Réseaux IP Européens Network Coordination Centre—covering Europe and the Middle East); and
- AfriNIC (African Network Information Centre). [13]

IANA/ICANN distributes blocks of IP numbers to the RIRs, which then distribute IP numbers to main Internet Service Providers (ISPs) in their respective regions. The ISPs further distribute the numbers to smaller ISPs, corporations, and individuals.

To fulfil ICANN's mission, a web of contracts and more informal agreements has been spun between the corporation and the bodies with which it deals. [14] These agreements are in three main categories: (*a*) agreements between ICANN and the US Department of Commerce (DOC); (*b*) agreements between NSI (later VeriSign) [15] and DOC; (*c*) agreements between ICANN and other bodies that are directly engaged in DNS operations (mainly domain name registries and registrars).

Of primary importance in the first category is the MOU—termed 'Joint Project Agreement'—that defines the relationship between ICANN and DOC. The MOU was first entered into on 25 November 1998 with an initial expiry date of 30 September 2000. [16] Under it, DNS management is essentially cast as a collaborative project of ICANN and DOC whereby they

will jointly design, develop, and test the mechanisms, methods, and procedures that should be in place and the steps necessary to transition management responsibility for DNS functions now performed by, or on behalf of, the US Government to a private-sector not-for-profit entity.

Thus, the MOU envisages the private sector gradually taking full responsibility for technical management of the DNS. At the same time, it gives DOC an oversight function to ensure that ICANN carries out its tasks as agreed.

---

[13] See generally <http://www.nro.net/>, last accessed 20 June 2008.
[14] For a full list, see <http://www.icann.org/general/agreements.htm>.
[15] VeriSign, Inc., acquired NSI in June 2000.
[16] Available at <http://www.icann.org/general/icann-mou-25nov98.htm>.

The MOU charters ICANN with five tasks:

a. Establishment of policy for and direction of the allocation of IP number blocks;
b. Oversight of the operation of the authoritative root server system;[17]
c. Oversight of the policy for determining the circumstances under which new top-level domains would be added to the root system;
d. Coordination of the assignment of other Internet technical parameters as needed to maintain universal connectivity on the Internet; and
e. Other activities necessary to coordinate the specified DNS management functions, as agreed by the Parties.

The MOU also lays down basic principles for DNS management; namely, ensuring (*a*) stability of the Internet; (*b*) competition and consumer choice in DNS management; (*c*) private, bottom–up coordination of policy; and (*d*) representation of Internet users (both in the United States and internationally).[18]

The MOU has since been renewed and amended several times. The latest version of the JPA was entered into in September 2006 and will expire in September 2009.[19] The overall result of the successive changes has been a gradual increase in ICANN's autonomy, particularly regarding its internal organizational affairs, yet DOC continues to have a supervisory role.[20] The basic principles of DNS governance have remained unchanged. As noted in Chapter 3 (Section 3.2.8), ICANN recently requested that the JPA be ended, but the official US response was not known at the time of writing.

The other main agreement in the first category is the ICANN/US Government Contract for the IANA Function.[21] Among other things, this contract gives ICANN the power to decide over additions to the gTLD

---

[17] The reference to 'authoritative root-server system' is to 'the constellation of DNS root-nameservers specified, from time to time, in the file <ftp://ftp.internic.net/domain/named.root>.' See .net Registry Agreement (25 May 2001), section 1.1, <http://www.icann.org/tlds/agreements/verisign/registry-agmt-net-25may01.htm>.

[18] These principles were emphasized already in the NTIA Green and White Papers.

[19] Available at <http://www.icann.org/general/JPA-29sep06.pdf>.

[20] See further Lindsay, *International Domain Name Law* [2.13]–[2.17].

[21] Additionally, there are several agreements that are now of largely historic interest only. One such agreement is the Cooperative Research and Development Agreement, entered into by ICANN and DOC in 1999, by which the parties undertook a joint project entitled 'Improvements to Management of the Internet Root Server System'. The project consisted of 'a study and process for making the management of the Internet (DNS) root server system more robust and secure' (Appendix A). The agreement appears to be no longer in effect. For a public summary of the project results issued in March 2003, see <http://www.icann.org/general/crada-report-summary-14mar03.htm>. Another agreement is the USC/ICANN Transition Agreement of December 1998 by which the University of Southern California agreed to transfer to ICANN all necessary resources for continued performance of the IANA functions.

namespace. The current number of gTLDs is set out in Table 5.1. Up until recently, ICANN's policy on gTLD extension has been restrictive. However, ICANN announced on 26 June 2008 that it will radically liberalize this policy.[22] The new plans are reported as permitting addition of gTLDs based on an extensive range of indicators, such as business names, cities, and geographical locations. Domains will be able to be based on any string of letters, and in any script.

The IANA functions contract is otherwise particularly noteworthy because of its explicit reservations against changes to the root zone file or associated information, or to root system responsibilities as set forth in the Cooperative Agreement between DOC and VeriSign (dealt with directly below), or to established methods for performing the IANA functions.[23]

The Cooperative Agreement between DOC and Verisign mentioned above comprises the second category of agreement for DNS management. It designates Verisign as the Registry Operator for the .com and .net TLDs and defines Verisign's relations with both DOC and ICANN. It builds on an agreement originally concluded between Network Solutions, Inc. (NSI)—which Verisign took over—and the National Science Foundation in January 1993 under which NSI was given sole rights to operate name and number registration services.[24] That agreement has been amended numerous times. Particularly important are Amendments 4, 11, and 19. Amendment 4 allowed NSI to charge a fee for registration services, thus enabling it (and later Verisign) to generate considerable revenue for itself during the domain name 'gold rush' that took off in the late 1990s. Amendment 11 is noteworthy as it constitutes the first formal assertion by the US government of ultimate authority over the root zone file:

> While NSI continues to operate the primary root server, it shall request written direction from an authorized USG [US Government] official before making or rejecting any modifications, additions or deletions to the root zone file.[25]

Amendment 19 is significant for defining the relationship between NSI, DOC, and ICANN. Tensions arose in the initial months of ICANN's existence as NewCo over the respective powers of the three bodies in

---

[22] See <http://www.icann.org/en/announcements/announcement-4-26jun08-en.htm>.

[23] See Clauses C.4.1–C.4.2. Similar reservations are found in the 1999 Cooperative Research and Development Agreement, Appendix A, Clause 10.

[24] Cooperative Agreement NCR-9218742 of 1 January 1993, <http://www.icann.org/nsi/coopagmt-01jan93.htm>.

[25] Amendment 11 to the Cooperative Agreement between NSI and US Government (7 October 1998), <http://www.icann.org/nsi/coopagmt-amend11-07oct98.htm>. That authority is further cemented by, *inter alia*, the reservations in the ICANN/US Government Contract for the IANA Function noted above.

relation to each other—particularly the ability of NSI to retain its authority to register domain names under the .com, .net, and .org TLDs.[26] Amendment 19 patched over these tensions and led to the conclusion of three other interdependent agreements: (*a*) a Registry Agreement between ICANN and NSI;[27] (*b*) a Registrar Transition Agreement between ICANN and NSI;[28] and (*c*) an amendment to the ICANN/DOC MOU.[29] Lindsay ably sums up the result as follows:

- The Department of Commerce and ICANN agreed to recognize NSI's continued operation as the registry for the open gTLDs, and to ensure that the authoritative root would point to a root server designated by NSI;
- NSI agreed to be subject to ICANN registry and registrar agreements; and
- ICANN agreed not to modify the NSI Registration Agreement, or to authorize the operation of other registries in the open gTLDs (.com, .net, and .org), without prior approval from the Department of Commerce.[30]

Verisign inherited this arrangement when it acquired NSI in June 2000. The arrangement has since been amended several times but its basic bones remain intact. Currently, Verisign operates registry services (through its Global Domain Registry) for the .com and .net TLDs.[31] Indeed, under its current registry agreement, Verisign has been given almost perpetual control over .com registry services, as renewal of its license is automatically granted unless it fundamentally breaches the agreement.[32]

The third category of ICANN-related agreements are those entered into between ICANN and other bodies directly engaged in DNS operations. These bodies are primarily domain name registries and registrars for gTLDs. In terms of registrars, ICANN accredits all registrars for the gTLDs, both sponsored and non-sponsored. Accreditation is pursuant to a Registrar Accreditation Agreement of May 2001.[33]

---

[26] Further on these tensions and their background, see, for example, Mueller, *Ruling the Root*, 194–5; Lindsay, *International Domain Name Law* [2.12].

[27] ICANN-NSI Registry Agreement (10 November 1999), <http://www.icann.org/nsi/nsi-registry-agreement-04nov99.htm>.

[28] ICANN-NSI Transition Agreement (10 November 1999), <http://www.icann.org/nsi/icann-nsi-transition-04nov99.htm>.

[29] Amendment 1 to ICANN/DOC Memorandum of Understanding (10 November 1999), <http://www.icann.org/nsi/amend1-jpamou-04nov99.htm>.

[30] Lindsay, *International Domain Name Law* [2.12].

[31] As noted in Section 3.2.1, registry responsibility for the .org TLD was allocated in 2003 to the Public Interest Registry set up by ISOC.

[32] See further Lindsay, *International Domain Name Law* [2.19].

[33] Registrar Accreditation Agreement (17 May 2001), <http://www.icann.org/registrars/ra-agreement-17may01.htm>.

All up, the contractual web for the DNS is immense, involving numerous actors. While there are a small number of agreements with actors 'upstream' of ICANN (i.e. the JPA and IANA functions contract), there are a relatively large number of 'downstream' agreements. The scale and complexity of the 'downstream' contractual web is illustrated in Figure 5.1.

It should be stressed, though, that this figure does not provide the full picture. It does not depict, for example, the agreements between ICANN and various ccTLD managers—though ICANN's relationship with the latter is not as uniformly laid down by contract as with the actors depicted in Figure 5.1. With respect to those actors, one sees how, for example, ICANN enters into a contract with a registry giving the latter a contractual right for the administration of a particular TLD. The registry may in turn contract with registrars, which in turn contract with a private legal or physical person who then gains certain rights to a domain within that namespace. The chain of agreements transmits obligations; many of the terms set by ICANN will filter down to the last link. And the agreements have a dynamic element, as they are revised where necessary on the adoption of new policies by ICANN.

5.1.4. ccTLD Governance

ICANN does not legally own the DNS or Internet, so it cannot transfer ownership rights to registries operating ccTLDs. As noted above, ICANN derives its powers from a contract with the US government and administers the powers according to the MOU with DOC. The latter has delegated aspects of DNS management to ICANN with the intention of 'privatizing' that management. As for ICANN's management over ccTLDs, this is governed in the background by the MOU but also by several other documents, most notably RFC 1591[34] and ICP-1 (Internet Coordination Policy 1).[35] Basically, the result is that ccTLD managers may develop their own structure and policy for their respective domains provided that this does not contravene any IANA requirement, as presently specified in ICP-1.

---

[34] RFC 1591: Domain Name System Structure and Delegation (author: Jon Postel) (March 1994), <http://www.ietf.org/rfc/rfc1591.txt>.

[35] ICP-1: Internet Domain Name System Structure and Coordination (ccTLD Administration and Delegation) (May 1999), <http://www.icann.org/en/icp/icp-1.htm>.

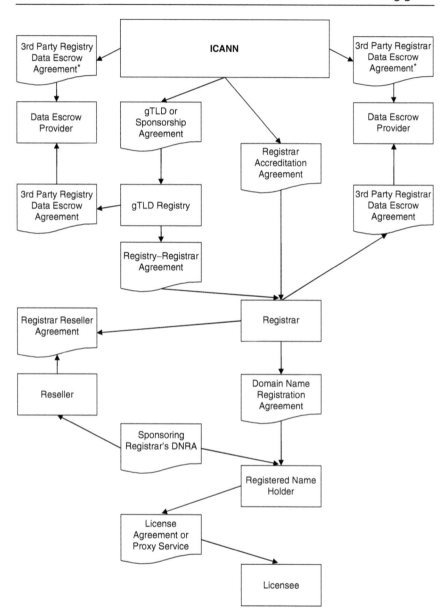

Figure 5.1. Contractual relationships of 'downstream' ICANN

*Data escrow refers here to third party provision of storage and back-up of registration data held primarily by registries and registrars. This service is to mitigate harm in the event that the data in the registry/registrar databases are lost, damaged, etc. Use of data escrow services is required by ICANN pursuant to its registrar and registry accreditation agreements. Iron Mountain Inc. is currently the dominant provider of escrow services in this regard and is indeed ICANN's approved escrow agent for registrar databases.

Historically, most ccTLDs were delegated by Jon Postel without written agreements.[36] However, in RFC 1591, Postel documented the general framework for the role of a ccTLD registry. This was done with fairly liberal, broad-brush prescriptions. For example, RFC 1591 stipulates that a ccTLD manager is to act as a 'trustee' for the domain, 'serve the community', 'act equitably', and do a 'satisfactory job'. RFC 1591 has been characterized as an anachronism partly because it allegedly embodies an outdated view of the goals and spirit of TLD administration and partly because it failed to resolve emerging conflicts over ccTLD governance.[37] Nonetheless, it continues to form the baseline for division of responsibilities between ccTLD administrators and ICANN

RFC 1591 can be seen as essentially manifesting a principle of subsidiarity for management of ccTLDs. That principle has since been lifted up and given explicit form by the Governmental Advisory Committee in its 'Principles and Guidelines for the Delegation and Administration of Country Code Top Level Domains':

> The main principle is the principle of subsidiarity. ccTLD policy should be set locally, unless it can be shown that the issue has global impact and needs to be resolved in an international framework. Most of the ccTLD policy issues are local in nature and should therefore be addressed by the local Internet Community, according to national law.[38]

Not surprisingly, then, the national regimes for ccTLD management vary considerably. One point of divergence is the extent of government involvement in operating the ccTLD registry. For example, in Finland, the ccTLD registry is a government agency.[39] In Norway, the equivalent body is a subsidiary of a non-profit shareholder company owned by the Norwegian state.[40] In the UK, it is a private company outside state ownership.[41] There are other points of divergence too which are elaborated in Section 5.3.

ICANN has long been concerned about the lack of formal agreements between itself and ccTLD managers. The concern revolves around delegation and redelegation of domain names, allocation of responsibility

---

[36] Froomkin, 'Habermas@discourse.net', 840.   [37] Mueller, *Ruling the Root*, 126–7.

[38] Governmental Advisory Committee, Principles and Guidelines for the Delegation and Administration of Country Code Top Level Domains (Mar del Plata, 5 April 2005), <http://gac.icann.org/web/home/ccTLD_Principles.rtf>.

[39] This being the Finnish Communications Regulatory Authority (FICORA) which is responsible for communications administration under the Finnish Ministry of Transport and Communications. Responsibility for managing the .fi TLD was transferred from the private sector to FICORA in 1997.

[40] See further Section 5.4.   [41] See further Section 5.5.

for global policy formulation, and the relationship between ccTLD managers and their respective governments. In order to meet this concern, ICANN has pushed for the creation of formal agreements between itself and ccTLD managers, but few such agreements have been signed to date.[42] The latest strategy implemented by ICANN is the construction of an 'Accountability Framework'. The framework has been negotiated between ccNSO and ICANN in order to establish the guidelines by which ccTLD managers should operate. There are two different avenues: one is to sign the Accountability Framework and thus reach an agreement; the other is to exchange formal letters, which is supposed to signify a simpler form of commitment but still contain elements from the Accountability Framework.[43]

ROLE OF EU

At present, there is no specific regulation by the EU of the DNS and IP address system. The preamble to the Framework Directive 2002/21/EC for electronic communications networks and services[44] states: 'The provisions of this Directive do not establish any new areas of responsibility for the national regulatory authorities in the field of Internet naming and addressing' (Recital 20). The Directive goes on to encourage EU Member States, 'where . . . appropriate in order to ensure full global interoperability of services, to coordinate their positions in international organisations and forums in which decisions are taken on issues relating to the numbering, naming and addressing of electronic communications networks and services' [Article 10(5)].

However, there may be indications that the Eu is preparing to depart from this hands-off policy in the near future. These indications are possibly manifest in a proposal from the Eu Commission issued in November 2007 for a new Directive to amend the regulatory package for electronic communications. Recital 37 in the preamble to the proposed Directive states that ' . . . power should be conferred on the Commission to adopt implementing measures in areas such as the regulatory treatment of new

[42] Currently eight ccTLD managers, together with the manager for the .eu TLD, have formalized their relationship with ICANN by contract. In addition, seven ccTLD managers have entered into MOUs with ICANN. See <http://www.icann.org/cctlds/agreements.html>.

[43] See letter of 9 January 2006 from ICANN CEO to ccNSO Chair, <http://icann.org/correspondence/twomey-disspain-09jan06.pdf>.

[44] Framework Directive 2002/21/EC of 7 March 2002 on a common regulatory framework for electronic communications networks and services (O.J. L 108, 24 April 2002, 33–50). For a comprehensive analysis of the EU regulatory framework for electronic communications generally, see Ian Walden and John Angel (eds.), *Telecommunications Law and Regulation* (Oxford: Oxford University Press, 2005, 2nd edn.).

services, *numbering, naming and addressing*, consumer issues . . . ' (emphasis added).[45] This increase in competence is proposed to be effectuated, in part, by amending the concept of 'associated facilities' (as defined in the current Framework Directive)[46] to embrace 'number and address translation systems' [Article 1(2)(c) in the proposed new Framework Directive]. Further, it is proposed that the Commission be given specific powers to introduce, when necessary, harmonizing measures for '[n]umbering, naming and addressing issues, including . . . number and address translation systems' [Article 19(1) and 19(4)(b) in the proposed new Framework Directive]. It is too early to reach firm conclusions on the significance of the proposal for the domain name and IP address systems. The Explanatory Memorandum for the proposal omits any substantial guidance on the proposal's possible impact on these systems. The Commission has claimed that the proposal will not change the current regime for these systems' management.[47] On their face, though, the proposed provisions will, if adopted, give the Commission greater potential to steer development of ccTLD policies in EU—and possibly EEA—Member States.

5.2. WHOIS and UDRP[48]

5.2.1. *WHOIS Databases*

In broad terms, WHOIS denotes a service allowing interested parties to address queries to a database containing information about registered domains, their registrants, and the servers used. Thus, 'WHOIS' is not an acronym but shorthand designation of the principal function/service of a type of database. Such a database is termed a WHOIS database. The

[45] See Proposal for a Directive of the European Parliament and of the Council amending Directives 2002/21/EC on a common regulatory framework for electronic communications networks and services, 2002/19/EC on access to, and interconnection of, electronic communications networks and services, and 2002/20/EC on the authorization of electronic communications networks and services [COM(2007) 697 final, Brussels, 13 November 2007].

[46] That is, 'those facilities associated with an electronic communications network and/or an electronic communications service which enable and/or support the provision of services via that network and/or service. It includes conditional access systems and electronic programme guides' [Article 2(e)]. 'Associated facilities' are specifically regulated in several provisions of the current Framework Directive [Articles 1(1), 8(2)–(3), 17(1)–(2)].

[47] See presentation on 'The EU Telecom Reform' by Isabelle Vandoorne (European Commission Directorate-General on Information Society and Media) for CENTR (Council of European National Top Level Domain Registries), Brussels, 7 March 2008, <https://www.centr.org/main/4201-CTR/version/default/part/AttachmentData/data>, last accessed 20 June 2008.

[48] Section 5.2 is co-authored by Susan Schiavetta and Lee A. Bygrave with assistance of Dana Irina Cojocarasu.

information displayed as a result of a query will have been provided by the registrant of the domain name as part of registration procedures. Originally, registrants were not legally required to provide information for the WHOIS service. After the establishment of ICANN, however, provision became obligatory.

This section provides an overview of the functions, regulatory framework, and principal policy issues associated with the WHOIS service.

FUNCTIONS

The WHOIS service has a multitude of functions. The primary function is to permit checking of a domain name's availability and status. For example, a registrant has the possibility to check if the domain has already been registered against its name or if the information regarding a domain is accurate. Businesses are able to monitor the expiry date of the registration of valuable domain names in order to re-register them for resale (so-called dropcatching). A consumer can check if the company operating an e-commerce site is legitimate.

The WHOIS service may be used for other purposes too. For instance, as part of ensuring the security and stability of the Internet, network operators are interested in obtaining information about the technical contact point for a domain name, in order to solve DNS errors, routing and/or interconnection issues, as well as other technical matters related to the configuration of records associated with the domain name. Additionally, through checking WHOIS records, anti-spam bodies can spot false data, identify the source of spam, and create block-lists. WHOIS records can also be used to identify a registrant who uses the domain name for illegitimate purposes (intellectual property infringement, fraud, child abuse, etc.).

At a more general level of abstraction, the WHOIS service can be seen as compensation for the paucity of identificational attributes in the TCP/IP.[49] The need for such attributes has increased in tact with the growth in the Internet's commercial significance.

REGULATORY FRAMEWORK: gTLDs

Information about registrants of names in gTLDs is first collected and stored in WHOIS databases created by registrars. This occurs pursuant to two types of contract. The first contract is the registration contract

[49] See further Milton Mueller and Mawaki Chango, 'The DNS as a Tool for Global Identity Policy: WHOIS, ICANN, and Global Internet Governance' (undated draft paper), <http://web.si.umich.edu/tprc/papers/2007/752/TPRC-WHOIS-DRAFT4.htm>, last accessed 20 June 2008.

between the registrant and the registrar. The collection of WHOIS data under that contract follows from the second type of contract, which is the Registrar Accreditation Agreement between the registrar and ICANN.[50] Under that agreement, ICANN's accreditation of a registrar is conditional upon the registrar providing a WHOIS service—more specifically, 'an interactive web page and a port 43 WHOIS service providing free public query-based access to up-to-date data concerning all active Registered Names sponsored by Registrar for each TLD in which it is accredited' (Article 3.3.1).

The agreement also specifies (in Article 3.3.1) the data elements that must be accessible upon request from the registrar's database:

- the name of the registered name;
- the names of the primary nameserver and secondary nameserver(s) for the registered name;
- the registrar's identity;
- the original creation date of the registration;
- the expiry date of the registration;
- the name and postal address of the registered name holder;
- the name, postal address, email address, voice telephone number, and (where available) fax number of the registered name's technical contact; and
- the name, postal address, email address, voice telephone number, and (where available) fax number of the registered name's administrative contact.

This information must be updated by the registrar upon request by the registrant (Article 3.3.2).

The registrar is also required to pass on the information (or elements of it) in two specified contexts. First, the registrar must forward certain technical information to a central directory known as the registry WHOIS (Article 3.3.4).[51] This information consists of the IP number corresponding to the registered domain name, together with the name of the registrar that registered the domain name, but not the registrant's name or contact

---

[50] Registrar Accreditation Agreement (adopted 17 May 2001), Article 3.3.1, <http://www.icann.org/registrars/ra-agreement-17may01.htm>.
[51] Ibid. Article 3.3.4.

details. The registry operates a WHOIS service that makes possible domain name searches on a gTLD-wide basis.[52]

Second, a registrar is under a qualified obligation to provide third parties with bulk access to all of the data on registrants it has stored in its WHOIS database (Article 3.3.6). Access may only be provided on condition that registrants who are natural persons be given the opportunity to opt-out from having their data available for marketing purposes. And access must otherwise be pursuant to agreement prohibiting the use of the data for purposes of mass, unsolicited, commercial marketing.

REGULATORY FRAMEWORK: ccTLDs

The situation with respect to WHOIS services for ccTLD registrations differs from that for the gTLD sector. Provision of such services is less standardized, partly due to the looser bonds between ICANN and ccTLD operators. Nevertheless, ccTLDs tend to operate with WHOIS databases containing the same data elements as ICANN requires of the gTLD registrars. However, for some ccTLDs, the WHOIS database is provided only by the registry not the individual registrars. This is the case, for instance, with the .eu, .uk, and .no domains.[53]

The key difference, though, is that the amount of registrant data that is publicly displayed by a ccTLD WHOIS can be less than under the gTLD regime. In this respect, for example, EURid (the .eu registry) distinguishes between registrants that are legal persons and registrants that are natural persons. For the former, all data collected is publicly displayed, whereas only the email address of a natural person is made publicly available (unless the registrant otherwise requests). The remaining information collected from natural persons is kept by the Registry for internal use. That information will be disclosed to third parties only following the request of a law enforcement authority or upon the request of a party that identifies both itself and the purpose of its request, and fills in an application form. Once the application is checked and approved by EURid, the information is transferred to the requesting party.[54] These restrictions on public

---

[52] The need for such a service arose once registry functions were separated from registrar functions and the latter functions were distributed among multiple registrars each maintaining their own customer account records. Under the aegis of ICANN, the Internet Network Information Center (InterNIC) maintains the registry WHOIS for the .com, .net, and .org domains.

[53] See further Sections 5.4 and 5.5.

[54] See .eu Domain Name WHOIS Policy (version 1.0), paragraphs 2.4 and 2.6, <http://www.eurid.eu/files/whois_en.pdf>. See too the Nominet policy, described in Section 5.5.2.

disclosure of registrant data follow from the relatively strict legal regime in Europe for privacy and data protection.[55]

PRIVACY AND DATA PROTECTION ISSUES

Clearly, the WHOIS Service can be viewed as a valuable asset to many Internet users. Yet it has also come under fire for violating the privacy interests and associated rights of domain name holders. Critics claim that too much personal information is disclosed from WHOIS databases and that the information can be easily misused by those who wish to send unsolicited commercial emails, engage in identity theft, or commit other crimes, such as stalking. Further, it is feared that disclosure may have a chilling effect on registration of websites offering controversial content.[56]

These concerns have been partially met by some of the ccTLD WHOIS services. This is particularly the case in Europe where fairly stringent rules for privacy and data protection apply. But stakeholders in other jurisdictions, especially the United States, are resistant to changing the present disclosure regime for gTLD WHOIS services. The cleavage here between the United States and Europe is part of a long pattern of trans-Atlantic disagreement over the setting of international privacy and data protection standards.[57]

The regulatory framework for providing WHOIS services at the gTLD level is currently being reviewed as part of a GNSO policy development process. That process began in 2001 but has currently ground to a halt due to fundamental disagreement between equally balanced factions within the Study Group charged with policy development. A key point of disagreement is the extent of weight to be given to privacy interests in a future WHOIS regime.[58] In the meantime, under the current Joint Project Agreement with the US Department of Commerce, ICANN shall 'continue to enforce existing policy relating to WHOIS, such existing policy requir[ing] that ICANN implement measures to maintain timely, unrestricted and public access to accurate and complete WHOIS information,

---

[55] See particularly Directive 95/46/EC on the Protection of Individuals with Regard to the Processing of Personal Data and on the Free Movement of Such Data (O.J. L 281, 23 November 1995, 31–50); adopted 24 October 1995.

[56] See, for example, the various comments collated on the CircleID website at <http://www.circleid.com/topics/whois>, last accessed 20 June 2008.

[57] Further on that pattern, see, for example, Lee A. Bygrave, 'International Agreements to Protect Personal Data', in James B. Rule and Graham Greenleaf (eds.), *Global Privacy Protection: The First Generation* (Cheltenham: Edward Elgar, 2008), 15–49.

[58] See *WHOIS Study Group Report to GNSO Council* (22 May 2008), <http://gnso.icann.org/issues/whois/gnso-whois-study-group-report-to-council-22may08.pdf>.

including registrant, technical, billing and administrative contact information'.[59]

5.2.2. *Uniform Domain Name Dispute Resolution Policy*

The Uniform Domain Name Dispute Resolution Policy (UDRP) came into force on 1 December 1999. It contains a very influential set of rules for resolving disputes over name registrations in gTLDs. The rules are tailored primarily to resolve conflicts between trademark owners and domain name holders. The purchase of the UDRP follows from the requirement by ICANN that the policy be applied by all registrars it accredits. This requirement is instituted by contract as a condition for registrar accreditation. Concomitantly, each registrar stipulates in its contract with a domain name registrant that the UDRP will form the basis for resolving a complaint alleging that the registrant, when registering the domain name, has acted in bad faith in relation to a trademark held by the complainant. Bad faith denotes, for example, a registrant deliberately registering a domain name so as to extort money from the complainant (so-called cybersquatting).

BACKGROUND

The UDRP has its origins in concern to protect the rights of trademark holders with respect to domain name registrations. Trademarks are unique signs used by businesses to identify their products and services to their customers, and thereby distinguish such products and services from the products and services of other businesses. A trademark can be a name, logo, symbol, sound, etc. To obtain trademark status, a business can either register the trademark, or, through legitimate use of a mark, establish and claim rights in that mark. Not only are trademarks important because they prevent confusion in the marketplace, but they are also deemed to be valuable commodities for businesses. In particular, the goodwill associated with a trademark can be a company's most valuable intellectual property asset.

In contrast to trademarks, domain names initially had a purely technical purpose—principally to allow Internet users to identify the website they were looking for without having to remember the underlying IP

---

[59] Joint Project Agreement (29 September 2006), Annex A, Affirmation of Responsibilities for ICANN's Private Sector Management, Clause 5, <http://www.icann.org/general/JPA-29sep06.pdf>.

number.[60] Nonetheless, since each IP number corresponded to a domain name, trademark holders began registering those domain names that were connected with their trademarks. The domain names thus gained trademark-like status. Indeed, it is possible to register a domain name as a trademark where the name is used to distinguish the goods or services of one entity from those of another entity, and to indicate the source of the goods or services.[61]

With the commercialization of the Internet, it became apparent that many potential registrants would seek the same domain name. While companies can have the same name in the offline context—so long as they offer different services or products, and/or they are based in different jurisdictions—the international nature of the Internet, and the ability to have, for example, only one <mcdonalds.com>, meant that conflicts were likely. In addition to trademark holders competing for certain domain names, other individuals and entities began registering domain names associated with trademarks. These registrations were often for illegitimate purposes—either to damage the reputation of the trademark holder, sell the domain name to the trademark holder, or take unfair advantage of the goodwill acquired by the trademark holder in connection with their trademark, by, for instance, passing off a product or service as associated with the trademark. Cybersquatting and other illegitimate registration practices were facilitated by the fact that registrars usually allocate domain names on a 'first come, first served' basis, without prior checking of the legitimacy of a registrant's claim.

The first attempts to tackle cybersquatting were through court litigation. While these cases were generally resolved in favour of trademark holders,[62] it was clear that litigation suffered from several weaknesses. One weakness was (and is) the expense and length of litigation. Another was that the law being applied by the courts—principally trademark law—was not tailored to deal specifically with domain name disputes. These weaknesses became evermore acute with the increasing scale of the cybersquatting problem together with companies' increasing perception that being able to properly represent themselves on the Internet was a *sine qua non* for their success.

---

[60] See Section 5.1.1.

[61] See, for example, US Patent and Trademark Office, *Examination and Guide No. 2-99: Marks Composed in Whole, or in Part, of Domain Names* (29 September 1999), <http://www.uspto.gov/web/offices/tac/notices/guide299.htm>.

[62] Leading US cases on point are *Intermatic Inc v. Toeppen*, 977 F. Supp. 1227 (ND Ill. 1996) and *Panavision International LP v. Toeppen*, 141 F. 3d 1316 (9th Cir. Ct. of Appeal 1998).

As a consequence, the US Government advocated the necessity of a dispute resolution system to deal specifically with trademark/domain name conflicts, and suggested that the World Intellectual Property Organization (WIPO) develop recommendations for a uniform approach to resolving such conflicts.[63] Subsequently, WIPO conducted extensive consultations with members of the Internet community and published a report that formed the foundation for the UDRP.[64]

THE PROVISIONS OF THE POLICY

The UDRP has two main manifestations: (*a*) the policy which is incorporated into the registration agreement between the registrar and the registrant (hereinafter 'the Policy'); (*b*) the rules which govern the administrative proceedings for resolving disputes under the policy (hereinafter 'the Rules'). In addition, each approved dispute resolution provider must have its own supplemental rules, which are implemented in accordance with the UDRP Policy and Rules. The supplemental rules cover topics such as fees, word and page limits, and the form of cover sheets.

Under Paragraph 4 of the Policy, a holder of a domain name is required to submit to UDRP proceedings where a complainant alleges that (*a*) the domain name is identical or confusingly similar to a trademark in which the complainant has rights; (*b*) the domain name holder has no rights or legitimate interests in respect of the domain name; and (*c*) the domain name registration process has been carried out in bad faith.

If the complainant proves all of the aforementioned points, the domain name will be transferred to the complainant or cancelled. The complainant is not entitled to damages under the scheme. If the respondent is also a trademark holder, it will be necessary for them to prove that they have a legitimate right to, or interest in, the domain name. To do this, they can show that they plan to use, or have used, the domain name in connection with a bona fide offering of goods or services prior to any notice of the dispute. Additionally, or alternatively, they can show that they have been commonly known by the domain name, via a registered or claimed trademark. If the respondent is not a trademark holder, they would need to prove that they have made, or intend to make, legitimate non-commercial or fair use of the domain name, without intent

[63] NTIA, *Statement of Policy on the Management of Internet Names and Addresses* (5 June 1998), <http://www.ntia.doc.gov/ntiahome/domainname/6_5_98dns.htm>.

[64] WIPO, *The Management of Internet Names and Addresses: Intellectual Property Issues, Final Report of the WIPO Internet Domain Name Process* (30 April 1999), <http://www.wipo.int/amc/en/processes/process1/report/finalreport.html#II>.

of commercial gain, misleadingly diverting consumers, or tarnishing the trademark at issue.

Complaints under the UDRP scheme are handled by dispute resolution providers (hereinafter 'Providers') appointed by ICANN. Four Providers are currently appointed.[65] These are the WIPO Arbitration and Mediation Center, the Asian Domain Name Dispute Resolution Provider (ADNDRP), the National Arbitration Forum (NAF), and, most recently, the Czech Arbitration Court (CAC). A complainant is free to choose which of these Providers shall treat their complaint. As elaborated below, they are also given some influence in determining the panellists whom the chosen Provider will appoint to decide their complaint.

When submitting their complaint, the complainant must provide the name of the domain name holder (the respondent) and any contact information they may have for the latter. In this context, the operation of the WHOIS service can be instrumental for the complainant's ability to lodge a valid complaint.[66]

Once the chosen Provider has received the complaint, it shall review it for administrative compliance with the Policy and Rules, and then forward the complaint on to the respondent. The date on which the Provider forwards the complaint to the respondent is the commencement date of proceedings.[67] Within 20 days of that date, the respondent must submit a response to the Provider if they are going to affect the outcome of the decision. In the event that the respondent misses the deadline, the panel(list) appointed to handle the dispute can reach a decision simply on the information produced by the complainant.[68]

Appointment of panellists to oversee the dispute is carried out by the Provider. Appointment must occur within five calendar days following the Provider's receipt of the response, or where the respondent has not responded, following the lapse of the deadline for submitting the response. Usually, the Provider will appoint a single panellist. The Provider chooses the person from a publicly available list. In the event that either the complainant or the respondent wishes to have a

---

[65] See further <http://www.icann.org/dndr/udrp/approved-providers.htm>, last accessed 30 May 2008. Two other bodies have previously functioned as approved providers: the CPR Institute for Dispute Resolution (CPR Institute) and eResolution.

[66] Rules, paragraph 3(a) and (b)(i)–(viii).   [67] Rules, paragraph 4.

[68] It is worth noting that respondents might default not just because they are a cybersquatter and realize there is little point in contesting the complaint. Respondents might simply be unavailable at the time the complaint was forwarded to them. Alternatively, they might not wish to respond because, for instance, the data in the WHOIS database incorrectly mark them as domain name holder.

three-member panel, both sides will present the Provider with a list of five panellists, and the Provider will choose a panellist from each list. The Provider will subsequently nominate five candidates to preside over the panel and ask both sides to indicate which candidate they prefer. Taking into account the preferences of both sides, the Provider will make a selection. If a Provider is unable to secure the appointment of a panellist from either side's list of candidates, it must make the appointment from the list of panellists it originally devised to complete the three-member panel.[69]

After hearing all the evidence, the panel(list) must submit a decision within 14 days of their appointment. The complaint must be decided on the basis of the statements and documents submitted in accordance with the Policy and Rules and any rules and principles of law that are deemed applicable. Where a three-member panel resides over the dispute, the majority decision shall take precedence. The decision shall be in writing, provide the reasons on which it is based, indicate the date on which it was rendered, and identify the name(s) of the panellist(s).[70]

Once the decision has been drafted, it must be sent to the Provider, which will then forward it to the disputants, the Registrars concerned and ICANN, within three calendar days. The Registrars concerned shall immediately communicate to each side, the provider, and ICANN, the date for implementing the decision.

There is no internal appeals process. However, neither the complainant nor the respondent is prevented from submitting the dispute to a court before, during, or after UDRP proceedings. With respect to initiating litigation directly after a panel(list) has reached a decision to cancel or transfer the domain name, a period of 10 business days will elapse before this decision is implemented. During this period, both the complainant and the respondent have the right to go to court on a de novo basis—that is, start the process afresh—thus staying the transfer or cancellation of the domain name until the litigation is over. If the 10-day period expires without official confirmation that a lawsuit has been commenced, the domain name will be transferred or cancelled.

If neither side opts for going to court, the whole UDRP process will last a total of 45 days. Thus, the procedure is relatively fast, especially compared with court litigation. It is also cheap relative to both litigation and customary arbitration fees. Generally, the complainant will pay the costs of the proceedings. Yet where the respondent has opted for a three-member

---

[69] Rules, paragraph 6.   [70] Rules, paragraph 15.

panel, the associated costs will be split between the complainant and respondent.

CRITICISMS OF UDRP

The UDRP is generally regarded as having been effective in achieving its principal aim of providing trademark owners with an expedient means to combat cybersquatting. It has been—and continues to be—extensively used, generating a wealth of new arbitration practice.[71] Questions have been raised, though, as to its ability to arrive at just results. More specifically, it has been alleged that the UDRP and associated panellists are biased towards the interests of trademark owners.[72] The fact that the vast majority of decisions taken under the UDRP favour the complainant is used to support the allegation, as is apparent evidence of forum shopping by complainants. However, it should be remembered that the bulk of UDRP decisions, particularly the early ones, deal with fairly clear cases of cybersquatting. Further, a significant number of respondents do not contest the complaint against them.

Nevertheless, there are aspects of the UDRP which manifest a procedural bias against respondents.[73] One such aspect, for instance, is the brevity of the procedure. In particular, the 20-day response period for the respondent is too short, especially if a respondent is caught off guard. It is also clear that the UDRP gives complainants procedural advantages over a respondent which they would normally not enjoy before a court. Under the UDRP, the complainant will pay a small fee in comparison to the fees associated with seeking a court-based injunction. Additionally, there is no discovery, no hearing to prepare for, and the extent of arguments provided for in the complaint are minimal in comparison to what would be the case if the complainant filed for an injunction in a court action. Moreover, in the event that the respondent does not agree with the outcome of the UDRP proceeding and appeals to a court, they (not the compliant) will have to pay the filling fees and shoulder the burden of proof—which

[71] For a comprehensive analysis, see Lindsay, *International Domain Name Law*, chapters 3–7.

[72] See, for example, Milton Mueller, 'Rough Justice: An Analysis of ICANN's Uniform Dispute Resolution Policy', (2000), <http://usacm.acm.org/usacm/IG/roughjustice.pdf>; Michael Geist, 'Fundamentally Fair.com? An Update on Bias Allegations and the ICANN UDRP', (2002), <http://aix1.uottawa.ca/~geist/fairupdate.pdf>.

[73] See further, for example, Elizabeth G. Thornburg, 'Going Private: Technology, Due Process, and Internet Dispute Resolution', 2000, *University of California at Davis Law Review*, vol. 34, 151, 188 *et seq*. A. Michael Froomkin, 'ICANN'S "Uniform Dispute Resolution Policy"—Causes and (Partial) Cures', *Brooklyn Law Review*, 2002, vol. 67, 605, 670 *et seq*.

would not have been the case had the complainant gone straight to court instead of first utilizing the UDRP process.[74]

5.2.3. *Other Dispute Resolution Procedures Specific to Domain Names*

The UDRP is not the only procedure tailored specifically to resolving domain name disputes. Equivalent procedures operate for disputes over names registered in ccTLDs. In many cases, ccTLD managers have implemented a policy modelled closely on the UDRP. WIPO has assisted this duplication by advising ccTLD managers on the establishment of appropriate dispute resolution procedures,[75] and by providing actual dispute resolution services for ccTLDs.

A few ccTLD managers have designed their own policy, taking into consideration criticisms made of the UDRP. For instance, Nominet, the .uk ccTLD manager, has implemented a system which departs from the UDRP in several respects.[76] It implements a 'cab rank' system for appointing third parties to hear disputes, such that neither the complainant nor the respondent can choose that party. It has also incorporated a mediation system, so that disputants can try to settle the dispute themselves on a relatively amicable basis. Further, it provides for an internal appeal process which may mitigate bias and the need for going to court afterwards. These features of the Nominet system make it less objectionable than the UDRP.

In the United States, legislation has been passed to deal specifically with domain name disputes. This takes the form of the AntiCybersquatting Consumer Protection Act 1999.[77] The Act gives trademark owners a civil right of action against defendants who register domain names that are identical or confusingly similar to the trademark, with the 'bad faith intent to profit from the mark'. If a trademark is well known, the same remedies are available if the domain name is identical or confusingly similar to the mark. A lawsuit brought under the Act must be filed in a US District Court. A complainant would typically sue under the Act, as opposed to using the UDRP, when they seek remedies, such as compensation, in

---

[74] A respondent's appeal possibilities will also be dogged by other factors. See further Froomkin, ibid., 678 *et seq.*

[75] WIPO, *ccTLD Best Practices for the Prevention and Resolution of Intellectual Property Disputes* (20 June 2001), <http://www.wipo.int/export/sites/www/amc/en/docs/bestpractices.pdf>.

[76] See further Section 5.5.

[77] Codified in US Code, Title 15, §1125(d). Further on the Act, see, for example, Steven J. Coran (Note), 'The Anticybersquatting Consumer Protection Act's *In Rem* Provision: Making American Trademark Law the Law of the Internet?', *Hofstra Law Review*, 2001–2002, vol. 30, 169, 183 *et seq.*

addition to cancelling or transferring the domain name. Alternatively, where the trademark owner suspects the domain name holder will file a claim in a court after a decision was reached via the UDRP, they may wish to sue in court to avoid the time and expense of a UDRP action. The downside with using the AntiCybersquatting Consumer Protection Act, of course, is that civil litigation is costly and time-consuming.

As noted above, it is also possible to launch UDRP proceedings and litigation simultaneously. However, the majority of trademark owners will generally choose to do one or the other.

5.3. Domain Name Policy Models[78]

5.3.1. *Introduction*

This section describes a system for categorizing domain name policies by identifying central aspects that form the way the policy is experienced, and sorting the policies according to those aspects. It is important to be aware that many other factors (prices, the possible organization of the top-level domain into second-level domains, etc.) may also play a part in how a specific domain name policy is experienced. Still, policies that are in the same category share some of the same advantages and disadvantages. Accordingly, the categorization may be useful.

When comparing different domain name policies there appears to be two central aspects which to a large degree form the policy. One aspect is the number of domain names each applicant may hold; the other is the requirements placed on the applicant at the time of registration of a domain name.[79] Based on these two aspects, domain name policies can be divided into four main categories (see Figure 5.2).

STRICT REQUIREMENTS FOR THE APPLICANT

Common to both of the upper categories is that priority is placed on preventing domain name registrations by applicants who have no rights to the name in question. To accomplish this, the applicants are subject to strict requirements, including that they are able to provide documentation showing that they have rights to the words they intend to register. Other requirements may be applied as well; for example, a requirement

---

[78] Section 5.3 is written by Hilde Thunem.
[79] Common requirements in this context are that the applicant is able to provide documentation showing that they have rights to the word they intend to register or a prerequisite that the applicant is an organization.

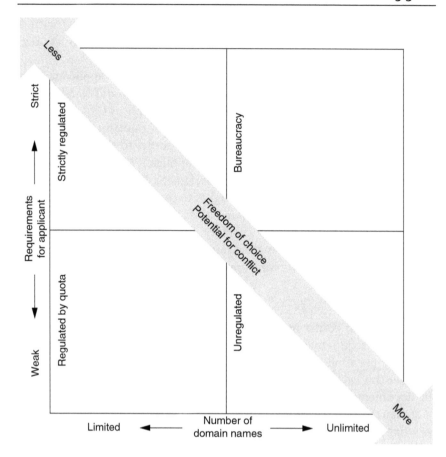

Figure 5.2. Domain name policy categories

for the applicant to have a local presence in the geographic area to which the top-level domain (TLD) corresponds.

Applicants are screened through the different requirements, and the 'first come, first served' rule does not apply until all requirements are met. This results in a lower potential for conflicts regarding domain names, but at the same time restricts the applicants' ability to freely choose their domain names.

STRICTLY REGULATED

In the upper left corner of the figure are the domain name policies based on the premise that the applicant may hold only a small number of domain names and that each domain name is evaluated against strict application requirements. Many TLDs started in this category, with a strictly regulated domain name policy, and then moved on to less regulated policies after a while.

The restrictions on the number of domain names per applicant limit the possibility for extensive domain name speculation and warehousing (the collection of many domain names by one applicant for later sale). Further, since there is a limit on the number of domains an applicant can have, some flexibility is possible when it comes to the requirements placed on the applicant (e.g. allowing the applicant to refer to the name of the organization, a trademark, a trade name, a logo, or other forms of documentation when documenting rights to the domain name).

The limit on the number of domain names also means that even though domain name policies in this category require manual evaluation for each application, the policies scale fairly well as there is no need for an extensive application-processing apparatus.

BUREAUCRACY

The upper right corner holds domain name policies that maintain strict application requirements, but allow an unlimited number of domains registered per applicant.

Under this category one of the essential tasks of the registry is evaluating documentation from applicants. When there is no cap on the number of domain names, the application requirements must be stricter compared to what is the case when there is a limited number of registrations. External evaluation of the documentation performed by lawyers or patent offices may therefore be an option.

Processing a large amount of applications requiring manual evaluation necessitates a large registry. The fact that several entities may be consulted could also result in longer processing times and higher costs per domain name. The advantage of this policy is that, unlike the strictly regulated policy, it does not limit an applicant that has many trademarks from registering all of them as domain names, no matter how many they are.

WEAK REQUIREMENTS FOR THE APPLICANT

Common to both the lower categories is that freedom of choice for the applicant is given a higher priority than the prevention of illicit registration of domain names. This means that the registry does not take into consideration whether the applicant has any rights to the domain name. There is no pre-screening of applicants; whoever applies first gets the name in question registered. The potential for post-registration conflict is higher under these domains than under the more restrictive domains.

For those TLDs where there are almost no requirements for the applicant, an additional drawback may be that it is more difficult to predict who operates the various domain names, as opposed to the case under a domain name policy that requires the applicant to have a local presence in the country connected with the TLD or requires the applicant to be a registered organization. On the other hand, fewer requirements put on the applicant also mean a greater flexibility for the applicants to choose the domain names they want.

REGULATED BY QUOTA

In the lower left corner are the domain name policies with weak application requirements, but with a limited number of domains allowed per applicant.

Here, the applicant's freedom of choice takes precedence over the desire to prevent illicit registration of domain names. Nonetheless, the limited quota per applicant is an attempt to place some restriction on speculation and warehousing. These policies require little bureaucracy, and may be implemented by a small registry.

UNREGULATED

The lower right corner holds domain name policies with few or no application requirements, and no restriction on the number of domain name registrations.

As in the previous category, precedence is accorded to the applicant's freedom of choice. The unlimited number of domain names allowed per applicant means that warehousing may be a problem unless other mechanisms, like pricing, are used to limit the number of domain names an applicant finds practical to hold. The policies in this category scale well and require little bureaucracy.

HANDLING OF CONFLICTS

Conflicts regarding the right to a domain name may arise under all domain name policy models shown above. Irrespective of the extent of the evaluation performed by the registry, the final responsibility for the choice of domain name resides with the applicant. Hence, the regular conflict procedure of most registries is to inform the parties how to get in touch with one another, but otherwise refrain from any involvement in the conflict.

If the parties cannot be reconciled, the conflict may be solved by means of the legal system in accordance with the applicable legislation on name rights. In this regard, domain name conflicts are no different from other conflicts regarding name rights. The drawback is that litigation can be time-consuming and, in some cases, it has been difficult to determine which laws apply. This is particularly so with regard to the gTLDs, but the problem has also occurred in the national domains. To alleviate these problems, some TLD managers have established some form of alternative dispute resolution that may be used instead of—and if necessary, in addition to—going to court.

It is also important to note that even under the unregulated domain name policies, few conflicts arise compared with the number of names that are registered.

MOVING FROM ONE CATEGORY TO ANOTHER

Unfortunately there is no 'perfect' domain name policy that will satisfy all needs. All of the domain name policy models have their advantages and disadvantages, and which model is chosen for a specific ccTLD depends on what the local Internet community judges to be the most important criteria. If flexibility and freedom of choice are given priority over the desire to stop illicit registrations, domain name policies with weak requirements will be chosen. If a desire to restrict warehousing—and to some degree domain name speculation—is predominant, a policy with a limit on the domain names allowed per applicant will be chosen.

As the needs of the local Internet community change, the domain name policy will be changed as well. A typical example is a ccTLD that starts with a restrictive domain name policy, and then later liberalizes the policy by either removing the limit on the number of names an applicant may hold (moving from the 'strictly regulated' category to 'bureaucracy') or decreasing the requirements put on the applicant (moving from 'strictly regulated' to 'regulated by quota') or doing both at once (moving from 'strictly regulated' to 'unregulated').

The important point to be aware of when changing from one model to another is that while liberalizing a restrictive policy is fairly easy, going back again and restricting a liberal policy is very hard. Thus, the local Internet community should be made aware of the consequences of such liberalization before it occurs.

5.3.2. Domain Name Policies among ccTLDs

Having learnt that there is no such thing as a 'perfect' domain name policy and that each ccTLD will modify their policy over time, it may still be interesting to examine whether there are global patterns as to which domain name policy model is most popular at present.

Figure 5.3 shows the domain name policies used by some of the ccTLDs mangers in the world as mapped into the four different policy categories.[80] To place the domain name policies correctly on the Y-axis (requirements for applicants) a value has been computed for each policy depending on how many of the three following items the policy requires from the applicant:

1. A requirement for the applicant to provide documentation showing that they have rights to the word they intend to register. This requirement is weighted more heavily than the other two. Any policy having this requirement ends up in one of the upper categories; any policy not having this requirement ends up in one of the lower categories.

2. A requirement for the applicant to be an organization.

3. A requirement for the applicant to have a local presence in the geographic area to which the TLD corresponds (requiring an administrative contact in the country counts as having half fulfilled this requirement).

While many TLDs started with a strictly regulated policy, few of the domain name policies in this Figure are currently in this category. This reflects a general move towards more liberalized domain name policies.

It is also clear that most ccTLDs within the survey seem to currently prefer a domain name policy that does not set limits on the number of names an applicant may hold. There are some exceptions; most of these have a policy regulated by quota.

While the majority of the TLD regimes in Figure 5.3 allow an unlimited number of domains per applicant, the degree of requirements for the

---

[80] The figure is a graphic representation of a survey conducted by Hilde Thunem in the period 2000–6. Survey results are continually accumulated, and updates are made when a ccTLD manager notifies that it has changed its domain name policy. There may be a few ccTLD managers that have changed their policies during the period without notification to the survey, but the overall distribution pattern of the domain name policies should still be correct. The survey is available at <http://www.norid.no/regelverk/rammer/policy-survey.en.html>.

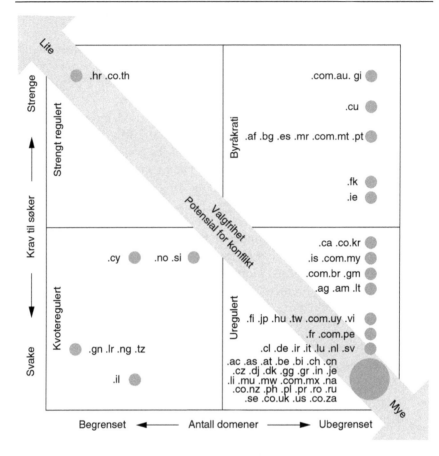

Figure 5.3. Domain name policies among some ccTLDs

applicant varies. A few require the applicant to document rights to the word they want to register. The large majority reside in the unregulated area and do not require any documentation of rights. Some still require either a local presence, or that the applicant is an organization (or both)—hence the spreading within the category.

With the steady growth in use of the Internet has come a steady push for changes in domain name policies. Unlike earlier, today's large companies are rarely satisfied with having only one Internet 'presence'. They want to have multiple domains each of which focuses on different services or customer groups, and they want an easy registration process with few hurdles. Interestingly too, many of them are increasingly intent on using a domain name not so much as an identifier for a service or a company, but rather as simply a device to generate and direct traffic towards a specific website or service.

In sum, these factors have resulted in a general move towards more liberalized and flexible domain name policies. The fact that liberalizing a policy is almost always a one-way change has served to reinforce this process.

5.4. The National Domain Name Regime for the .no Domain[81]

5.4.1. Introduction

Each national domain name regime can be divided into an administrative model and a domain name policy. The former defines roles and responsibilities in relation to the administration of the domain; the latter stipulates rules concerning the allocation of domain names. Over the years, most national domain name regimes have had to adjust both of these facets several times in order to adapt to new requirements emerging from the Internet becoming an important part of daily life. The .no domain is no exception.

When the Norwegian top-level domain (TLD) first came into existence in 1983 it was administered on a voluntary basis by Pål Spilling at the research institute of the old state-run telecommunications provider, Televerket. In 1987, however, the task had grown beyond what could be handled by one single person and the administration of the TLD was passed on to UNINETT AS, a non-profit shareholder company owned by the Norwegian state. UNINETT is the entity responsible for the research network in Norway and, as such, was considered to have both the requisite technical competence and neutrality to be a domain name registry. Today, the task of being the registry for the .no TLD rests with UNINETT Norid AS (hereinafter called simply Norid), which is a subsidiary non-profit company owned by UNINETT.[82]

While the administrative model has become more formalized over the years, the domain name policy has gone from being strictly regulated to more liberal. These adjustments have been made in response to the changing needs of the local Internet community in Norway, as it grew from its origins as a small group of expert users to the current situation

---

[81] Section 5.4 is co-authored by Hilde Thunem and Annebeth B. Lange, with the exception of section 5.4.9, which is authored by Lee A. Bygrave.

[82] For further information on Norid, see <http://www.norid.no/index.en.html>.

where it encompasses the overwhelming majority of Norwegian society. This section describes and explains the chosen administrative model and the current domain name policy,[83] along with the consequences that flow from these choices.

5.4.2. *Administrative Model for the .no Domain*

The administrative model defines the roles and responsibilities of the different entities involved in the administration of a TLD. In doing so, it delineates the relationship between the registry, the government, and the rest of the Internet community (whom the TLD should serve). The model also defines by whom and by which process the domain name policy is created and modified.

Administrative models come in many shapes and flavours. At one end of the spectrum we find the registries that are firmly placed within the public sector, some of them with a domain name policy set in law or regulation. These have the advantage of both stability and fitting in with the existing legal and governmental structure in a clear and well-defined way. However, the somewhat complex procedures required of all public-sector bodies (especially if they want to change a law/regulation) can make it a challenge for such registries to keep up with the demands of speed and flexibility from the ever-changing world of the Internet.

At the other end of the spectrum are the purely private-sector registries. Most of these define their domain name policy through some process of consultation with the local community, and enforce it through private law contracts. This gives room for flexibility and effectiveness. Although these registries have usually operated responsibly and in the service of society, the question is occasionally raised of how to ensure that this continues to be the case in the future.

The administrative model for the .no domain aims for the middle of the spectrum. It combines a domain name policy set by the registry (in consultation with the Norwegian community) with a high-level administrative framework set by the Norwegian government through regulation. Added to this mix is a private-sector registry that is owned by the Norwegian state. The model was formalized in 2003 through the creation of a Domain Name Regulation,[84] issued pursuant to the

---

[83] Available at <http://www.norid.no/navnepolitikk.en.html>.

[84] See Regulation No. 990 of 1 August 2003 on domain names under Norwegian country code top-level domains (*Forskrift om domenenavn under norske landkodetoppdomener*). The Regulation is anchored in sections 7-1 and 10-1 of the Electronic Communications Act. That Act

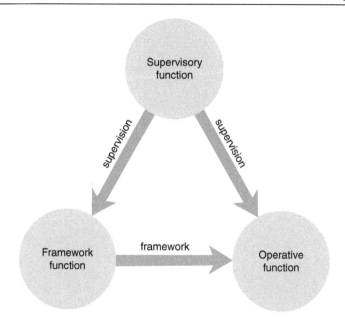

Figure 5.4. The three separate functions

Electronic Communications Act,[85] and continued the already existing practice developed during the years in which UNINETT had been the registry for .no.

The basis for the Norwegian administrative model is that there are three separate functions which interrelate in certain ways (Figure 5.4). First, there is an operative function which performs a given task. Second, there is a framework function which creates the framework for the operative function. Finally, there is a supervisory function which supervises both the other functions. This is, in principle, a three-way division of roles also seen in other contexts—the system comprising Parliament, government, and the judiciary being one of the more familiar tripartite divisions.

While the division into separate functions is not always as clear-cut as shown in Figure 5.4, the tripartite model may still provide a useful heuristic point of departure when considering the relationship between a set of entities.

also deals with limited resources other than domain names—namely telephone numbers and the frequency spectrum.

[85] Act No. 83 of 4 July 2003 (*Lov om elektronisk kommunikasjon*).

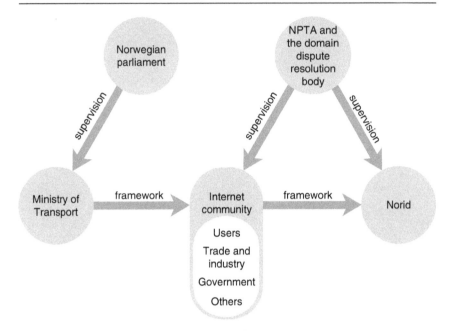

Figure 5.5. The administrative model for the .no domain

In the administrative model for the .no domain (Figure 5.5), the division takes place at two levels, linked by an entity which concurrently carries out both a framework and an operative function.

FRAMEWORK FUNCTION: NORWEGIAN AUTHORITIES

This function sets the high-level framework for the administration of all Norwegian TLDs. The main items covered in the framework are the requirements for the process used to develop the domain name policy, the minimum requirements that a registry administering a TLD has to fulfil, and the consequences if the registry does not fulfil those requirements.

The framework function is primarily performed by the Norwegian Ministry of Transport and Communications, which has laid the framework in the Domain Name Regulation. Additionally, limits beyond those laid down by the Ministry may follow from general Norwegian law, nationally transposed EU Directives, and any other applicable international standards with which Norway has undertaken to comply.

SUPERVISORY FUNCTION: NORWEGIAN PARLIAMENT

When laws are created, procedures exist to ensure that they are created through a proper process, and are consistent with the pre-existing legislation. These procedures inhere primarily in the Norwegian Parliament's enactment of new statutes. Regulations can only be created pursuant to the relevant Acts. This means that in principle the high-level supervisory function in relation to the Domain Name Regulation (and other relevant legislation making up the high-level framework) is held by the Norwegian Parliament. The judiciary may, of course, also play a supervisory role, though this is typically only after legislation is enacted.[86]

OPERATIVE FUNCTION/FRAMEWORK FUNCTION: THE LOCAL INTERNET COMMUNITY

This is the community that the .no domain should be serving. Use of the Internet in Norway has grown to such an extent that this community de facto encompasses the vast bulk of Norwegian society. The Internet community is, in effect, ultimately responsible for shaping the domain name policy for the .no domain within the high-level framework. As such, it performs an operative function in relation to the left semi-triangle in Figure 5.5. At the same time, it performs a framework function for the right triangle (since it creates the rules according to which the registry registers domain names).

As the Norwegian Internet community is not a legal entity, the task of drafting the domain name policy is formally placed with the .no domain registry. The latter is the organization legally responsible for the registration rules and other parts of the domain name policy for .no.

The high-level framework (the Domain Name Regulation) requires input to be gathered from the government and the user's representatives before changes are made in the domain name policy. In practice, this is implemented by the registry acting as a secretariat, drafting proposals for changes in the domain name policy which are then put forward for feedback from the Internet community.[87]

A policy advisory council (Norpol)[88]—with representatives from the private sector, the government, judiciary, Internet industry, consumer authorities, and other relevant parties—helps to ensure that the domain

---

[86] There is no case law dealing with the legislation relevant to administration of the Norwegian domain name regime.

[87] The process for changing the domain name policy is published at <http://www.norid.no/regelverk/rammer/regelverksprosess.en.html>.

[88] Further on Norpol, see <http://www.norid.no/omnorid/norpol.en.html>.

name policy is always adapted to the needs of the Internet community. In addition, a public enquiry is held before any major changes are made to the domain name policy.

SUPERVISORY FUNCTION: THE NORWEGIAN POST AND TELECOMMUNICATIONS AUTHORITY

The Norwegian Post and Telecommunications Authority (NPTA)[89] supervises the process whereby the domain name policy for .no is created or modified. It also checks that the registry complies with both frameworks applicable to it—the Domain Name Regulation and the domain name policy for .no.

In addition, a dispute resolution body has been created which functions as an appeal board in relation to the individual decisions that the registry makes regarding domain names under .no. The dispute resolution body also handles disputes between domain name holders and third parties who feel that their rights have been infringed upon, but this task is not part of its supervisory function in relation to the administration of the .no domain.[90] As the entity inhabiting the main supervisory role, the NPTA has a responsibility for checking that the dispute resolution body complies with the same frameworks as the registry.

OPERATIVE FUNCTION: NORID

This function administers the .no domain within the applicable frameworks. The primary tasks for the operative function are processing applications and operating the .no zone in a technically robust manner. The function is performed by the registry for the .no domain, Norid.

The registry follows a principle of only handling the essential core tasks in-house. The other tasks are left to companies that offer registrar services under contract with Norid and compete with each other to offer the best possible service to the applicants.[91]

5.4.3. *Consequences of the Chosen Model*

The result is a system that aims to incorporate 'the best of both worlds', where the government sets the high-level framework for the system but

---

[89] Further on the NPTA, see <http://www.npt.no>.

[90] The dispute resolution body is described in more detail in Section 5.4.9.

[91] For more information on the registrar model, see <http://www.norid.no/registrar/regrolle.en.html>.

does not dictate the details. Through its framework and supervisory functions, the government can safeguard that the service continues to operate
beneficially for the Norwegian community in the future. At the same
time, the model remains true to the principle of self-regulation, upon
which the successful growth of the Internet has been based. The people
who have a stake in the service—customers registering domain names,
registrars selling registration services, users accessing a website under a
domain, etc.—are the ones who set the rules for it. As in other areas,
market mechanisms regulate, to some degree, both prices and policy. If
registering a domain under .no becomes too expensive or the domain
name policy too arcane, people will simply stop using the TLD.

Even the way the registry is organized can be seen as an attempt to
combine the best of what the public and private sectors have to offer.
Although it was originally chosen for historical reasons, the fact that the
registry on the one hand is organized as a non-profit private company,
and on the other hand is owned by the State, results in a unique set of
advantages. The registry can be operated with the efficiency, flexibility,
and low costs made possible by being based within the private sector
while at the same time having the neutrality, legitimacy, and stability in
ownership provided by the State.

A registry with one foot in the private sector and one in the public is also
well-suited for understanding the interests of both. Such understanding
is useful when trying to create a domain name policy that serves the
entire community. One of the clearest examples of the advantages of the
chosen administrative model is the interaction around the domain name
policy. The Domain Name Regulation sets out certain basic principles,
such as transparency and non-discrimination, which all domain name
policies have to fulfil. Being placed within a regulation ensures that the
principles are not easily changed, which is important as they act as a final
'safety valve' for the domain name policy. The actual policy, however,
is a contract governed by private law. This means that the policy is
much more adaptable to the changing needs of the Norwegian Internet
community than it would have been if it also had been set down as a
regulation.

As with all compromises, the model has the disadvantage of being
complex and somewhat difficult to understand. If one crosses a bird
and a fish, the resulting hybrid may be able to both swim and fly but
will probably look weird to the uninitiated. Even so, in spite of its
complexity, the model is an instance of a very successful private–public
partnership.

5.4.4. *Other Factors Influencing Operation of the Registry*

Several other factors influence operation of the registry. First, the administration of the .no domain is a technically demanding task, requiring the registry to have close ties with the technical communities and to have personnel of high technical competence. In addition, operation of the registry is affected by its relationship with ICANN and the standards generated by IETF.

The mission and setup of ICANN and IETF respectively are dealt with elsewhere in this book and accordingly not discussed here. Further, as anyone participating in the IETF can only do so as an individual (and not as a representative of an organization), there are no formal agreements between the IETF and any registry. The following paragraphs deal, therefore, only with the formal relationship between Norid and ICANN.

When UNINETT became the registry for the .no domain in 1987, this was in agreement with IANA (Internet Assigned Numbers Authority)[92] which at that time held international responsibility for coordinating the administration of TLDs. As noted in Section 5.1.4 of this chapter, the framework for the role of a ccTLD registry was documented by Jon Postel in RFC 1591 in 1994.[93] Along with the informal acceptance of UNINETT as a registry by the Norwegian Internet community in 1987, RFC 1591 constitutes the factual and legal basis for Norid's administration of the .no domain.

After international responsibility for co-ordination of TLD administration was partly transferred from IANA to ICANN in 1998, ICANN has sought over the years a more formal and specific description of the relationship it has with each ccTLD registry than what is contained in RFC 1591. ICANN has chosen to provide several ways of doing this, taking into account that there are no identical registries. Some registries will not accept anything less formal than a contract, while others view a contract with a Californian private-sector corporation as inappropriate. ICANN's current solution is therefore to offer formal agreements or informal exchanges of letters depending on the preference of the registry concerned.

---

[92] In reality, the agreement was with Jon Postel, who ran IANA at the time. See Chapter 1 (Section 1.10) and Chapter 3 (Section 3.2.7).

[93] RFC 1591: Domain Name System Structure and Delegation (author: Jon Postel) (March 1994), <ftp://ftp.uninett.no/pub/rfc/rfc1591.txt>.

Norid exchanged letters with ICANN in July 2006.[94] These letters did not replace RFC 1591 as an agreement; instead, they elaborated the current distribution of roles between Norid and ICANN and documented a shared understanding of the roles. Both letters acknowledged that most ccTLD policy issues are local in nature and should be addressed by the local Internet community, unless it can be shown that the issue has global impact and needs to be resolved in an international framework. As noted in Section 5.1.4 of this chapter, this subsidiarity principle has been advocated by both the Governmental Advisory Committee and the ccTLD community in ICANN, and it is regarded by both Norid and the Norwegian government (through the Post and Telecommunications Authority) as one of the most important principles in relation to ICANN.

ICANN has also a support organization where ccTLD registries may become members—the Country Code Names Supporting Organization (ccNSO).[95] The latter provides a unique venue to deal with ccTLD issues within ICANN, especially in regard to the IANA policy—an issue which touches on the interests of every ccTLD registry. The ccNSO was constituted in 2004 and there has subsequently been discussion regarding its scope, tasks, and structure. For Norid, it was important that the ccNSO should accept the principle that most ccTLD policy issues should be addressed by the local Internet community and that, concomitantly, the ccNSO should limit its scope to those issues that must of necessity be dealt with on a global level. To this end, Norid actively participated in requesting changes to the ccNSO bylaws.[96] Several bylaw changes were implemented during 2005 and the first half of 2006, and while there are still some outstanding issues needing clarification, Norid decided to become a member of the ccNSO in December 2006.[97]

5.4.5. Domain Names in the World of Laws and Regulations

According to ISO 3166, Norway has three ccTLDs under its domain, namely, .no (for Norway), .bv (for Bouvet Island) and .sj (for Svalbard-Jan Mayen). All are formally administered by Norid, but only .no is currently open for registration.

---

[94] These letters are available at <http://www.norid.no/omnorid/icann/brev-fra-norid.pdf> and <http://www.norid.no/omnorid/icann/brev-fra-icann.pdf>.

[95] For the ccNSO bylaws, see <http://www.icann.org/general/bylaws.htm#IX>.

[96] A report of the process to change the ccNSO bylaws can be found at <http://ccnso.icann.org/about/pdp/ccpdp-members-report-07nov05.pdf>.

[97] Norid's membership application can be found at <http://www.norid.no/omnorid/icann/brev-icann-om-ccNSO.pdf>.

As described above, the Norwegian administrative model is based on a framework Regulation governing the relationship between the government and the administrator(s) of the Norwegian ccTLDs. In addition to that Regulation there are, of course, other rules and requirements applying to domain names. The rules for allocation of domain names (the domain name policy) take the form of a contract between Norid and the domain name holder, and bind the latter in the same manner as other contracts. The domain name holder must also comply with all relevant Norwegian law—for instance, the Personal Data Act,[98] the Trademark Act,[99] and the Electronic Communications Act—in addition to the contract with Norid.

It is a common misconception that there is something 'magic' about the Internet or domain names which exempts them from Norwegian law. No such exemption pertains, even if much of the law originally was designed to deal with the offline world. The law that already exists to deal with, for example, fraud, identity theft, or infringement of intellectual property rights is applicable to the online world as well, thus eliminating the need for a special law on domain names for these issues. This is why the Domain Name Regulation only deals with the administration—rather than the actual use—of the Norwegian ccTLDs.

5.4.6. *The High-Level Framework: Regulation on Domain Names under Norwegian ccTLDs*

The Domain Name Regulation is mainly a codification of an already existing practice, which the registry had established in co-operation with the authorities and the Internet community through 16 years of operation. The main content of the regulation is described below:

THE DOMAIN NAME POLICY FOR .no

The Regulation sets certain minimum requirements for the domain name policy: it needs to ensure cost efficiency and high technical quality, be non-discriminatory, promote transparency and predictability, protect the interests of Internet users and national interests, and take into account international development in the Internet area.

The registry has the formal responsibility for setting the domain name policy for .no, but before any significant changes are made in the policy,

---

[98] Act No. 31 of 14 April 2000 (*Lov om behandling av personopplysninger*).
[99] Act No. 4 of 3 March 1961 (*Lov om varemerker*).

input is asked for and received from the user's representatives and the government (both part of the Norwegian Internet community). The Norwegian Post and Telecommunications Authority is informed of all changes.

APPLICANT DECLARATION FORM

Before registering a domain name, the applicant must sign a declaration stating that the name applied for does not infringe on the rights of a third party, is not in breach of the domain name policy or Norwegian law, does not create an unwarranted impression of relating to government administration and that the applicant consents to participate in dispute resolution and accept the decisions of the dispute resolution body.

REGISTRAR SYSTEM

In addition to a registry for running the basic services, the Regulation provides for the existence of a number of registrars which act as an intermediary between the applicant and the registry and compete to offer the best possible service.

REQUIREMENTS FOR THE OPERATION

The registry must ensure that there are necessary backup copies of all registration data. In addition, the Regulation limits the use of the registration data to the area of registration and maintenance of domain names only.

DISPUTE RESOLUTION PROCEDURES

The registry is obliged to establish a dispute resolution body which can treat complaints that a registered name infringes on the rights of a third party, is in breach of Norwegian law or creates an unwarranted impression of relating to government administration. Moreover, the dispute resolution body is to treat complaints concerning the registry's processing of applications.[100]

SUPERVISION AND TERMINATION

The Regulation stipulates that the Norwegian Post and Telecommunications Authority is responsible for supervising compliance with the Regulation and may impose orders on the registry in the event of contravention. The Authority is also made responsible for taking over registered data from the registry in the case that the registry is dissolved without a new entity being ready to take over the task.

[100] See further Section 5.4.9.

5.4.7. *The Norwegian Domain Name Policy*

Like the administrative models, domain name policies also come in many shapes and flavours. The general rule is that the more restrictive a policy is, the harder it is for someone to get the domain name they want, but at the same time there is less potential for conflicts after the registration. In other words, a domain name policy will be more or less restrictive depending on whether the priority of the local Internet community is for low potential for conflicts or ease of registration.

The domain name policy for .no contains the rules for registering, holding, updating, transferring, and deleting .no domains, and is the actual contract between Norid and the domain name holders. The purpose of the policy is to ensure that the administration and allocation of domain names are conducted in the interests of Norwegian society as a whole. These interests are a moving target. What was considered to be a good policy in the early years of the TLD is not the same as what was needed to serve a more mature Internet community at a later date. Thus the policy has changed several times in order to keep up with the needs of its local Internet community.

A BRIEF LOOK AT THE PAST

The domain name policy for .no originally fell into the category of 'strictly regulated',[101] as did many of the other ccTLDs at that time. Common to these policies is that the priority is placed on preventing domain name registrations by applicants who have no rights to the name in question. To accomplish this, the applicants are subject to strict requirements, among them the requirement that they can document that they have rights to the words they intend to register. The 'first come, first served' rule does not apply until all requirements are met. This results in a lower potential for conflicts, but at the same time restricts the applicants' ability to freely choose their domain names.

In addition, policies of strict regulation limit the number of domain names each applicant may hold. This curtails domain name speculation and warehousing somewhat. It also means that even though domain name policies in this category require manual evaluation for each application, the policy scales fairly well and there is no need for an extensive application-processing apparatus.

---

[101] For more details on the consequences of different domain name policy models, see Section 5.3 above.

The original policy for .no allowed only one domain name per applicant and required the applicant to be a Norwegian organization. Individuals were not allowed to register domain names directly under .no, but could register domains under .priv.no.[102] Further, the policy required the applicant to be able to document some kind of affiliation with the desired name, but was somewhat more flexible than Sweden and Finland (which at that time also operated with a policy of strict regulation) regarding what was considered acceptable documentation.

In February 2001, a transition to a more liberal domain name policy was carried out. The changes were triggered by earlier feedback from the Norwegian Internet community which signalled that the previous policy was too restrictive. Hence, the basic premise for the changes was a desire to grant the applicants greater freedom of choice in registering domain names.

To achieve this, it was proposed to allow an increased number of domain names per applicant. Maintaining the strict application requirements while allowing a greater number of domain registrations would necessitate a larger and more bureaucratic apparatus for the evaluation of applications. Such a solution would result in increased processing time and cost per domain name, and was therefore not considered desirable. Moreover, feedback from the Internet community clearly signalled that the application requirements under the old policy were considered as too strict. It was therefore proposed that the requirement for applicants to document an affiliation with the domain names they wanted to register should be removed.

At the same time, the experience from Denmark (which stipulated few requirements for the applicant) showed that it was difficult to maintain updated contact information without requiring any form of unique applicant identification, and that individuals posed a greater challenge than organizations in this regard.

The need for a unique identifier follows from the fact that before any update to a domain can be made, the registry needs to ensure that the entity making the update is, indeed, the holder of the domain name. As indicated above, individuals tend to be more difficult than organizations to identify in this regard, partly because of privacy issues and the sheer number of individuals. In order to identify an individual, the

---

[102] The .no domain had (and still has) a series of generic sub-domains reserved for certain categories of domain name holders, such as .museum.no for museums and .mil.no for the military. Some of these sub-domains are administered by Norid, some by other entities. The sub-domain .priv.no is reserved for individuals.

registry can either create its own identifiers (e.g. a separate password for each domain) or use existing ones. Both of these solutions pose some challenges.

Creating a separate identifier per domain name makes it impossible to keep track of how many domains are being held by a single person, and thus cannot be used as an identification mechanism under a domain name policy that restricts the number of domains per applicant. On the other hand, existing unique identifiers like national identity numbers or passport numbers must be treated according to data protection law. This may require encryption of applications in order to protect the identifiers against exposure, certification for all registrars to allow them to handle such data, etc.

Moreover, contact information regarding individuals is harder to keep up to date—they tend to move more often than organizations and use fewer resources to keep their data updated.

Maintaining correct contact information was considered important both to ensure a high technical quality of the namespace under .no and to make it possible to identify and contact the entity responsible for a given domain. Accordingly, it was proposed that the requirement for the applicant to be an organization should be kept (with the exception of .priv.no).

It was assumed that the change in policy would lead to more conflicts concerning domain names. To keep the number of conflicts at a manageable level it was suggested to put a cap on the number of domain names each applicant could register. The proposal of a policy regulated by quota was also an attempt to place some restrictions on domain name speculation and warehousing.

When combined, the proposed changes would mean a major liberalization of the domain name policy for .no, moving it from the category of strictly regulated policies to policies regulated by quota. Were the changes to be implemented they would be almost impossible to reverse, so care was taken to ensure that the Norwegian Internet community both wanted the changes and understood the consequences that would ensue. A public hearing was conducted and a clear majority supported the proposed changes, resulting in a decision to proceed with the liberalization. The change in policy is shown in Figure 5.6.

Before the transition to the new domain name policy was implemented, consideration was given to whether there should be a 'sunrise period' during which applicants could document their rights to a name in order to register the corresponding domain name before all other applicants were given the opportunity to register. As a registry, Norid has neither mandate nor competence to judge which applicant has the strongest rights to a domain name, so if a sunrise period were to be implemented, a neutral third party would be needed to make such judgements.

Moreover, evaluating the documentation of thousands of applicants would increase the costs significantly for all applicants and slow down the whole process for several months. This was seen as undesirable, especiallyas one of the significant changes in the new domain name policy

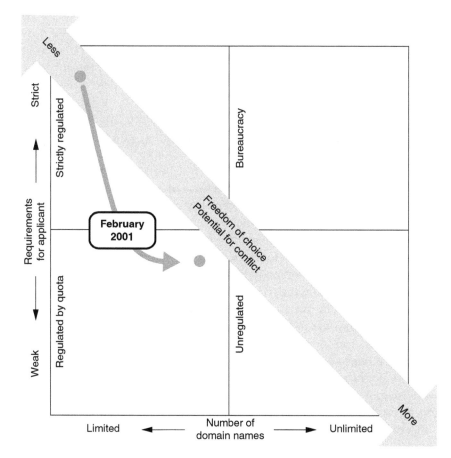

Figure 5.6. The liberalization of the domain name policy for .no[103]

---

[103] For an explanation of the categories in the figure, see Section 5.3.

was to remove the requirement for documentation. Discussion between Norid, Norpol, and the NPTA arrived at the conclusion that there would be no sunrise period.

As for the actual transition mechanism, two alternatives were considered. The first alternative (the 'big bang method') was to pick a date and time for the new domain name policy to be launched, and then open the floodgates and treat applications in the order which they arrived at the registry. This is the mechanism that is commonly used by registries when implementing a new domain name policy, but it has a serious drawback. The flood of applications may put a heavy strain on the registry system—in some cases it has even crashed the system. Also, it gives a false perception among applicants that they will be first in the queue if only they send their application at the exact second that the new policy is in force, while in reality there are a lot of random factors—for instance, the traffic on the way from their ISP to the registry—which determine which applications reach the registry first.

The other alternative (the 'lottery method') collects applications over a set period of time (usually a few days), and then processes them in a random order. After that, the 'first come, first served' principle pertains. To our knowledge, this mechanism had not been used by any registry at the time. The strength of this mechanism is that the registrars do not need to flood the system the very first moment the new policy is launched, since they know that they will have several days to send in the applications. Provided that the registry removes duplicates to ensure that each applicant only gets one application per domain name, it is a fair mechanism in which everybody has an equal chance to win, no matter how far their ISP is from the registry machines. The main drawback is that it takes some days to run a transition in this way, while just opening the floodgates can be over in hours.

There were clear indications from the Norwegian community that there would be a large amount of new applications as soon as the new domain name policy was launched. With that in mind, and after consultation with Norpol and the NPTA, Norid chose the lottery method for the transition. Norid then received and processed the applications while the NPTA created the random sequence in which they were processed.[104]

---

[104] Further information on the results of the transition can be found at <http://www.norid.no/regelverk/forslag/liberalisering-1999/index.en.html>.

THE CURRENT DOMAIN NAME POLICY FOR .no

There have been some further changes to the domain name policy since 2001, but it remains within the same policy category (regulated by quota). The main requirements of the current domain name policy for .no are as follows:

- The applicant is required to have a local presence in Norway.
- The applicant is required to be an organization. Currently this is defined as certain organization types registered in the Brønnøysund Register Centre.[105] Individuals are not allowed to register domain names directly under .no, but can register under .priv.no.
- Each domain name holder may have up to 20 domain names directly under .no. In addition, they may register domain names under geographical or generic subdomains.
- All domain names must be technically operative.[106]

While applicants do not have to document rights to the word they want to register as a domain name before registering it, they are required to sign a declaration stating, among other things, that they are responsible for their choice of domain name and do not infringe on anyone's right to the name or give a false impression of being a public authority. Further, there is an alternative dispute resolution body which deals with disputes concerning the infringement of third parties' rights, etc.[107]

There are both advantages and disadvantages to the chosen model. Indeed, this duality holds true for all policy models. To complicate matters further, there are separate advantages and disadvantages of each of the main requirements chosen within the single model. As the choice to put a limit on the number of domain names each applicant may hold is what places the Norwegian domain name policy into the policy category where it is currently situated, the following paragraphs will focus on the positive and negative effects that have been observed to result from the quota during the last five years.

[105] See further <http://www.brreg.no/english>.

[106] The domains need not have websites or email addresses connected to them, but each domain must be served by a minimum of two name servers configured according to the requirements stipulated in Appendix F to the policy; see further <http://www.norid.no/regelverk/vedlegg-f.en.html>.

[107] See further Section 5.4.9.

5.4.8. *Consequences of the Quota*

HIGH RENEWAL RATE

From 1 January 2005, domain name holders under .no have had to actively renew a domain name annually in order to keep it. The average renewal rate from January to October 2006 was 95 per cent, which is a high rate compared with comparable ccTLDs (e.g. .uk with a renewal rate of 70%,[108] and .fi with a renewal rate of 82%[109]). In other words, domains under .no are registered with the view to long-term use to a greater extent than under some of the other TLDs.

The high renewal rates are probably a result of three different factors:

- The fact that previous domain name policies under .no have been fairly restrictive means that a relatively high volume of early users had time to assess their needs and find good domain names that they intend to keep for a long time.

- Organizations mainly register domain names associated with products and enterprises that have a longer lifetime than would typically be the case were individual persons to register domain names. The fact that only organizations can register domain names directly under .no thus encourages a higher degree of domain name registration for long-term use.

- The quota limitation on the number of domain names per domain name holder contributes to the high renewal rates. While only 0.2 per cent of the domain name holders have filled the quota of 20 domain names, the fact that there is a limit at all appears to have an effect on the usage pattern.

The high renewal rates mean that the .no domain has a relatively stable namespace, and a user can expect a web address or an email address to function for a long period.

LESS SPECULATION

A quota system imposes some limits on the possibility of earning money on the domain market through purchases and sales of large numbers of domain names (domain name speculation). This phenomenon is

[108] Figure presented by Lesley Cowley (Chief Executive Officer, Nominet) at the ccNSO meeting 6 December 2006 in São Paulo.

[109] Figure presented by FICORA (the Finnish Communications Regulatory Authority which is responsible for operating the .fi registry) at a meeting between the Nordic registries held in Copenhagen on 22 November 2006.

especially common under the .com domain, in which there are no upfront restrictions on who can register what. Domain name speculation depends on a large enough market for the domain names in question. The problem may thus arise under other TLDs than .com as the market for their names develops sufficiently to be of interest to professional speculators.

To some extent, the quota also restricts registration of names that infringe on the rights of others (domain name piracy), or at least keeps the volume down sufficiently to enable an alternative dispute resolution mechanism to deal with the disputes without being overwhelmed.

Other effects of not having a quota include minimization of the problem observed in some other European countries, where the domain names that customers have requested are registered by certain registrars for themselves. This makes it almost impossible for the customer to change registrars, since the registrar is the de facto holder of the domain name. At the same time, the registry or others can do little about the situation, since it does not necessarily contravene local law as long as registrars explain to their customers what they are doing. The fact that .no has a quota helps to create obstacles to this kind of business model among Norwegian registrars.

LESS WAREHOUSING

Domain names are a limited resource. It is thus desirable to limit the number of domain names available to each applicant, to prevent a few early applicants from taking most of the names. This could have been solved by raising the price to make warehousing expensive, but this is in conflict with Norid's principles of providing a cost-effective service in accordance with the Domain Name Regulation. Instead, regulating by quota has been chosen to prevent warehousing.

The quota system probably also causes domain name holders to go through their domain names at regular intervals and delete the names they do not want, which releases names for other applicants.

A REAL OBSTACLE FOR SOME

It is a familiar principle that if you have no restrictions on a resource, a minority of the players will control the majority of the resources. When we compare the number of organizations with the number of domain names each organization controls, this principle seems to apply to domain names as well—as Figure 5.7 shows. In the distribution, the great majority has one or two domain names. If no quota for .no had

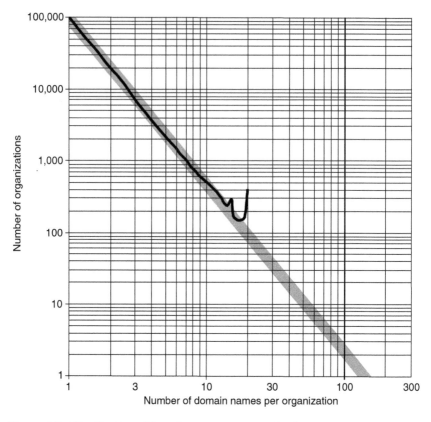

Figure 5.7. Distribution of domain names per organization

existed, we can assume that the distribution would have continued along the grey trend line (Figure 5.7).

A consequence of the quota is that certain organizations have stopped at a lower number of domain names than they would otherwise have had. This is reflected in the graph for organizations with 15 domain names (previous quota) and 18, 19, and 20 domain names (the area around the current quota). Analysis of the organizations in the upper region indicates that these are largely organizations that want domain names to meet their own needs.

In addition, the quota imposes a limit on how much a registrar can gain from the sale of domain names to a single customer, and how much the registry can earn in total. This means that removal of the quota would be in the registrars' interest.

SUPPORT FOR THE QUOTA IN THE NORWEGIAN INTERNET COMMUNITY

To obtain information about how the quota is perceived in the Norwegian community, Norid conducted two surveys during spring 2006. One of the surveys was directed at the public, represented by 1046 individuals, the other was directed at 500 organizations registered in the Brønnøysund Register Centre.

The result from the organization survey showed that a great majority of the organizations accept the quota and view it as being at an appropriate level: 6 per cent expressed that the quota should either be increased or be removed while 89 per cent felt that the quota was at the right level or should be decreased. The remaining 5 per cent did not take a position on the issue. The response from the public was almost identical to the response from the organizations except that the proportion of respondents who had not taken a position on the issue was higher. This is to be expected, as under the current domain name policy only organizations can register domain names directly under .no, and they are thus more likely to have an opinion about the size of the quota.

BALANCING THE DIFFERENT INTERESTS

For the great majority of the .no domain name holders, the quota system is no problem. It represents no real limit for them, while the quota makes it more likely that a given domain name will be available should the need for one more name arise.

Users of the .no domain—that is, people who visit .no websites or send emails to .no domain names—probably benefit from a quota, provided that the quota is not too low. A quota contributes to a more stable namespace and to registration of domain names for long-term use.

At the same time, whatever size is chosen for the quota, it will entail limitations for some parties. This applies to a clear minority of the domain name holders, but it may affect large organizations, such as large shareholder companies as well as government agencies at state and municipal level. The quota also has positive effects for them in the form of a more stable namespace, less domain name piracy, etc., but these are nonetheless the ones who pay the price for the advantages a quota system gives to the community.

As the choice of policy model depends heavily on what the Norwegian Internet community considers to be the most important policy criteria, and this is something that may change over time, the domain name policy for .no is evaluated continuously. Based on the analysis described above, it was concluded that the domain name policy regulated by quota still has broad support among the community in 2006, and the large majority experiences more advantages than disadvantages with the current model. The size of the quota also appears to be acceptable.

However, the fact that there currently is a fairly broad support for a domain name policy regulated by quota only means that the policy fulfils the *current* needs of the community. If the needs of the community change in the future, there might also emerge a need for a change in domain name policy. Since it is almost impossible to restrict a policy once it has been liberalized, it is likely that any new changes will be in order to meet a need for further liberalization. In that case, it will be imperative to ensure both that there is a real need for change and that the Internet community understands and accepts the consequences of the change before it is made.

So far it has been commonly accepted among the Internet community, including the government, that it is better to take small steps forward and evaluate the result, than to take giant steps and not be able to turn back. In the Internet world, it is very easy to reach the point of no return if one is too impatient. Therefore, the Norwegian policy has been, and still is, to 'hurry slowly'.

5.4.9. *Alternative Dispute Resolution*

As noted above, the Domain Name Regulation provides for the establishment of an extra-judicial scheme for resolving disputes over registrations in the .no namespace. The chief rationale for such a scheme is to provide a faster and cheaper alternative to settling conflicts than court litigation allows. The centrepiece of the scheme is the Alternative Dispute Resolution (ADR) body (Domeneklagenemnda—'DOK').[110] The ADR body may deal with complaints that a registered name infringes on a third party's rights, otherwise violates Norwegian law, or creates an unwarranted impression that it is associated with government administration or authority. The body may also handle complaints concerning Norid's processing of applications. In practice, the overwhelming majority of complaints come from third party right-holders.

---

[110] See further <http://www.norid.no/domenekonflikter/domeneklagenemnda.en.html>.

The ADR body has nine members most of whom have legal quali-fications. They are appointed by the Norid board in cooperation with Norpol and the NPTA. Norid provides the body with secretarial sup-port. However, the body is to exercise its decision-making powers independently.

Each case is handled by three members as appointed by the body head. Initial mediation by one of the members is possible if *both* parties to the complaint wish it. In practice, this is rarely the case.

In keeping with the aim of facilitating fast resolution of complaints at moderate cost, tight limits are put on the length of submissions and on the adjudication timeframe. For example, neither the complaint itself nor the response may exceed 2000 words. Most complaints are expedited solely by email and telephone. The system is also sufficiently simple to allow use by persons without legal qualifications. Nonetheless, the bulk of complainants are represented by lawyers. There is no internal appeals process; appeals from tribunal decisions go to the ordinary courts of law. No appeals have been mounted so far.[111] Parties are also free to initiate court proceedings at any time before or while the complaint is being handled by the body. If litigation is initiated, the body ceases to handle the complaint further. The body may also refuse to handle a complaint if it is too complex for the body to handle fairly in the set timeframe.

Complaints from third party right-holders are essentially dealt with by applying a test of 'bad faith' to the domain name registration in dispute. This is in keeping with the test laid down by ICANN's UDRP.[112] However, as a general rule, the test will be applied according to Norwegian law. The Domain Name Policy for .no defines 'bad faith' as basically covering cases where the registrant infringes on the complainant's rights either knowing of those rights or acting with gross negligence in respect of them.[113] In most cases, the ADR body has ruled in favour of the complainant. This reflects the fact that the scheme is directed at resolving relatively blatant instances of rights infringement.

---

[111] Independently of the scheme, there have so far been approximately 30 Norwe-gian court cases involving domain name disputes. Some of these, however, concern names registered outside the .no TLD. And most of the cases were mounted prior to the establishment of the ADR body. See further <http://www.norid.no/domenekonflikter/rettssaker/>, last accessed 20 June 2008.

[112] See Section 5.2.2.

[113] See Appendix H [Section 1.2(b)] to the .no domain name policy; available at <http://www.norid.no/regelverk/vedlegg-h.en.html>.

5.5. The National Domain Name Regime for the .uk Domain[114]

5.5.1. *Introduction*

Internet governance within the United Kingdom has traditionally been in the hands of the private sector, with the government taking an interested, but mainly 'hands-off' approach. This is particularly true of the Domain Name System. Since 1996, the .uk domain name has been under the control of Nominet, which is a neutral, non-profit company limited by guarantee, with approximately 3,000 members broadly representing the UK domain registration industry. Nominet's predecessor, the UK Naming Committee, did place some restrictions on who could have a .uk domain name, although these restrictions were minimal compared to the equivalent regimes operating in many other countries. Upon taking over the domain, Nominet liberalized the restrictions even further, and reduced registration fees. Not surprisingly, then, the .uk domain is heavily used, and is at the time of writing the ccTLD with the third largest number of registrations (after .de for Germany and .cn for China).[115]

Moreover, Nominet has long been seen by the community as a trustworthy, neutral body. The government has accordingly taken the view that since the system works well, the government need not intervene. Concomitantly, the relationship between Nominet and the government is currently very good. This has been of help to all parties during the international discussions about the future of Internet governance, both in terms of the discussions between ccTLD registries and ICANN, and the discussions at UN level.

5.5.2. *Relationship with State Agencies*

Nominet is a private company outside government ownership. Nonetheless, Nominet interacts closely with multiple government bodies and other state agencies. These are principally the following:

- The Department for Business, Enterprise, and Regulatory Reform (BERR) (formerly the Department of Trade and Industry).
- The Office of the Information Commissioner.
- The Office of Fair Trading.
- The Office of Communications.

---

[114] Section 5.5 is primarily written by Edward Phillips, with updates provided by Nick Wenban-Smith.
[115] See VeriSign, 'The Domain Name Industry Brief', June 2008, vol. 5, no. 3, <http://www.verisign.com/static/043939.pdf>.

- Law enforcement agencies.
- The Cabinet Office.
- The All Parliamentary Internet Group.

In addition, Nominet has a group called the 'Policy Advisory Body' (PAB), described below. While the PAB is not exclusively intended to communicate with government, various government-related people are part of it, and it provides a forum for the discussion of policy issues relating to the .uk TLD.

THE DEPARTMENT FOR BUSINESS, ENTERPRISE, AND REGULATORY REFORM (BERR)

BERR is the main department of central government with an interest in Nominet. BERR is responsible for infrastructure (other than transport), communications, and business. Therefore, it has responsibility for Internet-related matters. If the government is asked a question about the Domain Name System, it is BERR that has to answer it. It is BERR that sends the team to represent the UK at international conferences (such as WSIS) on the future of the Internet. BERR decides how Internet-related law should be implemented in the UK and, in particular, how EU Directives on this topic should be transposed into UK law. Finally, BERR also oversees the sector regulators—the Office of Fair Trading and the Office of Communications.

Thus, it helps Nominet and BERR to communicate with each other. BERR needs to be sure that Nominet is running the .uk domain properly, as a great deal of commerce depends on DNS stability. BERR also needs information to answer Parliamentary questions and to properly inform it in advance of conferences and legislative changes. Conversely, Nominet needs to understand the political climate, and what the future of legislation and regulation in this area is likely to be.

In the run-up to WSIS, Nominet staff briefed the UK minister attending the Summit and worked in close co-operation with the staff at BERR, helping to inform them about the Internet sector generally and DNS specifically.

THE OFFICE OF THE INFORMATION COMMISSIONER (OIC)

As a member state of the European Union, the UK has implemented Directive 95/46/EC on data protection and Directive 2002/58/EC on privacy of electronic communications.[116]

---

[116] The chief domestic rules on point being found in the Data Protection Act 1998 and Privacy and Electronic Communications (EC Directive) Regulations 2003 (SI 2003/2426).

The Information Commissioner is responsible for overseeing and enforcing data protection legislation in the UK, and is answerable directly to Parliament (i.e. the OIC is not part of the Government, and thus not answerable to BERR).

Nominet maintains a database of several million domain names, and, in accordance with normal practice of ccTLD registries, maintains a WHOIS database, the effect of which is to make available the names and addresses of the registrants of .uk domain names. The WHOIS database is available for use by persons both inside and outside the European Economic Area, making it of particular interest in data protection terms.

Additionally, Nominet has altered how it releases its WHOIS data, with a bigger emphasis on providing specific information tools for specific users, and a move away from a 'one-size-fits-all' WHOIS system. Nominet now provides four methods of obtaining data about domain names and registrants: the WHOIS system, the Domain Availability Checker (DAC) system, the Public Register Search Service (PRSS) system, and the Extensible Provisioning Protocol (EPP) system. Each of these systems is tailored to meet the access and information requirements of different people. For example, the DAC is designed for use by registrars that would like quickly to check the availability of a domain name and do not need to see the other WHOIS data (e.g. name and address of registrant).

For all these reasons, Nominet has long consulted with the OIC. This relationship has been a success, resulting in, *inter alia*, the implementation of privacy-enhancing options for WHOIS output. Nominet used to show the registrant's name in the WHOIS, but did not give an address. In 2002, Nominet proposed that inclusion of an address in the WHOIS would make the data more useful, as it would allow the person concerned to be contacted. When this idea was made public, there was some public resistance to it on privacy grounds. In consultation with the OIC, Nominet then decided to allow consumers (i.e. non-trading individuals, as opposed to those in business either as a company or in their own name) to opt-out of having their address shown in the WHOIS, but that those trading should not have this option. This would help private individuals to retain privacy yet allow Nominet to release the address of businesses, which is particularly helpful for identifying disreputable traders. While the Data Protection Act 1998 grants data protection rights to all individuals (i.e. whether they trade or not), a number of other UK laws require trading individuals to make their name and postal address known to potential customers.[117] The Office of the Information Commissioner therefore took the view that the rights of data subjects were adequately protected by this proposed scheme, and that it was permissible to show these addresses in the WHOIS.

THE OFFICE OF FAIR TRADING (OFT)

The Office of Fair Trading has two main roles. It enforces competition law and it enforces consumer protection law. Complaints about Nominet have been made to the OFT in the past, in particular about the system for issuing second-level domains (SLDs).[118] These complaints have led to changes in Nominet's procedures, and Nominet's relations with the OFT remain friendly.

THE OFFICE OF COMMUNICATIONS (OFCOM)

The Office of Communications is the national regulatory authority for communications, and much of its authority and remit are derived from the UK implementation of the four principal EU Directives on electronic communications.[119] As part of the implementation of those Directives, UK law[120] was changed so that OFCOM would have been authorized to allocate 'numbers', originally defined to include domain names. However, the government used secondary legislation to prevent this occurring.[121] As a result, domain name allocation policy remains with Nominet, but the government could obtain control of such policy by making a fairly minor change in the law.

Aside from this area, Nominet is not subject to regulation by OFCOM and has minimal interaction with it.

LAW ENFORCEMENT

As a registry, Nominet holds information which may be of interest to the police and other state bodies engaged in law enforcement [such as the Home Office and Trading Standards offices (local fair-trading regulators)].

---

[117] Currently including the Business Names Act 1985, the Companies Act 1985 (both of which are being replaced by the gradual implementation of the recent Companies Act 2006, which will be fully in force by October 2008), and laws on distance selling and e-commerce (implementing, *inter alia*, Directives 1997/7/EC and 2000/31/EC).

[118] Note that, under .uk, domains are usually issued at the third level.

[119] Directives 2002/21/EC (Framework Directive), 2002/20/EC (Authorisation Directive), 2002/19/EC (Access and Interconnection Directive), and 2002/22/EC (Universal Services Directive).

[120] Specifically, section 56 of the Communications Act 2003.

[121] The Telephone Number Exclusion (Domain Names and Internet Addresses) Order 2003 (SI 2003/3281).

Nominet provides statements and information to these bodies on a regular basis, and includes provisions in its domain name contract with registrants to allow this.

THE CABINET OFFICE

As the office of government associated with the Prime Minister, the Cabinet Office has two reasons to be interested in Nominet. The first is that the Cabinet Office includes the civil servants that oversee the government's acquisition and application of ICT (as opposed to BERR, which oversees ICT usage by other bodies). The Cabinet Office influences, therefore, the way in which government runs its own websites and other Internet applications.

The second reason is that the Cabinet Office oversees the use of the .gov.uk SLD, which is reserved for government use (see Section 5.5.3).

THE ALL PARLIAMENTARY INTERNET GROUP (APIG)

The All Parliamentary Internet Group consists of Members of Parliament and Members of the House of Lords from all parties. Thus, it represents a broader group of parliamentarians than just the government. A representative from APIG sits on the Policy Advisory Body (see below).

THE POLICY ADVISORY BODY (PAB)

The Policy Advisory Body (previously 'Policy Advisory Board') was established in 1999 chiefly in order to provide Nominet's Board of Directors with advice on policy matters. It is composed of eight representatives elected by Nominet's members (i.e. the Internet community), up to two (non-voting) representatives from Nominet's Board of Directors, and up to eight representatives appointed from organizations with an interest in the .uk domain. These appointed representatives include, or have included, representatives from consumer organizations, business groups (such as the Confederation of British Industry), intellectual property interests (The Institute of Trade Mark Agents), other registries (Companies House), operators of SLDs (The Cabinet Office), the government (BERR), parliamentary politicians (APIG), and regulators (OIC).

As such, the PAB is a mechanism for dialogue with the whole .uk community, including the government. If there is a matter which the Nominet Board of Directors views as raising policy issues, that matter is passed to the PAB. The PAB then makes a recommendation using its relatively broad range of experience and representation. The Nominet Board takes this recommendation seriously and will usually implement it. However, the Nominet Board deals with operational matters and occasionally has altered or delayed the implementation of a PAB recommendation that would have had significant operational ramifications for Nominet.

5.5.3. *Domain Name Allocation Policy for .uk*

SECOND-LEVEL DOMAINS

The .uk namespace has always been subdivided by second-level domains (SLDs). These domains have charters, some of which are enforced strictly, some of which are not. The actual rules for allocation of .uk domains are on Nominet's website.[122]

In summary, these SLDs are as follows:

Group A:
　.co.uk—intended for commercial bodies (though anyone can register);
　.org.uk—intended for non-profit bodies (again, though, anyone can register);
　.me.uk—restricted for individuals (names not registered to an individual can be cancelled);
　.net.uk—restricted to Internet Service Providers (checked manually on application);
　.ltd.uk—restricted to Limited Companies from the UK;
　.plc.uk—restricted to Public Limited Companies from the UK.

Group B:
　.nic.uk—reserved for the .uk network information centre (Nominet);
　.sch.uk—restricted to schools in the UK.

Group C:
　.ac.uk—restricted to tertiary education establishments in the UK (e.g. universities);
　.mod.uk—restricted to the UK Ministry of Defence and UK Armed Forces;
　.nhs.uk—restricted to the UK National Health Service;
　.police.uk—restricted to UK Police forces and related organizations;
　.gov.uk—restricted to the UK Government and regional government in the UK.

---

[122] See further <http://www.nominet.org.uk/registrants/aboutdomainnames/rules/>.

Domain names in Group A are run by Nominet, and are subject to publicly accessible rules. They are available on a 'first registered, first served' basis (i.e. the first valid application processed by the registration system is allocated the registration).

GENERAL NAMING RULES

There are some general restrictions which result from the DNS itself, or similar factors:

- Because Nominet does not (yet) support Internationalised Domain Names (IDN), the character set is restricted to 'a'-'z', '-' and '0'-'9'.
- Third-level domains usually cannot reflect a .uk SLD or a gTLD (thus, com.co.uk or mod.org.uk are not allowed).
- One-character domains are prohibited (for instance, x.co.uk or 3.co.uk are not permitted).
- Two-letter domains are generally prohibited (such as xx.co.uk), but one-letter one-character domains are permitted (e.g. a9.co.uk or 2a.co.uk). There remain a small number of two-letter domains that predate Nominet's incorporation (such as bt.co.uk).
- Domains cannot start or end with a hyphen (e.g. -2.co.uk and 2-.me.uk are prohibited).
- The domain is subject to a length limit.

THE SPECIFIC RULES FOR EACH SLD

For .co.uk, and .org.uk, no requirements whatsoever pertain, and the 'intended' usage in the rules is purely advisory.

For .me.uk, there is a requirement that the registrant is a natural/physical person (in other words, not a company or other corporate body). If the registrant is not a natural/physical person, the domain name can be cancelled. However, this rule was introduced on 25 October 2004 and some exemptions pertain for .me.uk domain names registered before that date.

For .ltd.uk and .plc.uk, there are a strict set of rules determining eligibility. These domains are restricted to companies registered under the (UK) Companies Acts. The rules set out an algorithm: the company's name as recorded at Companies House (the government register of companies) is processed through this algorithm, and if a registerable domain name can be obtained at the end, the registrant is entitled to that domain name. The original purpose of these SLDs was that, because each name on Companies House is unique, every company would be guaranteed a domain name. In practice, because domain names do not support the same character set as Companies House, it is possible for two companies to qualify for the same domain name but this is rare. The registrations are not manually checked on application, but are periodically reviewed.

For .net.uk, there is a strict requirement that the user be a UK Internet Service Provider. Each application is checked by hand.

The domains in Group B above are operated by Nominet, but the rules are not public. Essentially, .nic.uk is used for network use only (e.g. Nominet uses it for the .uk nameservers). The .sch.uk domains are allocated in accordance with agreements with UK education authorities (since most schools in the UK are operated by the state). They are generally allocated at the fourth level, with the third level reserved for a geographical location (e.g. aldro.surrey.sch.uk).

The domains in Group C are not operated by Nominet. They all relate to state undertakings of one sort or other, and the policies and rules for them are accordingly set by the relevant bodies. These bodies are the following:

.mod.uk—The Ministry of Defence
.gov.uk—The Cabinet Office
.police.uk—The Police IT Organisation
.nhs.uk—The National Health Service IT Organisation; and
.ac.uk—UKERNA (United Kingdom Education and Research Networking Association).

As the intended target user groups for these SLDs is small and the rules for them are strictly enforced, we refrain from elaborating these rules here.

REGISTRATION VOLUMES AND PRACTICE

As of November 2007, there were 6,445,465 .uk domains[123] on Nominet's register, of which 92 per cent were .co.uk, about 5 per cent were .org.uk, 1.5 per cent were .me.uk, and the remaining 1.5 per cent were made up of .ltd.uk, .plc.uk, .net.uk, and .sch.uk. The registration rate for .uk domains is approximately 200/hour.

[123] For the latest count, see <http://www.nominet.org.uk/intelligence/statistics/registration/>, last accessd 30 April 2008.

In terms of volume, the SLDs not operated by Nominet (i.e. Group C) are comparatively small domains. Only .gov.uk, .nhs.uk, and .ac.uk have more than a few hundred registrations. The .mod.uk SLD (which is only used for public sites, and not for military operations) and .police.uk have only a handful of registrations.

In general, therefore, when people are talking about .uk domain names, they are really talking about .co.uk and, to some degree, .org.uk domain names. The large registration volumes of these SLDs are due to a multiplicity of factors:

- the lack of any substantive pre-conditions on registrants;
- their ease of availability;
- their low cost (currently £5 + sales tax for a fixed two-year term);
- the ability to resell them; and
- the ability to register as many as one wishes (with some registrants having over 15,000 domain names).

Allocation of .co.uk and .org.uk thus mirrors the allocation of .com and .org, and the take-up has been correspondingly high. By contrast, .net.uk has remained extremely restrictive (both in terms of national requirements, registrant requirements, and because of the manual application process) and so has seen only a tiny number of registrations, while its international cousin, .net has become very popular (although still not as popular as .com).

WHY NOMINET HAS NOT HAD MORE RESTRICTIVE REQUIREMENTS

There are two main reasons why Nominet does not, and has never had, more restrictive requirements for .co.uk and .org.uk. The first is that, in part, Nominet took over the operation of .uk precisely because pre-vetting of domain names was not working. Nominet's predecessor, the Naming Committee, used to vet each application by committee. This was a workable approach when registration volumes were very small in the early 1990s, but it became unworkable by 1995 as volumes increased, and one of the core decisions involved in the creation of Nominet was the general adoption of an automated 'first come, first served' registration system. By way of illustration, at the end of 1996 and 1997, Nominet was processing about 5,000 registrations a month. By the end of 1998, this number was 10,000 and, by the end of 1999, it was 100,000. While this number fell after the dot-com bubble burst, it is now returning to those levels.

The second reason is that the number of 'problem' registrations is actually very low, with less than 0.1 per cent of registrations leading to a dispute. Given this low number, and since only some of these problems could be stopped even if they were manually vetted, the prevailing attitude in the UK Internet community has been that *ex post facto* (after the event) remedies are sufficient. Nominet developed a Dispute Resolution Service (see directly below), which it relaunched in 2001, drawing on ICANN's experience with the UDRP and including a free mediation stage. Nominet has found this service to be very successful, and versions of it have been emulated in a number of countries, including New Zealand, Norway, Switzerland, and South Africa.

5.5.4. *The Dispute Resolution Service*

The Dispute Resolution Service (DRS) is a relatively quick, cheap, and effective means of handling complaints over domain name allocation.[124] Essentially, the complaints-handling process is initiated when a complainant makes out a complaint online, using up to 2,000 words. Nominet acts as a neutral administrator for the complaint, taking no sides. The complaint is forwarded to the registrant concerned, who is given a chance to respond. If they do so, a trained member of the Nominet staff acts as a mediator to try to resolve the complaint. More than half the cases which are mediated result in a private confidential settlement. Complaints settled at this stage do not cost either party any money, making the DRS extremely accessible.

If mediation is unsuccessful, or in cases where no response is filed by the registrant, then the complainant can elect to pay (£750 + VAT) for an Independent Expert to decide the case, or withdraw from the process. The Expert is chosen by Nominet from an approved list, and will always be the next person on the list who is available and who can confirm that they have no conflict of interest. The Expert will return a decision, ordering no action, suspension, or transfer of the domain name in dispute. There is a chance to appeal, to a panel of three Experts, although this is rarely used.

The rules of the DRS are set out in the DRS Policy and Procedure, which form part of the contract of domain name registration. The DRS requires

---

[124] See further <http://www.nominet.org.uk/disputes/drs/>, last accessed 30 April 2008.

the complainant to prove, on the balance of probabilities, that they have rights in a name or mark which is identical or similar to the domain name, and to prove that the registration in the hands of the registrant is 'abusive'. A non-exhaustive list of examples of what amounts to 'abuse' is given in the Policy.

The DRS is updated roughly every three years, and new Experts are appointed from time to time. The service grows in popularity each year, providing a large number of users, many of whom are individuals or small businesses, with access to a system that actually works. For most of these users, recourse to the UK courts is too expensive and time-consuming. The DRS has proved to be very successful and is being copied elsewhere. In 2004, the DRS won an industry award for Excellence in Alternative Dispute Resolution from CEDR (Centre for Effective Dispute Resolution).

6

Internet governance goes global

Amanda Hubbard* and Lee A. Bygrave

6.1. Introduction

One of the most ambitious international undertakings to resolve friction regarding governance of the Internet was the World Summit on the Information Society (WSIS). The WSIS was a series of international conferences for governments, businesses, and civil society, developed and organized by the International Telecommunications Union (ITU) under the aegis of the United Nations (UN). Organizing these efforts was a gargantuan undertaking spanning more than six years. It involved completing a two-phase World Summit, along with numerous preparatory workshops, regional conferences, and topical consultations. The entire process was instrumental in lifting policy discourse on Internet governance from the sphere of the technical community, flanked by a relatively small number of special interest groups and government agencies, into a truly global arena. Internet governance now engages a vast number of heterogeneous actors. Concomitantly, the concept of 'multi-stakeholder' has come to dominate current discourse in the field.[1]

This chapter provides background on the organizational structure and thematic composition of the Summit. It describes the origin of the Summit, the various stakeholders and their principal viewpoints, and the main content of the Summit negotiations. It also describes the outcomes

---

* Amanda Hubbard wishes to emphasize that she has co-authored this chapter in her personal capacity and that the views expressed herein do not as such represent the opinion of the US government or any other national government.

[1] See, for example, Wolfgang Kleinwächter (ed.), *The Power of Ideas: Internet Governance in a Global Multi-Stakeholder Environment* (Berlin: Marketing für Deutschland, 2007); Malcolm, *Multi-Stakeholder Governance and the Internet Governance Forum.*

of the two phases of WSIS in terms of the content of the final negotiated documents and the organizational structures created to continue
work specifically in the field of Internet governance. It concludes with
a brief outline of some of the lessons that may be learned from the
process and that can be applied in addressing future challenges in the
field.

6.2. Origin of the WSIS

The ITU launched the idea for the World Summit on the Information Society in the late 1990s. At its 1998 Plenipotentiary Meeting in
Minneapolis, Minnesota, the ITU passed Resolution 73. The resolution
directed the ITU to take steps towards coordinating both within the UN
organizational structure and through activities within the ITU efforts
to hold an international summit on telecommunications and Internet
issues. It explained the rationale for such an event by, *inter alia*, citing
the growth of telecommunications structures globally and the fact that
'telecommunications are playing an increasingly decisive and driving role
at the political, economic, social and cultural levels'. In the resolution,
the ITU cast itself as 'the organization best able to seek appropriate ways
to provide for development of the telecommunication sector geared to
economic, social and cultural development'.

The goals of the envisaged process, as stated in the resolution, were the
following:

- establishing an overall framework identifying, with the contribution of all partners, a joint and harmonized understanding of the information society;
- drawing up a strategic plan of action for concerted development of the information society by defining an agenda covering the objectives to be achieved and
  the resources to be mobilized; and
- identifying the roles of the various partners to ensure smooth coordination of
  the establishment in practice of the information society in all Member States.

The first part of this process was to engage the UN with a view to determining whether the UN Secretary-General would support such a proposal
and whether the subject was appropriate for a UN World Summit. The
UN had already sponsored a series of such summits on topics of fundamental political, cultural, and economic importance. Prominent examples
include the World Summit for Children (held in New York, 1990), the

Earth Summit on Environment and Development (held in Rio de Janeiro, 1992), and the Millennium Summit (held in New York, 2000). The World Summit on the Information Society sought to build on the principles from these prior summits, such as the need to use ICT to achieve the Millennium Development Goals.[2]

In 1999, the Office of the UN Secretary-General endorsed the idea of the World Summit on the Information Society and appointed a High-level Summit Organization Committee (HLSOC) composed of the senior executives from other UN bodies and affiliated organizations. Other international bodies, such as the Organization for Economic Cooperation and Development (OECD) and Inter-American Development Bank, were offered observer status.

The next part of the process involved the ITU developing the substantive and procedural elements necessary for the success of such an ambitious undertaking. The ITU Council proposed that the Summit take place in two phases. The first phase, in Geneva, would be held in December 2003, and create a framework for future developments in ICT by formulating a Declaration of Principles that all members could agree upon and a Plan of Action for future efforts. The second phase, in Tunis, was scheduled for late 2005 in order to review and evaluate the progress on the Plan of Action and develop a concrete agenda for achieving specific goals by 2015 (the same target year for realizing the Millennium Development Goals).

The UN General Assembly endorsed the ITU proposal in Resolution 56/183 of 21 December 2001. Through this Resolution, the General Assembly invited the ITU to assume primary organizational responsibility for all aspects of the Summit and preceding preparatory processes. The Resolution recommended that Summit preparations occur through an 'open-ended intergovernmental preparatory committee'.

6.3. Development of Summit Topics

Remarkably, even though Internet governance was really one of the central—and, indeed, most controversial—topics at issue, it did not receive specific mention in the initial list of themes prepared by the ITU

---

[2] Part of the Millennium Development Goals is to '[d]evelop a global partnership for development:... [i]ncluding making available, in cooperation with the private sector, the benefits of new technologies—especially information and communications technologies—to all'. See further <http://www.un.org/millenniumgoals/> (under Goal 8).

Council for the Summit. Rather, the themes were couched in a more general nomenclature. They were divided into six main categories as follows:[3]

A. *Building the infrastructure.* This category included the roles of telecommunications, investment, and technology in creating the infrastructure of the information society and bridging the 'Digital Divide'.

B. *Opening the Gates (to all users).* This category included the topics of 'universal and equitable access' to the information society as well as the various needs of the developing world. Another discussion topic falling under this category was the notion of information as a common public good instead of a private commodity.

C. *Services and applications.* This category encompassed both substantive and procedural issues inherent in the software, hardware, and telecommunications services used on and through the Internet.

D. *The Needs of Users.* This category dealt mainly with content and user issues, rather than technical functions of the communications infrastructure. Falling into this category were consumer protection, ethics, privacy, security, training, and worker protection. Additional topics included 'relevant content', cultural diversity, and rights to communicate.

E. *Developing a Framework.* This category embraced arguably the core issue that spawned the ITU's initiative to hold a worldwide conference—that is, challenges in developing the structure of the information society itself, as opposed to the content or uses of the infrastructure. Five specific issues fell into this category, as quoted from the ITU's 'List of Proposed Themes':

E.1. The roles of government, private sector, and civil society in shaping the 'Information Society'

E.2. Information as a common public good (public domain information)

E.3. Intellectual property rights and legal exceptions

E.4. Freedom of expression

E.5. Telecommunication and Internet access tariff policies

E.6. Others

---

[3] See ITU Council, *WSIS—List of Proposed Themes* (22 January 2002), <http://www.itu.int/osg/spu/wsis-themes/com04/com04.html>.

F. *ICT and Education.* Although the topic of education could have fallen under Category D ('Needs of Users'), the ITU decided instead to devote an entire theme to education. The topics under this category included using ICT as a catalyst for change, using ICT in schools, and the educational needs of 'current workers'.

It is important to note that each of the above main categories of themes included a subcategory termed 'others'. As described below, the inclusion of 'other' topics, including topics already under review in other UN or intergovernmental forums, became a significant hurdle to achieving consensus on technical and infrastructure issues. What began as discussions over problems surrounding technical development quickly transformed into an open-ended agenda covering every possible problem arising out of or in any way tangentially related to the 'information society'. While the agenda was a success in terms of being broad and inclusive in a very democratic way, the inclusion of so many topics had some negative consequences. For national representatives, the inclusion of a myriad of diverse, controversial, and specialized topics required a tremendous body of expertise in order to effectively negotiate the conference document language and participate in the discussions. For all participants, the extensive meeting and preparation schedule also required significant expenditure of resources and commitment. The next part of this chapter looks at the army of representatives who mobilized to address the plethora of issues, specifically focusing on the parties most active in the debate surrounding the fifth theme category in the above-cited ITU listing of topics. That category eventually evolved into discussion specifically on Internet governance.

6.4. WSIS Stakeholders and Procedures

Under the directions of both the UN and the ITU, the Executive Committee organizing the Summit made significant efforts to invite as many representative stakeholders as possible. The results of these efforts, in terms of number of participants and diverse viewpoints, were impressive.

According to official WSIS reports,[4] more than 11,000 individuals representing over 1,400 different stakeholder groups attended the Geneva phase of the Summit. Of those 11,000 individuals, approximately half were official country representatives from 175 countries, including nearly

---

[4] See statistics at <http://www.itu.int/wsis/basic/about.html>.

50 Heads of State. Fifty UN bodies and agencies sent nearly 1,000 representatives. Other international organizations sent more than 200 representatives. In terms of non-governmental organizations (NGOs), 481 sponsored over 3,000 participants, and 631 media organizations sent nearly 1,000 media personnel.

Two years later in Tunis, the crowd had nearly doubled. Official figures report nearly 20,000 people attending Phase Two of the Summit in Tunis.[5] Almost 6,000 representatives were sent by 173 countries, the EU, and (then) Palestinian Authority. Ninety-two different international organizations[6] sent more than 1,500 people; over 600 NGOs and civil society entities sent more than 6,000 people, and the business sector sponsored nearly 5,000 people from more than 200 different groups. The media returned for Phase Two at similar levels, with nearly 1,000 representatives from 642 different organizations.

The purpose of providing these statistics is to demonstrate that the ITU's success in encouraging the participation of groups with different viewpoints created a distinct challenge for the WSIS committees—how to incorporate so many divergent (and often diametrically opposed) views into the discussion to create an outcome that was and is both democratically legitimate and technologically productive, without stifling the innovation that has made the Internet grow into the robust infrastructure it is today.

At the same time, it is important to note that only official country representatives may negotiate text in documents that go before the full assembly for consideration in a UN-led effort. Many NGO and civil society groups complained about this process, believing that their views would not be accounted for in the final drafts. Nevertheless, non-state representatives were given opportunity to speak to the congregation but, in accordance with the UN rules, their statements were limited. An example of this process is the list of speakers for the final sessions of Phase Two of the Summit. During the high-level meetings held each day of the summit, Prime Ministers, Presidents, and Heads-of-Delegations delivered speeches. The conference organizers, in accordance with UN practice, reserved time at the end of each session to allow for statements by non-state representatives. Over 50 entities took advantage of this opportunity, ranging from the International Federation on Human Rights to Intel

[5] See statistics at <http://www.itu.int/wsis/basic/about.html>.
[6] The statistical breakdown of the data is slightly different from that for the Geneva Summit, however, in that the ITU has not categorized the international organizations in terms of UN affiliation.

Corporation and speaking on topics as diverse as the rights of children and the need for improved literacy programs to the need for greater native language capability on the Internet to support the preservation of indigenous cultures.

While it is beyond the scope of this chapter to attempt to recite or even summarize the widely divergent views of the hundreds of groups represented at the WSIS conferences, it is important to note that several groups provided the majority of the input on several important issues, particularly those related specifically to Internet governance. The following provides a brief overview of the main groups.

Executive Committee. The first group is the organizing group itself. Often overlooked in the literature to date, the organizing Executive Committee had a significant stake in ensuring that all of the effort and expense going into holding WSIS had some positive outcome. The difficulty for the Committee and the representatives selected to head subcommittees or other WSIS organizational structures was to walk a very high tightrope between fulfilling the mandate from the ITU and UN Secretary General to be broad-reaching and at the same time pushing the participants' discussion forward towards establishing realistic goals.

Nation States and Supranational Bodies. The second major group of stakeholders were the nation states of the UN system. Every country brings to the negotiating table its unique political agenda and linguistic peculiarity as well as economic, philosophical, and cultural bias. Controversy arose between the countries throughout the negotiations, not only because of the topics at hand but also because only country representatives could propose and approve language in the negotiated texts.

Intergovernmental Organizations. The third major group of participants represented intergovernmental organizations (IGOs) of several types. It included the Council of Europe and OECD. It also included UN bodies devoted to specific issues such as the UN Educational, Scientific, and Cultural Organization (UNESCO). Finally, regional groups, such as the Organization of American States and the Arab League, contributed by forging common positions among member states and streamlining the negotiations by speaking through a single representative on common positions.

Non-governmental groups. The fourth major group consisted of hundreds of entities representing specific topical or organizational goals. These groups contributed to the Summit by providing valuable insight into topics with greater detail and research than often available to a member state or IGO responsible for every issue on the agenda. NGOs also play a critical role in implementing any solutions developed at the Summit within their respective areas of expertise and practice. NGOs come in many shapes and sizes. The two categories of NGOs most often referenced at WSIS were the civil society groups and business and industry groups.

'Civil society' includes a host of groups that focus on topics such as privacy, freedom of speech and expression, women and children's rights, and development issues. Not all of them support the same ideals, viewpoints, or implementation plans. Many press reports on WSIS treated 'civil society' as a relatively homogeneous entity, yet this failed to reflect the myriad of positions of the NGOs in this category. Insufficient organization, unfamiliarity with UN practice and procedure, and a lack of a common unified message hindered effective lobbying throughout the process and diluted the impact any one group had on the development of Summit principles. In order to alleviate some of these problems, civil society groups formed a Civil Society Bureau. The Bureau represented regional and topical groups. It allowed civil society groups to provide consolidated contributions to the discussions, recommend amendments to drafts, and acted as a conduit to disseminate information to the hundreds of groups participating in the Summit activities.

Business and industry NGOs and other commercial entities also played a critical role. The main actor at WSIS representing the private business sector was the Coordinating Committee of Business Interlocutors (CCBI), chaired by the International Chamber of Commerce (ICC). As elaborated in Section 6.5, the CCBI attempted consistently to remind WSIS participants of the need to focus negotiations on infrastructure and investment issues.

Media groups. Media groups played two roles throughout WSIS. First, the media served its traditional function by reporting to the public as events unfolded. Second, media groups played an important role as a stakeholder in the outcome of WSIS beyond that of the civil society category in which they fit. Freedom of expression via the press was a critical and contentious topic throughout the negotiations. Media groups stood particularly for the principle that fostering ICTs for development could not be successful in an atmosphere of censorship or state control of information.

The variety of opinions does not end with the number of official representative groups; observers of the WSIS process not in attendance also expressed views through Internet-based outreach initiatives. Unfortunately, more is not necessarily better. The UN and ITU success in achieving a forum that included a multitude of divergent groups may have been (ironically) the principle cause of the lack of concrete progress on reaching consensus on the difficult issues that so many entities hoped to resolve. With so many voices shouting in the marketplace of ideas, valuable signals were often lost in the noise. Additionally, because the United Nations works on a consensus-building basis, only the views that could gain unanimous consent appeared in the final documents. The UN principle to seek consensus is critical to remember when looking at the WSIS outcomes.

In considering these outcomes it is also important to note that the bulk of policy negotiations took place in meetings prior to each phase of the Summit. The meetings in Geneva and Tunis—that is, the actual Summit—really just ratified policy agreed to at meetings beforehand. Chief among the latter were the Preparatory Committee meetings (PrepComs). The PrepComs were a combined set of meetings of full committees, subcommittees, and drafting groups convened on specific topics. At times, multiple groups would meet simultaneously, especially towards the end of the final PrepCom before each phase of the Summit. Often, this structure created great difficulty for smaller delegations and civil society groups who could not be in two or three places at once nor attend all the international and regional meetings. When such events occurred, in accordance with UN tradition, either the chairperson or a national delegate would reopen discussions on topics or draft language already completed in the full committee to allow the delegate not present during the negotiations to express views. In practical terms, this process led to tremendous frustration and delays in reaching consensus on any language in the documents. Any national representative could block consensus language by asking that [brackets] appear around any disputed text, even if the language was the result of delicate compromises between groups of national representatives. The benefit of this procedure, however, was that no delegation, regardless of size, could be excluded from participating in the open debate on any topic under the WSIS agenda.

6.5. Agenda for WSIS Phase One

The first PrepCom, held in July 2002, was the main organizing meeting where the delegations produced a tentative agenda for WSIS in the form of a draft 'Proposed themes for the Summit and possible outcomes'. This draft included the following list of topics: 'Building the infrastructure; Opening the gates; Services and applications; The needs of users; Developing a framework; ICTs and education; The role of ICTs in good governance'. Note that the use of the term 'governance' here did not refer to governance of the Internet but the concept of good governance in national matters generally.

Already at this stage, many realized that the agenda was growing beyond what could reasonably be accomplished in the Summit process. Further, it became quickly clear that reaching consensus on what the agenda ought to focus upon would be difficult. In particular, there was disagreement on the extent to which discussion should focus on issues related directly to technology and infrastructure. The principal business and industry group, CCBI, urged delegates to focus on these issues—in particular, 'the building of an appropriate policy framework that creates an environment that attracts investment, both domestic and foreign, in technology and infrastructure, including the experiences we have had around the world in telecommunications liberalization'.[7] According to this group, without the necessary infrastructure and private investment in telecommunications networks, other interests regarding use and content were purely academic. Other civil society bodies disagreed, with one coalition stating that 'what matters is human interaction and the exchange of information and content', and urging, concomitantly, that 'communication and information-sharing...should be the focus of the Summit'.[8] A second civil society statement, this time by the Global Information Infrastructure Commission, returned to the infrastructure development theme, stressing that '[w]ithout infrastructure there can be no connectivity or access. And if there is no private sector investment, there will be, for all intents and purposes, no infrastructure deployment'.[9] These opening exchanges of opinion were the harbinger of long-running disputes to come.

Another stumbling block concerned definition of the term 'Internet governance'. Despite being omitted from the initial list of proposed topics for discussion, the term was commonly mentioned in most official statements and in the prepared remarks of non-governmental speakers. Yet a clear meaning of the term was elusive and shifted depending on the participant. Indeed, much of the saga of WSIS is the syntactic struggle over attempts to provide a common working definition of that term. By the

---

[7] Statement of 4 July 2002, <http://www.itu.int/wsis/docs/pc1/statements_content/ccbi.doc>.

[8] *Putting People First in the Information Society: A Statement on WSIS Content and Themes Endorsed by 22 NGOs and Civil Society Entities* (undated), <http://www.itu.int/wsis/docs/pc1/statements_content/cs_group.doc>.

[9] Statement of 4 July 2002, <http://www.itu.int/wsis/docs/pc1/statements_content/giic.doc>.

first phase of the Summit, in Geneva, there was still no broad consensus on the term's ambit.

6.6. Outcome of Geneva Phase with Regard to Internet Governance

The principal formal outcome of the Geneva phase was the adoption of a Declaration of Principles,[10] together with a Plan of Action for following up the Declaration. Adoption of these documents was the result of numerous late-night compromises and last-minute modifications. In many cases, the delegates achieved compromises only by deferring contentious issues to the second phase of the Summit. One such issue was Internet governance. The Declaration of Principles included the following three paragraphs on specifically that issue.

48. The Internet has evolved into a global facility available to the public and its governance should constitute a core issue of the Information Society agenda. The international management of the Internet should be multilateral, transparent and democratic, with the full involvement of governments, the private sector, civil society and international organizations. It should ensure an equitable distribution of resources, facilitate access for all and ensure a stable and secure functioning of the Internet, taking into account multilingualism.

49. The management of the Internet encompasses both technical and public policy issues and should involve all stakeholders and relevant intergovernmental and international organizations. In this respect it is recognized that:

(a) Policy authority for Internet-related public policy issues is the sovereign right of States. They have rights and responsibilities for international Internet-related public policy issues.

(b) The private sector has had and should continue to have an important role in the development of the Internet, both in the technical and economic fields.

(c) Civil society has also played an important role on Internet matters, especially at community level, and should continue to play such a role.

(d) Intergovernmental organizations have had and should continue to have a facilitating role in the coordination of Internet-related public policy issues.

---

[10] WSIS, *Declaration of Principles. Building the Information Society: A Global Challenge in the New Millennium* (adopted 12 December 2003) (WSIS-03/GENEVA/DOC/4-E), <http://www.itu.int/wsis/docs/geneva/official/dop.html>.

(e) International organizations have also had and should continue to have an important role in the development of Internet-related technical standards and relevant policies.

50. International Internet governance issues should be addressed in a coordinated manner. We ask the Secretary-General of the United Nations to set up a working group on Internet governance, in an open and inclusive process that ensures a mechanism for the full and active participation of governments, the private sector and civil society from both developing and developed countries, involving relevant intergovernmental and international organizations and forums, to investigate and make proposals for action, as appropriate, on the governance of Internet by 2005.

The Plan of Action set out a detailed list of actions for the period between the two phases of the Summit. It also addressed Internet governance (under the heading 'enabling environment'), proposing the establishment of a 'working group on Internet governance' [paragraph 13(b)]:

(b) We ask the Secretary General of the United Nations to set up a working group on Internet governance, in an open and inclusive process that ensures a mechanism for the full and active participation of governments, the private sector and civil society from both developing and developed countries, involving relevant intergovernmental and international organizations and forums, to investigate and make proposals for action, as appropriate, on the governance of Internet by 2005. The group should, inter alia:

a. develop a working definition of Internet governance;

b. identify the public policy issues that are relevant to Internet governance;

c. develop a common understanding of the respective roles and responsibilities of governments, existing intergovernmental and international organisations and other forums as well as the private sector and civil society from both developing and developed countries;

d. prepare a report on the results of this activity to be presented for consideration and appropriate action for the second phase of WSIS in Tunis in 2005.

6.7. Working Group on Internet Governance

In line with the wishes expressed in Geneva, the UN Secretary-General created the Working Group on Internet Governance with a limited executive and support staff based at the UN Offices in Geneva. However, it took almost a year from the adoption of the Geneva Plan of Action to determine the structure, schedule, membership, and methodology for achieving the group's mandate. Eventually, 40 individuals were appointed to serve on the WGIG in their personal capacities. The group included representatives of all of the WSIS stakeholder groups. The newly appointed WGIG members, along with an army of observers, gathered in four subsequent meetings in Geneva to prepare their report.[11]

At the same time as the WGIG efforts, other groups sponsored a variety of events that added differing viewpoints and dimensions to existing public policy topics that the WGIG also examined. Among the most important of these events was a series of workshops and Thematic Meetings sponsored by the ITU. The first such event was a workshop on Internet Governance held in Geneva in late February 2004. At this workshop, the ITU invited experts to help the ITU develop its position on the WGIG efforts. The goal was to collect all the contributions and presentations made at the Workshop along with the Chairman's report into a book for all the ITU members. Invited experts, several countries, Siemens, and the Internet Society also provided written contributions.

The UN ICT Task Force staged yet a third grouping of events. Chief among these was organization of a Global Forum on Internet Governance in New York in March 2004 to bring interested parties from all the stakeholder groups together in one place. A large number of participants from all the stakeholder groups met at UN headquarters in New York to review progress on internet governance topics and take another look at the issues arising out of WSIS and other events such as the ITU workshops. The Global Forum also created working groups to look at a broad range of Internet-related issues.

At first glance, all of these efforts may seem to have duplicated each other, and indeed, the agendas for the groups, as well as the participant lists, overlapped considerably. One wonders what types of resource constraints smaller delegations and civil society groups faced when confronted with three sets of similar events. One wonders too what progress could have been made by streamlining, at the very least, the events sponsored by UN-affiliated groups. One benefit of the overlap was that all of the events succeeded in airing a plethora of viewpoints in different

---

[11] For insight into the internal dynamics of the WGIG, see generally William J. Drake (ed.), *Reforming Internet Governance: Perspectives from the Working Group on Internet Governance (WGIG)* (New York: United Nations Information and Communication Technologies Task Force, 2005).

forums. The WGIG had the opportunity to listen to the ideas expressed in those forums and incorporate them into the final report. Another benefit of the concurrent events was that each provided significant output in terms of website content, white papers, and reports—output that helped to educate all parties as to each other's positions prior to Phase Two of the WSIS Summit, and thereby reduce gaps in definitional coverage.

The WGIG Final Report was presented in July 2005. A significant achievement of the WGIG is its agreement on a 'working definition of Internet governance' in section II of the report:

Internet governance is the development and application by Governments, the private sector and civil society, in their respective roles, of shared principles, norms, rules, decision-making procedures, and programmes that shape the evolution and use of the Internet.[12]

Feedback on this definition was generally positive, and the definition ended up being inserted *verbatim* into paragraph 34 of the Tunis Agenda (described in Section 6.8).

In terms of long-term policy impact, another significant achievement of the WGIG was its proposal to create an open, multi-stakeholder forum, attached to the UN, for addressing Internet governance issues.[13] Again, this proposal ended up being endorsed in the Tunis Agenda (as elaborated in Section 6.8).

The WGIG Final Report is otherwise notable for canvassing several alternative models for 'Global Public Policy and Oversight'. Three of these models would involve major changes to the current structure for DNS management, either replacing ICANN or transferring oversight functions from the US Department of Commerce (DOC) to a new international body.[14] None of these three models ended up being endorsed in the Tunis Agenda, though they were the subject of much discussion both during and after the life of the WGIG. One such model envisages an intergovernmental 'Global Internet Council' (GIC) anchored in the United Nations. That council would assume the current functions of DOC with respect to international Internet management and also replace the ICANN Governmental Advisory Committee (GAC).[15] As related below, this model was to gain particular prominence in the ensuing debate.

---

[12] WGIG, *Report of the Working Group on Internet Governance* (Château de Bossey, June 2005), 4.
[13] Ibid. 10–11.   [14] Ibid. 13–16.   [15] Ibid. 13.

6.8. Outcome of Tunis Phase with Regard to Internet Governance

The objective of the second phase of the summit was to review all of the progress towards reaching the goals in the Geneva Plan of Action and to find solutions for the two most contentious issues during the Geneva phase: Internet governance and financing mechanisms. The increased attention on these two issues drew an even larger crowd to Tunis than that which converged on Geneva.

The PrepCom process leading up to the Tunis phase proceeded along the same path as the prior phase in Geneva with one significant advantage—an understanding among parties reached during the first PrepCom that consensus language already agreed in the Geneva phase was not to be reopened. Additionally, since the Geneva phase had already completed a Statement of Principles and a Plan of Action, the delegates decided that the final result of the Tunis phase should be some written product (or products) that also comprised two elements: a political statement or declaration and an action-oriented part to further the progress made in Geneva. The parties also agreed that the spirit of cooperative, transparent, open, and inclusive representation begun in Geneva should continue, augmented by actions to make the preparations for Tunis efficient. These understandings allowed negotiators to focus their efforts on Internet governance and financial mechanisms. Even so, the negotiations remained quite contentious throughout the preparations. At various stages, delegates and observers expressed concerns as to whether Summit attendees would have any documents to endorse.

The second round of the PrepCom process, held in Geneva in February 2005, was successful in reaching consensus on a funding mechanism that would enable greater aid to countries trying to develop ICT infrastructures and programmes to meet WSIS commitments.[16] With the funding mechanism impasse bridged, the remaining topic of Internet governance took centre stage for debate in the third and final PrepCom round, beginning in late September 2005 in Geneva. That debate nearly destroyed the negotiation process.

The WGIG Final Report provided an important focal point and catalyst for the debate. Much of the debate revolved around reform of ICANN and DOC responsibilities for management of critical Internet resources. A

---

[16] Reflected in paragraph 28 of the Tunis Agenda.

group of developing countries, including Saudi Arabia, Iran, Brazil, China, and Pakistan, rallied around the GIC model canvassed in the WGIG report.[17] On the opposite side, the United States adamantly resisted any changes, particularly changes that could affect DNS security or stability. In a major policy statement issued 30 June 2005, the US government announced, *inter alia*:

Given the Internet's importance to the world's economy, it is essential that the underlying DNS of the Internet remain stable and secure. As such, the United States is committed to taking no action that would have the potential to adversely impact the effective and efficient operation of the DNS and will therefore maintain its historic role in authorizing changes or modifications to the authoritative root zone file.[18]

Other delegations from the developed world, such as Australia, Japan, and—at least initially—the EU, also urged caution in advocating drastic changes. Later in the heated negotiations, the EU representative suddenly changed tack, proposing a new international government structure with an expansive jurisdiction over both structural and policy issues.[19] More specifically, the EU proposed a 'new cooperation model' which

should include the development and application of globally applicable public policy principles and provide an international government involvement at the level of principles over the . . . naming, numbering and addressing-related matters. . . .

At the same time, the proposal stated that the new model 'should not replace existing mechanisms or institutions, but should build on the existing structures of Internet Governance'. In other words, it was not calling for ICANN's replacement, rather a new oversight regime. Neither did it specifically call for that oversight to be exercised by an existing international body, such as the ITU. The other main prong of the proposal was for the creation of a new discussion forum along the lines suggested by the WGIG.

The EU did not flesh out its proposal with explanatory detail and little information has emerged on the political basis for the EU's abrupt

[17] See further William J. Drake, 'Why the WGIG Process Mattered', in Drake (ed.), *Reforming Internet Governance*, 249, 261; Declan McCullagh, 'Power Grab could Split the Net', CNET News, 3 October 2005, <http://news.cnet.com/2010-1071_3-5886556.html>.

[18] National Telecommunications and Information Administration, *US Principles on the Internet's Domain Name and Addressing System* (30 June 2005), <http://www.ntia.doc.gov/ntiahome/domainname/usdnsprinciples_06302005.htm>.

[19] European Union, 'Proposal for Addition to Chair's Paper Sub-Com A Internet Governance on Paragraph 5 "Follow-up and Possible Arrangements"' (30 September 2005) (WSIS-II/PC-3/DT/21-E), <http://www.itu.int/wsis/docs2/pc3/working/dt21.pdf>.

shift in position. An EU representative is cited as calling the move an attempt to break the stalemate between the United States and developing countries.[20] It had, however, little positive effect on the negotiating climate—one US official describing it as a 'very shocking and profound change'.[21] The US response was to reiterate the elements of US policy which it had communicated in June.

The negotiations in the third PrepCom ended without agreement. It was only in the last-minute negotiations right before the Tunis meeting that consensus text on all points was finally drafted. It took the form of two documents: first, the 'Tunis Commitment', a high-level political statement;[22] and second, the 'Tunis Agenda for the Information Society', which sets out in broad terms the need to develop international implementation mechanisms to match the various action items in the Geneva Plan of Action. The final text of the language on Internet governance in the Tunis Commitment reads as follows:

7. We reaffirm the commitments made in Geneva and build on them in Tunis by focusing on financial mechanisms for bridging the digital divide, on Internet governance and related issues, as well as on follow-up and implementation of the Geneva and Tunis decisions, as referenced in the Tunis Agenda for the Information Society.

As for the Tunis Agenda, the final language in the section on Internet governance is long (comprising over 50 paragraphs), broad, duplicative, and includes nearly all of the themes from the prior assemblies. If volume alone is the measure of effectiveness, the 50 plus paragraphs of text include enough words that the section could be deemed a success, whether by states, civil society, business and industry, or the media. Depending on one's viewpoint, it provides enough coverage of every Internet governance-related topic to please almost everyone (or no one). Every group can point to something positive (or negative) about the process and substance to please superiors and constituents, and justify the expense of hosting a delegation of representatives throughout the marathon summit process.

---

[20] See Tom Wright, 'EU Tries to Unblock Internet Impasse', *New York Times*, 30 September 2005, <http://www.nytimes.com/iht/2005/09/30/business/IHT-30net.html>. For further analysis, see Victor Mayer-Schönberger and Malte Ziewitz, 'Jefferson Rebuffed: The United States and the Future of Internet Governance', *Columbia Science and Technology Law Review*, 2007, vol. 8, 188–228.
[21] Wright, 'EU Tries to Unblock Internet Impasse'.
[22] World Summit on the Information Society, *Tunis Commitment* (18 November 2005) (WSIS-05/TUNIS/DOC/7-E), <http://www.itu.int/wsis/docs2/tunis/off/7.html>.

Particularly relevant to this chapter are the following three paragraphs:

55. We recognize that the existing arrangements for Internet governance have worked effectively to make the Internet the highly robust, dynamic and geographically diverse medium that it is today, with the private sector taking the lead in day-to-day operations, and with innovation and value creation at the edges.

68. We recognize that all governments should have an equal role and responsibility for international Internet governance and for ensuring the stability, security and continuity of the Internet. We also recognize the need for development of public policy by governments in consultation with all stakeholders.

69. We further recognize the need for enhanced cooperation in the future, to enable governments, on an equal footing, to carry out their roles and responsibilities, in international public policy issues pertaining to the Internet, but not in the day-to-day technical and operational matters, that do not impact on international public policy issues.

Also particularly noteworthy is paragraph 72 (elaborated in the next section) requesting the UN Secretary-General to create a 'new forum for multi-stakeholder policy dialogue—called the Internet Governance Forum'.

Taken together, the above four paragraphs comprise the key formal elements of the compromise reached to bridge the disagreement between the United States and other stakeholders. While paragraph 55 echoes the policy statement issued by the US government on DNS management, the other paragraphs seek to make room for greater involvement by other states (and other stakeholders) in policy development, first through a process of 'enhanced cooperation' and second through the Internet Governance Forum. Exactly how this compromise will cut remains to be seen.

In terms of 'enhanced cooperation', paragraph 71 stipulates that this process is to be initiated by the UN Secretary-General 'by the end of the first quarter of 2006', and 'involving all relevant organizations' (paragraph 71). Using 'relevant international organizations', it is to 'include the development of globally-applicable principles on public policy issues associated with the coordination and management of critical Internet resources' (paragraph 70). As of June 2008, little publicly visible progress has been made on this front.[23]

---

[23] For an overview of developments, see Malcolm, *Multi-Stakeholder Governance and the Internet Governance Forum*, 348–9.

Most public attention has turned to the Internet Governance Forum, regarded by many as the principal organizational outcome of WSIS. The mandate and operations of the Forum are described in the next section.

6.9. Internet Governance Forum

The Internet Governance Forum (IGF) has a lengthy mandate, set out in paragraph 72 of the Tunis Agenda:

The mandate of the Forum is to:

(a) Discuss public policy issues related to key elements of Internet governance in order to foster the sustainability, robustness, security, stability and development of the Internet.

(b) Facilitate discourse between bodies dealing with different cross-cutting international public policies regarding the Internet and discuss issues that do not fall within the scope of any existing body.

(c) Interface with appropriate intergovernmental organizations and other institutions on matters under their purview.

(d) Facilitate the exchange of information and best practices, and in this regard make full use of the expertise of the academic, scientific and technical communities.

(e) Advise all stakeholders in proposing ways and means to accelerate the availability and affordability of the Internet in the developing world.

(f) Strengthen and enhance the engagement of stakeholders in existing and/or future Internet governance mechanisms, particularly those from developing countries.

(g) Identify emerging issues, bring them to the attention of the relevant bodies and the general public, and, where appropriate, make recommendations.

(h) Contribute to capacity building for Internet governance in developing countries, drawing fully on local sources of knowledge and expertise.

(i) Promote and assess, on an ongoing basis, the embodiment of WSIS principles in Internet governance processes.

(j) Discuss, inter alia, issues relating to critical Internet resources.

(k) Help to find solutions to the issues arising from the use and misuse of the Internet, of particular concern to everyday users.

(l) Publish its proceedings.

The key point from this list is that the IGF is essentially a discussion body not a decision-making body. Concomitantly, it has no oversight function or involvement in technical operations of the Internet.[24] As a discussion body, it is to be 'multilateral, multi-stakeholder, democratic and transparent', with a 'lightweight and decentralized structure subject to periodic review'.[25]

As a point of departure, the IGF is to conduct five annual meetings. The inaugural meeting was held in Athens from 30 October to 2 November 2006; the second meeting in Rio de Janeiro from 12 to 15 November 2007. The third meeting is scheduled to take place in Hyderabad, India, from 3 to 6 December 2008.

What have been the practical results so far? It is tempting to answer that the results are long on rhetoric and short on concrete proposals. Initially at least, the IGF appears to be plagued by the same problem as the WSIS—opening up for extremely broad and unstructured discussion, much of which overlooks infrastructure and investment issues, such as the future of root-server administration, sustainable growth patterns for telecommunications networks, or investment incentives for public–private partnerships.

At the inaugural meeting in Athens, four general themes were used to structure discussion: (*a*) 'Openess'; (*b*) 'Security'; (*c*) 'Diversity'; (*d*) 'Access'. Discussion under the first three listed themes was framed to focus mainly on content that flows through the Internet, with debate over censorship and spam stealing much of the limelight. While the themes could also have been framed to encourage discussion of infrastructure issues, the latter were really only treated under the theme of 'Access'. That theme addressed matters such as interoperability, interconnection costs, and the role of open standards. The workshops organized under this rubric also included management of the DNS root zone file. Yet, significantly, naming and numbering issues were largely left out of the formal framework for discussion.[26] This omission was not repeated at the second IGF meeting, which added the theme 'Critical Internet Resources' to the list of main discussion themes.[27]

---

[24] Tunis Agenda, paragraph 77.   [25] Ibid. paragraph 73.

[26] For a comprehensive analysis of the Athens meeting, see further Malcolm, *Multi-Stakeholder Governance and the Internet Governance Forum*, 366–84.

[27] See further, for example, the Chairman's Summary of the Rio de Janeiro meeting, <http://www.intgovforum.org/Rio_Meeting/Chairman%20Summary.FINAL.16.11.2007.pdf>.

It would be wrong to say that the IGF has hitherto achieved nothing. At the opening of the Athens meeting, Markus Kummer, the Executive Coordinator of the UN Secretariat on Internet Governance, was asked what he expected from the forum. He answered that '[t]he value of the meeting is the meeting itself. There will be no negotiated outcome'.[28] In many ways, this statement sums up the value of international forums such as WSIS, WGIG, and the IGF—progress is the narrowing of gaps in information and viewpoints between widely divergent groups. Only through exchange of views can national, topical, technological, business, and civil groups hope to find common ground. And arguably, the IGF is achieving progress elusive to the participants in WSIS because the nature of the forum is not to negotiate policy. Moreover, all IGF participants are, in principle, placed on an equal footing.

Participation levels at the IGF meetings are healthy. Over 1,500 delegates attended the Athens meeting, that number growing to over 2,000 for the Rio de Janeiro meeting. Participants represent a broad range of interest groups, though corporate interest in attending IGF meetings has been slow to take off.[29] As one UN official stated in the Opening Session of the second IGF meeting, '[t]he Forum is...unique in that it brings together people who normally do not meet under the same roof'.[30] Moreover, the IGF is increasingly attracting public attention, not least in the 'blogosphere',[31] and is already the subject of at least one lengthy academic treatise.[32] Finally, IGF-related forums are springing up at regional and national levels.[33]

6.10. Lessons and Challenges

What may be learned from the history of the WSIS, WGIG, and IGF? We wish to highlight the following. First, the broad range of topics collected under a single umbrella term loosely called 'Internet governance' will

---

[28] See citation at <http://www.apc.org/en/news/governance/world/openness-activist-s-eye>, last accessed 28 June 2008.

[29] It is reported that less than a sixth of the participants at the Athens meeting came from the corporate world. See Chris Williams, 'IGF 2007: Rio here we come', The Register, 12 June 2007, <http://www.theregister.co.uk/2007/06/12/igf_nominet_2007/>.

[30] Sha Zukang (UN Under-Secretary-General for Economic and Social Affairs), Opening Session Address at the second IGF meeting, <http://www.intgovforum.org/Rio_Meeting/IGF2-opening-12NOV07.txt>.

[31] The principal blogsite being 'IGF Watch', <http://igfwatch.org/>.

[32] Jeremy Malcolm, *Multi-Stakeholder Governance and the Internet Governance Forum.*

[33] For example, the East African IGF; see <http://www.eaigf.or.ke>.

continue to defy simplistic solutions based on a single precept, categorization, or oversight body.

Second, the underlying political, economic, and cultural differences inherent in a wide range of involved stakeholders will continue to challenge any attempt at reaching complete agreement on questions of Internet governance. Nevertheless, each of the stakeholder groups has something constructive to contribute to the evolution of the Internet.

Third, the way in which each stakeholder group conveys its message will either hinder or advance the reception of that message. For groups to be effective, they must craft their message to meet the needs and limitations of the intended recipients. If they can craft their message appropriately, then even where common positions or concrete measurable progress are not yet possible, stakeholders can learn from each other. And in doing so, they can better meet the challenges raised by Internet governance.

Bearing in mind the latter point, our final observation is that much of the WSIS and IGF dialogue has been plagued by an apparent disjuncture between policy discourses. One discourse focuses on governance of the DNS—with ICANN as the central target—and tends to frame Internet governance as largely a debate about DNS management. The other discourse not only covers DNS management but also covers a host of other issues, including accessibility of the Internet in developing countries (the 'digital divide'), spam, information security, intellectual property rights, freedom of expression, and privacy. It tends to frame Internet governance as enveloping all of these topics and more, and tends in the process to lose sight of engineering and infrastructure issues. While the former discourse can be criticized for being overly narrow, the latter discourse can be criticized for being overly broad. In short, the former misses the big picture; the latter paints the picture too big. As one observer aptly comments, '[t]o proceed assuming that the primary challenge for Internet governance is narrowly one of managing administrative functions or is broadly one of deploying the network to additional people is to overlook the most important questions facing the Internet's future'.[34]

For that observer, those questions relate essentially to the continued ability of the Internet to facilitate and engender innovation—what he terms, in short, the 'generativity' of the Internet.[35] We agree entirely. In

[34] Jonathan Zittrain, 'The Generative Internet', *Harvard Law Review*, 2006, vol. 119, 1974, 2033.

[35] 'Generativity is a function of a technology's capacity for leverage across a range of tasks, adaptability to a range of different tasks, ease of mastery, and accessibility.' Ibid. 1981. See also Zittrain, *The Future of the Internet*, chapter 4.

doing so, we also agree that there is a pressing need to reframe the Internet governance debate so that it engages more directly with the issue of how to maintain the Internet's generativity in the face of growing pressures—some legitimate, others less so—to clamp down on its supposed 'excesses'. In other words, policy discourse on Internet governance ought to focus more on achieving the appropriate balance between Internet government and Internet generativity.

Bibliography

Abbate, J., *Inventing the Internet* (Cambridge, Massachusetts: MIT Press, 1999).

Baran, P., 'On Distributed Communications: I. Introduction to Distributed Communications Networks', Memorandum RM-3420-PR (Santa Monica: Rand Corporation, 1964).

Berners-Lee, T., *Weaving the Web* (London/New York: Texere, 2000).

Bing, J., *Handbook of Legal Information Retrieval* (Amsterdam: North-Holland, 1984).

——*Ansvar for ytringer på nett*: *særlig om formidlerens ansvar* (Oslo: Universitetsforlaget, 2008).

Boyd Rayward, W., *The Universe of Information: The Work of Paul Otlet for Documentation and International Organization* (Moscow: International Federation of Documentation (FID), 1975).

——'The Origins of Information Science and the International Institute of Bibliography/International Federation for Information and Documentation (FID)', *Journal of the American Society for Information Science*, 1997, vol. 48, no. 4, 289–300.

Buono, F. M. and Friedman, J. A., 'Maximizing the Enforceability of Click-Wrap Agreements', *Journal of Technology Law & Policy*, 1999, vol. 4, issue 3, available at <http://grove.ufl.edu/~techlaw/vol4/issue3/friedman.html>.

Bush, V., 'As We May Think', *Atlantic Monthly*, July 1945, available at <http://www.theatlantic.com/doc/194507/bush>.

Bygrave, L. A., 'International Agreements to Protect Personal Data', in James B. Rule and Graham Greenleaf (eds.), *Global Privacy Protection: The First Generation* (Cheltenham: Edward Elgar, 2008), 25–84.

Cerf, V. G. and Kahn, R. E., 'A Protocol for Packet Networks Intercommunication', *IEEE Transactions on Communication Technology*, May 1974, vol. Com-22, no. 5, 627–41.

Chander, A., 'The New, New Property', *Texas Law Review*, 2002–3, vol. 81, 715–97.

Cheng, T. S. L., 'Recent International Attempts to Can Spam', *Computer Law & Security Report*, 2004, vol. 20, 472–9.

Clark, D. D., 'The Design Philosophy of the DARPA Internet Protocols', *Computer Communication Review*, August 1988, vol. 18, 106–14.

Cojocarasu, D. I., *Anti-Spam Legislation between Privacy and Commercial Interest: An Overview of the European Union Legislation Regarding the E-Mail Spam*, CompLex 1/06 (Oslo: Unipub, 2006).

Coran, S. J. (Note), 'The Anticybersquatting Consumer Protection Act's *In Rem* Provision: Making American Trademark Law the Law of the Internet?', *Hofstra Law Review*, 2001–2, vol. 30, 169–96.

Deibert, R. J., Palfrey, J. G., Rohozinski, R., and Zittrain, J. (eds.), *Access Denied: The Practice and Policy of Global Internet Filtering* (Cambridge, Massachusetts: MIT Press, 2008).

Drake, W. J. (ed.), *Reforming Internet Governance: Perspectives from the Working Group on Internet Governance (WGIG)* (New York: United Nations ICT Task Force, 2005).

Easterbrook, F. H., 'Cyberspace and the Law of the Horse', *University of Chicago Legal Forum*, 1996, vol. 11, 207–16.

Edwards, L. (ed.), *The New Legal Framework for E-Commerce in Europe* (Oxford/ Portland: Hart Publishing, 2005).

Felten, E., 'Zfone Encrypts VoIP Calls', Freedom to Tinker, 23 May 2006, <http://www.freedom-to-tinker.com/?p=1019>.

Fogo, C. E., 'The Postman always Rings 4,000 Times: New Approaches to Curb Spam', *John Marshall Journal of Computer & Information Law*, 2000, vol. xviii, 915–44.

Froomkin, A. M., 'Wrong Turn in Cyberspace: Using ICANN to Route around the APA and the Constitution', *Duke Law Journal*, 2000, vol. 50, 17–184.

——'ICANN's "Uniform Dispute Resolution Policy"—Causes and (Partial) Cures', *Brooklyn Law Review*, 2002, vol. 67, 605–718.

——'Habermas@discourse.net: Toward a Critical Theory of Cyberspace', *Harvard Law Review*, 2003, vol. 116, 749–873.

Geist, M., 'Fundamentally Fair.com? An Update on Bias Allegations and the ICANN UDRP', <http://aix1.uottawa.ca/~geist/fairupdate.pdf>.

Hafner, K. and Lyon, M., *Where Wizards Stay Up Late: The Origins of the Internet* (New York: Simon & Schuster, Touchstone ed., 1996).

Haraldsen, A., *50 år: og bare begynnelsen* (Oslo: Cappelen, 2003).

Hauben, M. and Hauben, R., *Netizens: On the History and Impact of Usenet and the Internet* (Los Alamitos: IEEE Computer Society Press, 1997).

Hughes, J., 'The Internet and the Persistence of Law', *Boston College Law Review*, 2003, vol. 44, 359–98.

ITU Council, *WSIS: List of Proposed Themes* (22 January 2002); available at <http://www.itu.int/osg/spu/wsis-themes/com04/com04.html>.

Johnson, D. R. and Post, D. G., 'Law and Borders: The Rise of Law in Cyberspace', *Stanford Law Review*, 1996, vol. 48, 1367–402.

Kesan, J. P. and Shah, R. C., 'Shaping Code', *Harvard Journal of Law & Technology*, 2005, vol. 18, 319–99.

Kleinwächter, W., 'Beyond ICANN vs. ITU', in D. MacLean (ed.), *Internet Governance: A Grand Collaboration. An Edited Collection of Papers Contributed to the United Nations ICT Task Force Global Forum on Internet Governance, New York, March 25–26, 2004* (New York: United Nations ICT Task Force, 2004), 31–52.

—— (ed.), *The Power of Ideas: Internet Governance in a Global Multi-Stakeholder Environment* (Berlin: Marketing für Deutschland, 2007).

Komaitis, K., 'ICANN: Guilty as Charged?' *The Journal of Information, Law and Technology*, 2003, Issue 1, <http://elj.warwick.ac.uk/jilt/03-1/komaitis.html>.

Koops, B.-J. and Brenner, S. W. (eds.), *Cybercrime and Jurisdiction: A Global Survey* (The Hague: T. M. C. Asser Press, 2006).

Leib, V., 'ICANN—EU Can't: Internet Governance and Europe's Role in the Formation of the Internet Corporation for Assigned Names and Numbers (ICANN)', *Telematics and Informatics*, 2002, vol. 19, 159–71.

Lenard, T. M. and May, R. J. (eds.), *Net Neutrality or Net Neutering: Should Broadband Internet Services Be Regulated?* (New York: Springer Publishing, 2006).

Lessig, L., *Code, and Other Laws of Cyberspace* (New York: Basic Books, 1999).

—— 'The Law of the Horse: What Cyberlaw Might Teach', *Harvard Law Review*, 1999, vol. 113, 501–46.

Levie, F., *L'homme qui voulait classer le monde: Paul Otlet et le Mundaneum* (Brussels: Les Impressions Nouvelles, 2006).

Licklider, J. C. R., 'Man-Computer Symbiosis', *IRE Transactions on Human Factors in Electronics*, March 1960, vol. HFE-1.

—— *Libraries of the Future* (Cambridge, Massachusetts: MIT Press, 1965).

Lindsay, D., *International Domain Name Law* (Oxford/Portland, Oregon: Hart Publishing, 2007).

MacLean, D. (ed.), *Internet Governance: A Grand Collaboration. An Edited Collection of Papers Contributed to the United Nations ICT Task Force Global Forum on Internet Governance, New York, March 25–26, 2004* (New York: United Nations ICT Task Force, 2004).

Macrae, N., *John von Neumann* (New York: Pantheon Books, 1992).

Malcolm, J., *Multi-Stakeholder Governance and the Internet Governance Forum* (Perth: Terminus Press, 2008).

Mayer-Schönberger, V. and Ziewitz, M., 'Jefferson Rebuffed: The United States and the Future of Internet Governance', *Columbia Science and Technology Law Review*, 2007, vol. 8, 188–228.

Mueller, M., *Ruling the Root: Internet Governance and the Taming of Cyberspace* (Cambridge, Massachusetts: MIT Press, 2002).

—— 'Rough Justice: An Analysis of ICANN's Uniform Dispute Resolution Policy', <http://usacm.acm.org/usacm/IG/roughjustice.pdf>.

—— Mathiason, J., and McKnight, L. W., *Making Sense of 'Internet Governance': Defining Principles and Norms in a Policy Context* (April 2004), <http://dcc.syr.edu/miscarticles/SU-IGP-rev2.pdf>.

Murray, A. D., *The Regulation of Cyberspace: Control in the Online Environment* (Milton Park: Routledge, 2007).

Mühlberg, A., 'Users and Internet Governance: The Structure of ICANN's At-Large Advisory Committee (ALAC)', in W. Kleinwächter (ed.), *The Power of Ideas: Internet Governance in a Global Multi-Stakeholder Environment* (Berlin: Marketing für Deutschland, 2007), 249–53.

National Telecommunications and Information Administration, *Improvement of Technical Management of Internet Names and Addresses*, Federal Register, 1998, vol. 63, no. 34, 8825–33.

——*Management of Internet Names and Addresses*, Federal Register, 1998, vol. 63, no. 111, 31,741–51.

——*Statement of Policy on the Management of Internet Names and Addresses* (5 June 1998), <http://www.ntia.doc.gov/ntiahome/domainname/6_5_98dns.htm>.

——*US Principles on the Internet's Domain Name and Addressing System* (30 June 2005), <http://www.ntia.doc.gov/ntiahome/domainname/usdnsprinciples_06302005.htm>.

Nicoll, C., 'Concealing and Revealing Identity on the Internet', in C. Nicoll, J. E. J. Prins, and M. J. M. van Dellen (eds.), *Digital Anonymity and the Law* (The Hague: T. M. C. Asser Press, 2003), 99–119.

Nørretranders, T., *Stedet som ikke er: Fremtidens nærvær, netværk og internet* (Copenhagen: Aschehoug, 1997).

O'Neill, J., 'The Role of ARPA in the Development of the ARPANET', *IEEE Annals of the History of Computing*, 1995, vol. 17, no. 4, 76–81.

Rawls, J., *Political Liberalism* (New York: Columbia University Press, 1993).

Reidenberg, J. R., 'Lex Informatica: The Formulation of Information Policy Rules through Technology', *Texas Law Review*, 1998, vol. 76, 553–93.

——'Yahoo and Democracy on the Internet', *Jurimetrics Journal*, 2002, vol. 42, 261–80.

Russell, A. L., ' "Rough Consensus and Running Code" and the Internet-OSI Standards War', *IEEE Annals of the History of Computing*, 2006, vol. 28, no. 3, 48–61.

Saltzer, J. H., Reed, D. P., and Clark, D. D., 'End-to-End Arguments in System Design', *ACM Transactions on Computer Systems*, 1984, vol. 2, 277–88.

Saxby, S., *Public Policy and Legal Regulation of the Information Market in the Digital Network Environment*, CompLex 2/96 (Oslo: TANO, 1996).

Shea, V., *Netiquette* (San Rafael, California: Albion Books, 1994).

Shy, O., *The Economics of Network Industries* (Cambridge: Cambridge University Press, 2001).

Sohmen, P., 'Taming the Dragon: China's Efforts to Regulate the Internet', *Stanford Journal of East Asian Affairs*, 2001, vol. 1, 17–26.

Svantesson, D. J. B., 'Geo-Location Technologies and Other Means of Placing Borders on the "Borderless" Internet', *John Marshall Journal of Computer & Information Law*, 2004, vol. XXIII, 101–39.

—— ' "Imagine There's No Countries . . . ": Geo-Identification, the Law and the Not so Borderless Internet', *Journal of Internet Law*, 2007, vol. 10, no. 9, 1, 18–21.

Tanenbaum, A. S., *Computer Networks* (Upper Saddle River, New Jersey: Prentice Hall, 1996, 3rd edn.).

Thornburg, E. G., 'Going Private: Technology, Due Process, and Internet Dispute Resolution', *University of California at Davis Law Review*, 2000, vol. 34, 151–220.

van Schewick, B., 'Towards an Economic Framework for Network Neutrality Regulation', *Journal of Telecommunications and High Technology Law*, 2007, vol. 5, 329–83.

Walden, I. and Angel, J. (eds.), *Telecommunications Law and Regulation* (Oxford: Oxford University Press, 2005, 2nd edn.).

Weinberg, J., 'ICANN and the Problem of Legitimacy', *Duke Law Journal*, 2000, vol. 50, 187–260.

Windhausen, J., Jr., *Good Fences Make Bad Broadband: Preserving an Open Internet through Net Neutrality* (Public Knowledge White Paper, 6 February 2006), <http://static.publicknowledge.org/pdf/pk-net-neutrality-whitep-20060206.pdf>.

Working Group on Internet Governance, *Report of the Working Group on Internet Governance* (Château de Bossey, June 2005); <http://www.wgig.org/docs/WGIGREPORT.pdf>.

World Intellectual Property Organization, *The Management of Internet Names and Addresses: Intellectual Property Issues. Final Report of the WIPO Internet Domain Name Process* (30 April 1999), <http://www.wipo.int/amc/en/processes/process1/report/finalreport.html#II>.

World Summit on the Information Society, *Declaration of Principles. Building the Information Society: A Global Challenge in the New Millennium* (adopted 12 December 2003)(WSIS-03/GENEVA/DOC/4-E), <http://www.itu.int/wsis/docs/geneva/official/dop.html>.

—— *Plan of Action* (12 December 2003) (WSIS-03/GENEVA/DOC/0005), <http://www.itu.int/wsis/docs/geneva/official/poa.html>.

—— *Tunis Agenda for the Information Society* (18 November 2005) (WSIS-05/TUNIS/DOC(6(rev. 1)-E), <http://www.itu.int/wsis/docs2/tunis/off/6rev1.html>.

—— *Tunis Commitment* (18 November 2005) (WSIS-05/TUNIS/DOC/7-E), <http://www.itu.int/wsis/docs2/tunis/off/7.html>.

Yoo, C. S., 'Network Neutrality and the Economics of Congestion', *Georgetown Law Journal*, 2006, vol. 94, 1847–908.

—— 'Beyond Network Neutrality', *Harvard Journal of Law & Technology*, 2005, vol. 19, no. 1, <http://jolt.law.harvard.edu/articles/pdf/v19/19HarvJLTech001.pdf>.

Zittrain, J., *The Future of the Internet and How to Stop It* (New Haven: Yale University Press, 2008).

—— 'The Generative Internet', *Harvard Law Review*, 2006, vol. 119, 1974–2040.

Index

Lightning Source UK Ltd.
Milton Keynes UK
UKHW010648130223
416869UK00004B/324